W9-CCE-524

Absolute Beginner's Guide

TO

Second Edition

Project Management

Greg Horine

QUE®

800 East 96th Street,
Indianapolis, Indiana 46240

Absolute Beginner's Guide to Project Management, Second Edition

Copyright © 2009 by Que Publishing

All rights reserved. No part of this book shall be reproduced, stored in a retrieval system, or transmitted by any means, electronic, mechanical, photocopying, recording, or otherwise, without written permission from the publisher. No patent liability is assumed with respect to the use of the information contained herein. Although every precaution has been taken in the preparation of this book, the publisher and author assume no responsibility for errors or omissions. Nor is any liability assumed for damages resulting from the use of the information contained herein.

ISBN-13: 978-0-7897-3821-0
ISBN-10: 0-7897-3821-X

Library of Congress Cataloging-in-Publication Data:

Horine, Greg.
Absolute beginner's guide to project management / Greg Horine. — 2nd ed.
p. cm.
Includes index.
ISBN 978-0-7897-3821-9
1. Project management. I. Title.
HD69.P75H67 2009
658.4'04—dc22
2008052475

Printed in the United States of America

First Printing: January 2009

Trademarks

All terms mentioned in this book that are known to be trademarks or service marks have been appropriately capitalized. Que Publishing cannot attest to the accuracy of this information. Use of a term in this book should not be regarded as affecting the validity of any trademark or service mark.

PMBOK is a registered trademark of the Project Management Institute, Inc.

Warning and Disclaimer

Every effort has been made to make this book as complete and as accurate as possible, but no warranty or fitness is implied. The information provided is on an "as is" basis. The author and the publisher shall have neither liability nor responsibility to any person or entity with respect to any loss or damages arising from the information contained in this.

Bulk Sales

Que Publishing offers excellent discounts on this book when ordered in quantity for bulk purchases or special sales. For more information, please contact

U.S. Corporate and Government Sales
1-800-382-3419
corpsales@pearsontechgroup.com

For sales outside of the U.S., please contact

International Sales
international@pearson.com

Associate Publisher
Greg Wiegand

Acquisitions Editor
Loretta Yates

Development Editor
Todd Brakke

Managing Editor
Kristy Hart

Project Editor
Lori Lyons

Copy Editor
Editorial Advantage

Senior Indexer
Cheryl Lenser

Proofreader
Jennifer Gallant

Technical Editor
Todd Meister

Publishing Coordinator
Cindy Teeters

Book Designer
Ann Jones

Compositor
Nonie Ratcliff

Contents at a Glance

Table of Contents

About the Author

Gregory M. Horine is a certified (PMP, CCP) business technology and IT project management professional with more than 20 years of successful results across multiple industries using servant leadership principles. Primary areas of expertise and strength include

- Project management and leadership
- Complete project lifecycle experience
- Regulatory and process compliancet
- Package implementation and integration
- Quality and risk management
- Enterprise solution development
- Effective use of project management tools
- MS Project
- Project and portfolio management tools
- Complex application developmen
- Data analysis and transformation
- Business process analysis and improvement
- Vendor and procurement management
- Mind mapping tools

In addition, Mr. Horine holds a master's degree in computer science from Ball State University and a bachelor's degree in both marketing and computer science from Anderson College (Anderson, IN).

Through his "servant leadership" approach, Mr. Horine has established a track record of empowering his teammates, improving project communications, overcoming technical and political obstacles, and successfully completing projects that meet the targeted objectives.

Mr. Horine is grateful for the guidance and the opportunities that he has received from many mentors throughout his career. Their patience and influence has resulted in a rewarding career that has been marked by continuous learning and improvement.

When not engaged in professional endeavors, Mr. Horine hones his project management skills at home with his lovely wife, Mayme, and his five incredible children: Michael, Victoria, Alex, Luke, and Elayna.

Dedication

This book is dedicated to the "students" that I constantly visualized in my mind as I developed this book—the bright and caring family that surround my life, including my wife, parents, siblings, in-laws, aunts, uncles, cousins, and grandparents.

This book is also dedicated to the parents, families, practitioners, and researchers who are diligently fighting to rescue children from autism spectrum and bipolar disorders.

This book is dedicated to my key inspirational sources: my incredible wife, Mayme (I still wake-up everyday with a smile in my heart knowing I am married to her), and my "fabulous five" children: Michael, Victoria, Alex, Luke, and Elayna (each one is a hero to me).

Acknowledgments

I am grateful for the patience, support, and teamwork demonstrated by the following individuals: my editor, Loretta Yates; the Que Publishing team of Todd Brakke, Lori Lyons, Cheryl Lenser, Nonie Ratcliff; my family; and my parents, Carla and Bud.

In addition, I wish to acknowledge the talents and professionalism of Mr. Craig Thurmond for his graphical design contributions to this book.

We Want to Hear from You!

As the reader of this book, *you* are our most important critic and commentator. We value your opinion and want to know what we're doing right, what we could do better, what areas you'd like to see us publish in, and any other words of wisdom you're willing to pass our way.

As an associate publisher for Que Publishing, I welcome your comments. You can email or write me directly to let me know what you did or didn't like about this book—as well as what we can do to make our books better.

Please note that I cannot help you with technical problems related to the topic of this book. We do have a User Services group, however, where I will forward specific technical questions related to the book.

When you write, please be sure to include this book's title and author as well as your name, email address, and phone number. I will carefully review your comments and share them with the author and editors who worked on the book.

Email: feedback@quepublishing.com

Mail: Greg Wiegand
Associate Publisher
Que Publishing
800 East 96th Street
Indianapolis, IN 46240 USA

Reader Services

Visit our website and register this book at informit.com/register for convenient access to any updates, downloads, or errata that might be available for this book.

INTRODUCTION

As organizations continue to move toward "project-based" management to get more done with fewer resources, and as the demand for effective project managers continues to grow, more and more individuals find themselves with the opportunity to manage projects for the first time.

In an ideal world, every new project manager candidate would complete certified project management training programs and serve as an apprentice before starting his or her first project manager opportunity, but...this is the real world. In many cases, a quicker, more accessible, and more economical alternative is needed to guide these candidates in managing projects successfully the first time.

The *Absolute Beginner's Guide to Project Management, Second Edition,* is intended to provide this alternative with a helpful, fun, and informative style.

About This Book

Let's review the objectives and approach of this book.

Objectives

The objectives of this book include the following:

- To be an easy-to-use tutorial and reference resource for any person managing their first project(s).
- To teach the key concepts and fundamentals behind project management techniques. If these are understood, they can be applied effectively independent of toolset, environment, or industry.
- To reduce the "on-the-job" learning curve by sharing the traits of successful projects and "lessons learned" from less-than-successful projects.
- To balance the breadth of topics covered with adequate depth in specific areas to best prepare a new project manager.
- To review the skills and qualities of effective project managers.
- To emphasize the importance of project "leadership" versus just project "management."

Approach

Consistent with the *Absolute Beginner's Guide* series, this book uses a teaching style to review the essential techniques and skills needed to successfully manage a project. By teaching style, we intend the following:

- A mentoring, coaching style.
- A fun, easy-to-read, practical style.
- Assumes that the reader does not have previous hands-on experience with project management.
- Teaches the material as if an instructor were physically present.
- Task-oriented, logically ordered, self-contained lessons (chapters) that can be read and comprehended in a short period of time (15–30 minutes).
- Emphasis on understanding the principle behind the technique or practice.
- Teaches the material independent of specific tools and methodologies.
- Teaches the material with the assumption that the reader does not have access to organizational templates or methodologies.
- Provides a summary map of the main ideas covered at the end of each chapter. Research has shown that this type of "mind-map" approach can drive better memory recollection when compared to traditional linear summary approaches.

OUT-OF-SCOPE

The scope of this book is clearly outlined in the table of contents, but as we will cover later, it is always good to review what is out of scope to ensure understanding of the scope boundaries. Because the field of project management is extremely broad, and we needed to draw the line somewhere, this book focuses on the proper management of a single project. As a result, the following advanced project management subjects are not covered in this book:

- Program management
- Enterprise portfolio management
- Enterprise resource management
- Advanced project risk management topics
- Advanced project quality management topics
- Advanced project procurement management topics

Table 1.1 Comparing Projects and Operations

Feature	Projects	Operations
Key Similarities	Planned, executed, and controlled. Performed by people. Resource constrained.	Planned, executed, and controlled. Performed by people. Resource constrained.
Purpose	Attain objectives and terminate.	Sustain the organization.
Time	Temporary. Definite beginning and end points.	Ongoing.
Outcome	Unique product, service, or result.	Non-unique product, service, or result.
People	Dynamic, temporary teams formed to meet project needs. Generally not aligned with organizational structure.	Functional teams generally aligned with organizational structure.
Authority of Manager	Varies by organizational structure. Generally minimal, if any, direct line authority.	Generally formal, direct line authority.

After reviewing this comparison, you are beginning to see the inherent challenges involved with project management. Projects are less predictable and are constantly impacted by the dynamic, uncertain nature of most organizational environments. We will detail the typical challenges later in this chapter. For now, let's better define "project management."

PMI definition of "project": A temporary endeavor to produce a unique product or service

"Managing" Projects

What do we mean when we say "managing" projects?

- We mean applying both the science and art to planning, organizing, implementing, leading, and controlling the work of a project to meet the goals and objectives of the organization.
- We mean the process of defining a project, developing a plan, executing the plan, monitoring progress against the plan, overcoming obstacles, managing risks, and taking corrective actions.
- We mean the process of managing the competing demands and trade-offs between the desired results of the project (scope, performance, quality) and the natural constraints of the project (time and cost).

- We mean the process of leading a team that has never worked together before to accomplish something that has never been done before in a given amount of time with a limited amount of money.

Sounds like fun, doesn't it? We will explain each of these key aspects of project management in subsequent chapters, and we will discuss many of the specific tasks and responsibilities performed by the project manager in Chapter 2, "The Project Manager," but for now we just want to align our general understanding of project management.

PMI definition of project management—The application of knowledge, skills, tools, and techniques to project activities to meet project requirements.

An Academic Look

To further assist this alignment process, let's look at project management from a more academic level. The Project Management Institute (PMI), the globally recognized standards organization for project management (www.pmi.org), defines project management as a set of five process groups (see Table 1.2) and nine knowledge areas (see Table 1.3). These references are taken from the PMI 's *A Guide to the Project Management Body of Knowledge, Third Edition (PMBOK® Guide – Third Edition).*

Table 1.2 Description of Project Management Process Groups

#	Process Group	Description per *PMBOK® Guide – Third Edition*	Common Terms
1	Initiating	Authorizing the project or phase.	"preliminary planning" "kicking off"
2	Planning	Defining and refining objectives of the project and selecting the best course of action to attain those objectives.	"defining" "developing the plan" "setting the stage"
3	Executing	Coordinating the people and resources to implement the plan.	"making it happen" "getting it done" "coordinating"
4	Controlling	Ensuring project objectives are met by monitoring and measuring progress regularly to identify variances from the plan so that corrective actions can be taken.	"tracking progress" "keeping on course"
5	Closing	Formalizing acceptance of project or phase and bringing to an orderly end.	"client acceptance" "transition" "closeout"

Figure 1.1 summarizes the relationships among the project management process groups, which is based on *PMBOK® Guide – Third Edition* (Figure 3-2 page 40).

FIGURE 1.1
Project management process relationships.

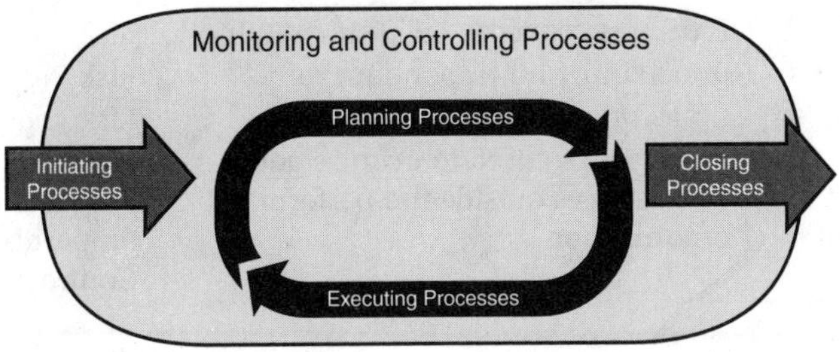

Table 1.3 Description of PMBOK Knowledge Areas

#	Knowledge Area	Description per *PMBOK® Guide, Third Edition*	Common Deliverables
1	Project Integration Management	Processes required to ensure the elements of the project are properly coordinated.	Project Charter Project Plan Change Requests Work Results
2	Project Scope Management	Processes required to ensure that project includes all the work that is required and only the work that is required to complete the project successfully.	Scope Statement Work Breakdown Structure Formal Acceptance
3	Project Time Management	Processes required to ensure timely completion of the project.	Network Diagram Task Estimates Project Schedule
4	Project Cost Management	Processes required to ensure the project is completed within the approved budget.	Resource Requirements Cost Estimates Project Budget
5	Project Quality Management	Processes required to ensure the project will satisfy the needs for which it was undertaken.	Quality Management Plan Checklists Quality Reviews
6	Project Human Resources Management	Processes required to make the most effective use of the people involved with the project.	Role and Responsibility Matrix Organization Chart Performance Evaluations
7	Project Communications Management	Processes required to ensure the timely and appropriate generation, collection, dissemination, storage, and ultimate disposition of project information.	Communication Plan Status Reports Presentations Lessons Learned

Table 1.3 (continued)

#	Knowledge Area	Description per *PMBOK® Guide, Third Edition*	Common Deliverables
8	Project Risk Management	Processes concerned with identifying, analyzing, and responding to project risk.	Risk Management Plan Risk Response Plan Risk Log
9	Project Procurement Management	Processes required to acquire goods and services outside the performing organization.	Procurement Plan Statement of Work Proposals Contracts

Again, depending on your experiences, you may not have realized that project management consisted of all this, and you may not actually perform all these activities as a project manager in your organization. However, it is important and helpful to understand how big your playing field is when learning something new. This book will not completely educate you on each of these process groups nor each of the nine knowledge areas, but it will provide you with the knowledge, essential tools, and "real-world" insights to improve your effectiveness on your first project management assignment.

Project management is a broad field with great potential for specialized and in-depth study. There are entire books and training classes focused solely on advanced analysis of individual process groups and knowledge areas.

What Is the Value of Project Management?

As the organizational operating environment continues to become more global, more competitive, and more demanding, organizations must adapt. They must become more efficient, more productive—they must "do more with less." They must continually innovate. They must respond rapidly to a fast-changing environment. *How can they do this? How can they do this in a strategic manner? How can they do this and still have the proper management controls?* They can do this with effective project management. The strategic value points that effective project management can offer an organization the following:

- Provides a controlled way to rapidly respond to changing market conditions and new strategic opportunities
- Maximizes the innovative and creative capabilities of the organization by creating environments of focus and open communication

- Allows organizations to accomplish more with less costs
- Enables better leverage of both internal and external expertise
- Provides key information and visibility on project metrics to enable better management decision-making
- Increases the pace and level of stakeholder acceptance for any strategic change
- Reduces financial losses by "killing off" poor project investments early in their life cycles

In addition to providing apparent value to any organization, project management also offers tremendous value to each of us as individuals. At a personal level, the value of effective project management

- Ensures that our work is put to the best use for the organization and properly recognized
- Provides a career path that offers unique, challenging opportunities on each new project
- Provides a career path that requires all of our abilities and knowledge, including our management, business, people, and technical skills
- Provides a career path that is high in demand, and generally, an increase in income
- Provides a career path that prepares you for organizational leadership positions
- Provides a career path that is recognized more each year as excellent preparation for CxO positions (as more CxO positions are filled by individuals with project management experience)
- Provides a career path that allows you to be on the front lines of strategic organizational initiatives and have major impact on the organization's future

Stakeholder is the term used to describe individuals and organizations who are actively involved in the project, or whose interests may be impacted by the execution or completion of the project.

Why Are Projects Challenging?

From what we've covered so far, from your own experiences, or from your reading of trade publications, you likely have some appreciation for the difficulty of completing a successful project. While we address many common challenges in more detail throughout this book, let's review the key reasons why projects are challenging to manage:

- **Uncharted territory**—Each project is unique. The work to be done has likely never been done before by this group of people in this particular environment.
- **Multiple expectations**—Each project has multiple stakeholders that each have their own needs and expectations for the project.
- **Communication obstacles**—Due to natural organizational boundaries, communication channels, and team development stages, communication of project information must be proactively managed to ensure proper flow.
- **Balancing the competing demands**—Every project is defined to produce one or more deliverables (scope) within a defined time period (time), under an approved budget (cost) with a specified set of resources. In addition, the deliverables must achieve a certain performance level (quality) and meet the approval of the key stakeholders (expectations). Each of these factors can affect the others, as Figure 1.2 illustrates. For example, if additional functionality (scope, quality) is desired, the time and cost (resources needed) of the project will increase. This is a key focus of an effective project manager.

FIGURE 1.2

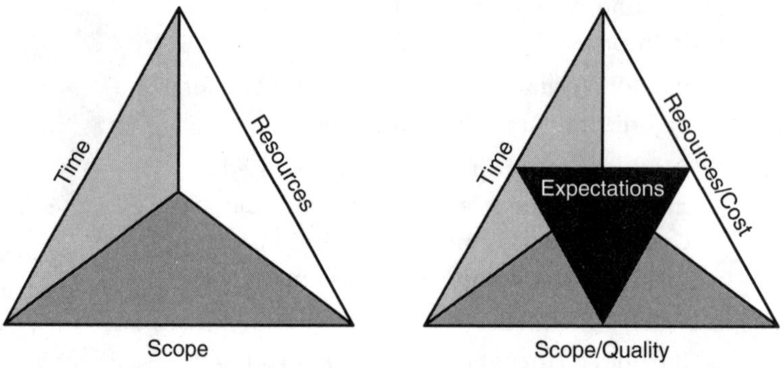

Competing project demands (traditional model on left, modern model on right), summarizing the relationships between the natural competing demands of projects.

- **Cutting Edge**—Often, projects have a strategic, innovative focus. As a result, they will often deal with new, leading edge technologies. In these cases, the project has more risks, more unknowns, and is much more difficult to estimate accurately.
- **Organizational Impacts**—In addition to overcoming natural communication obstacles created by the project structure, the project manager must also

manage overlaps in organizational approval and authority domains, contend with competing priorities for shared resources, deal with annual budget cycles that may not be aligned with the project's funding needs, and ensure that the project is aligned with the focus of the organization.

- **Collaboration**—Depending on the strategic level and scope of your project, your project team will consist of stakeholders across the organization from different functional areas that are likely not accustomed to working together. For project success, these different stakeholders must learn to work together and to understand the others' perspectives in order to make the best decisions for the project. Often, the project manager plays a key facilitating role in this collaboration process.
- **Estimating the Work**—Estimating project work is difficult, yet the time and cost dimensions of the project are built upon these work effort estimates. Given the facts that the work of the project is often unique (never been done before at all, never been done with these tools, and never been done by these people), and most organizations do not maintain accurate historical records on previous projects (that may have similar work components), it is difficult to accurately estimate the effort for individual work items, not to mention the entire project. For the entire project, you need to anticipate the quantity and severity of the issues and obstacles that are likely to surface. We'll cover this in more detail in Chapters 7, "Estimating the Work," and 14, "Managing Project Risk."

The competing project demands are often referred to as the *triple constraint of project management*. Time and Cost (or Resources) are always two sides of the triangle. Depending on where you look, the third side is either Scope, Performance, or Quality. In either case, it's the "output" of the project. Additionally, many recent variations of this model have included the additional demand of Client Expectations.

Growing Demand for Effective Project Managers?

With the value that project management offers any organization, it is easy to understand why more and more industries are adopting project management as the way to do business. As a result, if you check nearly any recent hiring survey or "hot" careers forecast, you will find project management near the top of this list.

With the business trends of global competition and increased worker productivity continuing for the foreseeable future, the demand for successful project managers will only increase. Even in industries and organizations that are experiencing staff reductions, the individuals who have the knowledge, the people skills, and the management competence to solve problems and get projects done will be the individuals most valued and retained by the parent organization.

In addition, many organizations have either compliance or competitive drivers requiring them to make process improvements to meet process standards set forth by acts of Congress (Sarbanes-Oxley act), government agencies (such as the federal Food and Drug Administration or Environmental Protection Agency), industry standards bodies (such as International Organization for Standards), or industry process models (such as Six Sigma Quality Model, or the Capability Maturity Model Integration for software engineering or project management). In all these cases, effective project management is a requirement to ensure these process improvements are made, sustained, and can be repeated.

As the demand for effective project managers continues to grow and organizations continue to experience varying degrees of success with project management, more organizations are requiring their project managers to be certified. Specifically, they are requesting PMI's Project Management Professional (PMP) certification. Much like a master's of business administration (M.B.A.) degree does not guarantee a person can run a profitable, growing business, the PMP certification does not guarantee a person can successfully manage a project. However, it does provide assurance that the individual does have a baseline level of knowledge and experience, and it does indicate that the person takes their profession seriously.

Trends in Project Management

In addition to the focus on organizational process improvements, there are other trends in business and project management that a first-time project manager is likely to encounter (that they may not have just a decade or less ago).

- **Managing Vendors**—With the increased outsourcing of non-core activities, more projects leverage one or more vendors (suppliers) to get work done. More on this in Chapter 21, "Managing Vendors."
- **Facilitating a Selection Process**—In order to determine which vendors you will partner with to get work done, a selection and evaluation process is normally conducted.

- **Risk Management**—Coinciding with the focus on enterprisewide process improvements and in response to past project experiences, more organizations are placing additional emphasis and formality on their project risk management processes. More on this in Chapter 14, "Managing Project Risks."
- **Quality Management**—Much like the factors driving the emphasis on risk management, the link between rigorous quality management procedures and improved project management practices continues to strengthen. More on this in Chapter 15, "Managing Project Quality."
- **Managing Virtual, Cross-Functional, and Multi-Cultural Teams**—With the continuous advancements in workgroup and communications tools, the increased integration of processes within an organization, and the continuous drive for increased organizational efficiencies, it is very likely that your project team will consist of members from different physical locations (virtual), different functional departments (cross-functional), or different cultures (multi-cultural, global). More on this in Chapter 20, "Managing Differences."
- **Working with PMOs and Corporate Governance Processes**—If you are working in any type of corporate or multiple business unit environment, you will most likely deal with Project Management Office (PMO) or other corporate governance processes. More on this in Chapter 25.
- **Change Agent**—Since most projects represent a "change" to business as usual, the project manager is expected to play a key role in leading the stakeholders through the change and acceptance process. More on this in Chapter 16, "Leading a Project," and Chapter 18, "Managing Expectations."
- **Servant Leadership**—Due to a lack of formal authority; the need to understand the requirements of all stakeholders; and the importance of facilitation, collaboration, and managing expectations; there is a growing awareness that a servant leadership style is paramount for effective project management. More on this in Chapter 16.

THE ABSOLUTE MINIMUM

At this point, you should have a high-level understanding of the following:

- The elements of project management.
- The common challenges of managing projects.
- The value of effective project management to an organization.
- The merits of project management as a career choice.
- The latest business and project management trends that may impact your first opportunity.

In addition, I recommend the following online resources for insightful articles on project management:

- www.pmi.org
- www.gantthead.com/
- www.niwotridge.com/
- www.maxwideman.com/pmglossary/
- http://projectmanagement.ittoolbox.com/
- www.pmforum.org
- www.pmousa.com
- www.cio.com

The map in Figure 1.3 summarizes the main points we reviewed in this chapter.

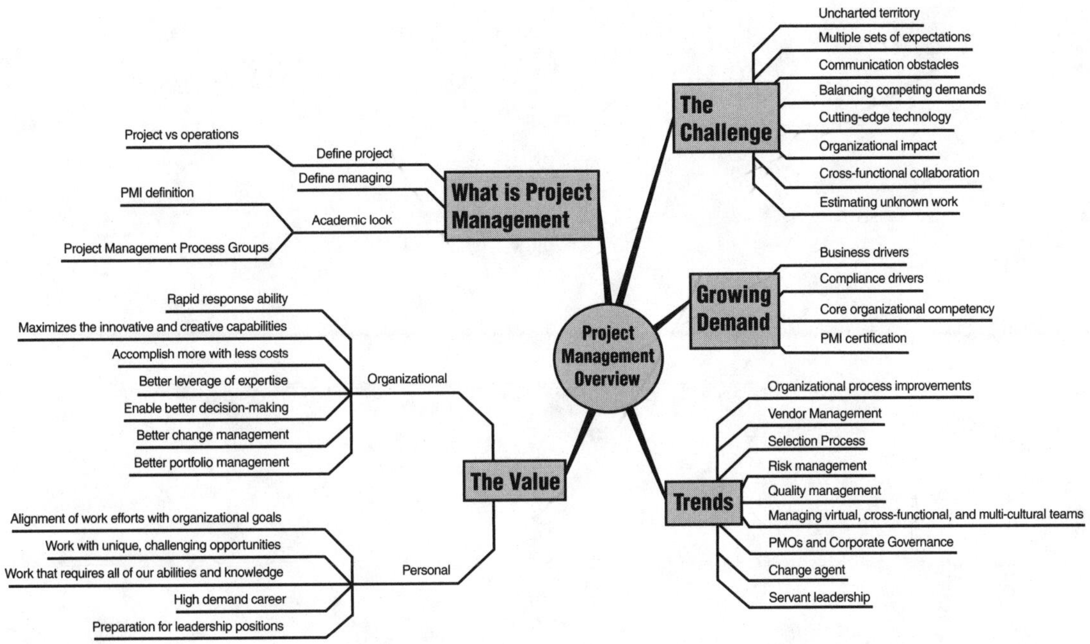

FIGURE 1.3

Project management overview.

In This Chapter

- Review the different roles played by the project manager
- Review the key skills every project manager should possess
- Learn why some project managers are much more successful than others
- Understand the common mistakes made by many project managers

2

The Project Manager

As we reviewed in Chapter 1, the project manager has many activities to perform, challenges to overcome, and responsibilities to uphold over the life of a project. Depending on your individual experiences, your industry background, and the manner in which project management has been implemented, this review may have been quite enlightening to you.

To ensure that we have a common understanding on what a project manager does, we'll review the different roles a project manager plays over the life of a project, and we'll discuss the prerequisite skills that are needed to perform those roles. Most importantly, we'll accelerate your learning curve by sharing the characteristics of successful project managers and the common mistakes made by many others.

One Title, Many Roles

You've likely heard many of the analogies before to describe the role of project manager—the "captain" of the ship, the "conductor" of the orchestra, the "coach" of the team, the "catalyst" of the engine, and so on. There's truth and insight in each of the analogies, but each can be incomplete as well. To gain better understanding of what a project manager does, let's briefly discuss each of the key roles played by the project manager:

- **Planner**—Ensures that the project is defined properly and completely for success, all stakeholders are engaged, work effort approach is determined, required resources are available when needed, and processes are in place to properly execute and control the project.
- **Organizer**—Using work breakdown, estimating, and scheduling techniques, determines the complete work effort for the project, the proper sequence of the work activities, when the work will be accomplished, who will do the work, and how much the work will cost.
- **Point Man**—Serves as the central point-of-contact for all oral and written project communications.
- **Quartermaster**—Ensures the project has the resources, materials, and facilities it needs when it needs it.
- **Facilitator**—Ensures that stakeholders and team members who come from different perspectives understand each other and work together to accomplish the project goals.
- **Persuader**—Gains agreement from the stakeholders on project definition, success criteria, and approach; manages stakeholder expectations throughout the project while managing the competing demands of time, cost, and quality; and gains agreement on resource decisions and issue resolution action steps.
- **Problem-Solver**—Utilizes root-cause analysis process experience, prior project experiences, and technical knowledge to resolve unforeseen technical issues and to take any necessary corrective actions.
- **The Umbrella**—Works to shield the project team from the politics and "noise" surrounding the project, so they can stay focused and productive.
- **Coach**—Determines and communicates the role each team member plays and the importance of that role to the project success; finds ways to motivate each team member; looks for ways to improve the skills of each team member; and provides constructive and timely feedback on individual performances.

- **The Bulldog**—Performs the follow-up to ensure that commitments are maintained, issues are resolved, and action items are completed.
- **Librarian**—Manages all information, communications, and documentation involved in the project.
- **Insurance Agent**—Continuously works to identify risks and to develop responses to those risk events in advance.
- **The Police Officer**—Consistently measures progress against the plan; develops corrective actions; reviews quality of both project processes and project deliverables.
- **Salesman**—An extension of the Persuader and Coach roles, but this role is focused on "selling" the benefits of the project to the organization, serving as a "change agent," and inspiring team members to meet project goals and overcome project challenges.

While there is consensus that the disciplines and techniques used in project management can be applied in any industry, there is no consensus on whether individual project managers can be effective in a different industry.

There is no doubt that the more knowledge and experience that a project manager has in the subject matter area of the project, the more value that he/she can offer. However, depending on the size of the initiative and the team composition, a project manager with different industry experience can bring tremendous value if they are strong in the other four skill categories discussed in here.

Key Skills of Project Managers

While there is a broad range of skills needed to effectively manage the people, process, and technical aspects of any project, it becomes clear there is a set of key skills that each project manager should have. While these skill categories are not necessarily exclusive of each other, let's group them into five categories to streamline our review and discussion:

1. **Project Management Fundamentals**—The "science" part of project management, covered in this book, including office productivity suite (such as Microsoft Office, email, and so on) and project management software skills.
2. **Business Management Skills**—Those skills that would be equally valuable to an "operations" or "line-of-business" manager, such as budgeting, finance, procurement, organizational dynamics, team development, performance management, coaching, and motivation.

3. **Technical Knowledge**—The knowledge gained from experience and competence in the focal area of the project. With it, you greatly increase your "effectiveness" as a project manager. You have more credibility, and you can ask better questions, validate the estimates and detail plans of team members, help solve technical issues, develop better solutions, and serve more of a leadership role.

tip

Active listening is one of the secret weapons of effective project managers.

4. **Communication Skills**—Since communication is regarded as the most important project management skill by the Project Management Institute (PMI), I feel it is important to separate these out. Skills included in this category include all written communication skills (correspondence, emails, documents), oral communication skills, facilitation skills, presentation skills, and the most valuable—active listening. Active listening can be defined as "really listening" and the ability to listen with focus, empathy, and the desire to connect with the speaker.
5. **Leadership Skills**—This category overlaps with some of the others and focuses on the "attitude" and "mindset" required for project management. However, it also includes key skills such as interpersonal and general people skills, adaptability, flexibility, people management, degree of customer-orientation, analytical skills, problem-solving skills, and the ability to keep the "big picture" in mind.

The specific combination of skills that are required for a project manager to be successful on a given project vary depending on the size and nature of the project. For example, as a general rule, on larger projects, technical knowledge will be less important than competence in the other four skill categories.

I know, I know...after reading this, you are probably thinking either one or more of the following:

- "You must be kidding! I need to be good in all those areas to manage a project?"
- "Wait! I've been on projects before, and I've yet to see a project manager who could do all that."
- "Wait, you must be kidding! If anyone was excellent in all those areas, they'd be a CxO of our company."

To help answer all these questions, please understand two important observations:

1. Many projects are not successful.
2. You do not need to get an "A" in all these categories to be successful as a project manager.

The key is that the project manager has the right mix of skills to meet the needs of the given project. In addition, a self-assessment against these skill categories allows you to leverage your strengths, compensate for your deficiencies, and focus your self-improvement program.

Qualities of Successful Project Managers

Given the many roles played by a project manager, the broad range of skills needed, and the inherent challenges in successfully delivering a project, we need to find ways to accelerate the learning process. Two key ways to accelerate our learning are understanding the qualities of successful project managers, and understanding the common mistakes made by project managers.

Successful project managers do not share personality types, appearances, or sizes, but they do share three important features.

1. They excel in at least two of the five key skill categories (Project Management Fundamentals, Business Management Skills, Technical Knowledge, Communication Skills, Leadership Skills) and are either "good enough" in the other categories or staff their teams to compensate for their deficiencies.
2. They avoid the "common" mistakes described in the next section.
3. They bring a mindset and approach to project management that is best characterized by one or more of the following qualities:
    - **Takes Ownership**—Takes responsibility and accountability for the project; leads by example; brings energy and drive to the project; without this attitude, all the skills and techniques in the world will only get you so far.
    - **Savvy**—Understands people and the dynamics of the organization; navigates tricky politics; ability to quickly read and diffuse emotionally charged situations; thinks fast on the feet; builds relationships; leverages personal power for benefit of the project.
    - **Intensity with a Smile**—Balances an assertive, resilient, tenacious, results-oriented focus with a style that makes people want to help; consistently follows up on everything and their resolutions without "annoying" everyone.

- **Eye of the Storm**—Demonstrates ability to be the calm eye of the project hurricane; high tolerance for ambiguity; takes the heat from key stakeholders (CxOs, business managers, and project team); exhibits a calm, confident aura when others are showing signs of issue or project stress.
- **Strong customer-service orientation**—Demonstrates ability to see each stakeholder's perspective; ability to provide voice of all key stakeholders (especially the sponsor) to the project team; strong facilitation and collaboration skills; and excellent active listening skills.
- **People-focused**—Takes a team-oriented approach; understands that methodology, process, and tools are important, but without quality people it's very difficult to complete a project successfully.
- **Always keeps "eye on the ball"**—Stays focused on the project goals and objectives. There are many ways to accomplish a given objective. Especially important to remember when things don't go as planned.
- **"Controlled passion"**—Balances passion for completing the project objectives with a healthy detached perspective. This allows him or her to make better decisions, to continue to see all points of view, to better anticipate risks, and to better respond to project issues.
- **Healthy paranoia**— Balances a confident, positive outlook with a realism that assumes nothing, constantly questions, and verifies everything.
- **"Context" understanding**—Understands the context of the project—the priority that your project has among the organization's portfolio of projects and how it aligns with the overall goals of the organization.
- **Looking for trouble**—Constantly looking and listening for potential risks, issues, or obstacles; confronts doubt head-on; deals with disgruntled users right away; understands that most of these situations are opportunities and can be resolved up-front before they become full-scale crisis points.

15 Common Mistakes of Project Managers

While we review many of the common errors made in each of the fundamental areas of project management throughout this book (so you can avoid them), understanding the most common project management mistakes helps focus our efforts and help us to avoid the same mistakes on our projects. The following are some of the most common mistakes made by project managers:

1. Not clearly understanding how or ensuring the project is aligned with organizational objectives.
2. Not properly managing stakeholder expectations throughout the project.
3. Not gaining agreement and buy-in on project goals and success criteria from key stakeholders.
4. Not developing a realistic schedule that includes all work efforts, task dependencies, bottom-up estimates, and leveled assigned resources.
5. Not getting buy-in and acceptance on the project schedule.
6. Not clearly deciding and communicating who is responsible for what.
7. Not utilizing change control procedures to manage the scope of the project.
8. Not communicating consistently and effectively with all key stakeholders.
9. Not executing the project plan.
10. Not tackling key risks early in the project.
11. Not proactively identifying risks and developing contingency plans (responses) for those risks.
12. Not obtaining the right resources with the right skills at the right time.
13. Not aggressively pursuing issue resolution.
14. Inadequate requirements definition and management.
15. Insufficient management and leadership of project team.

The Absolute Minimum

At this point, you should have a high-level understanding of the following:

- The different roles played by the project manager
- The five key skill areas every project manager should master
- The common qualities of successful project managers
- The common mistakes made by project managers

The map in Figure 2.1 summarizes the main points we reviewed in this chapter.

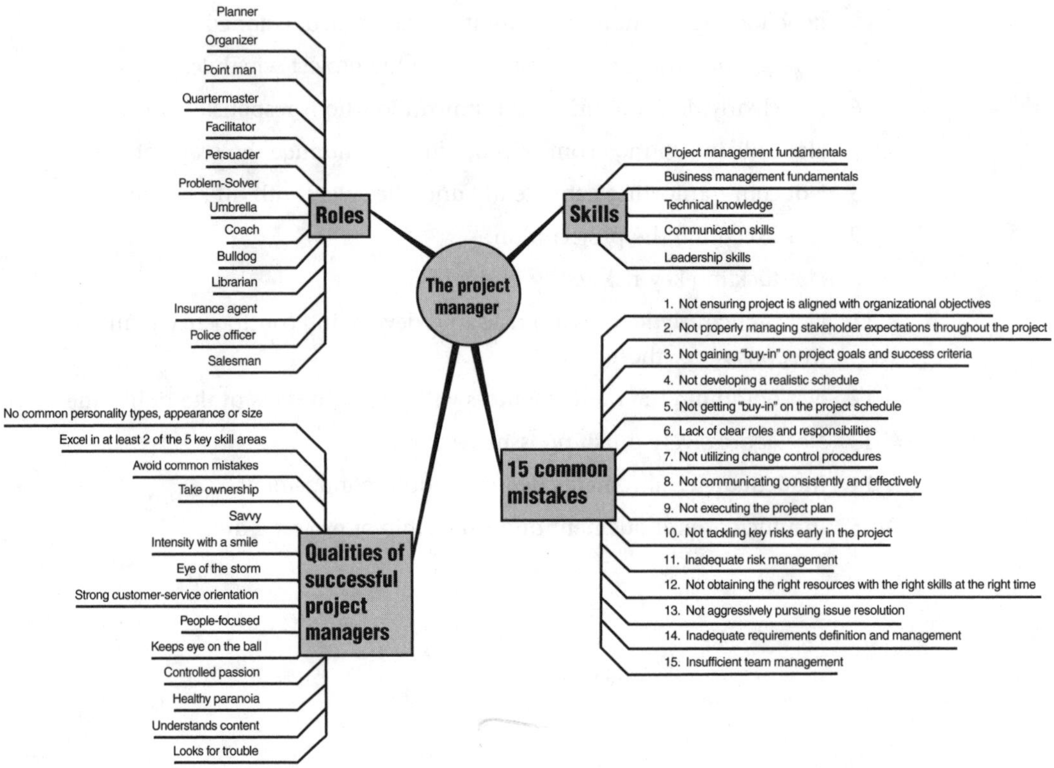

FIGURE 2.1

The Project manager overview.

IN THIS CHAPTER

- Learn what comprises a "successful" project
- Understand the common characteristics of "troubled" projects
- Review the common characteristics of successful projects
- Learn which tools are indispensable to most project managers

3

ESSENTIAL ELEMENTS FOR ANY SUCCESSFUL PROJECT

In this chapter, we want to continue the accelerated learning approach we started in the previous chapter. Anytime you are learning a new skill set, especially one that is as broad as project management, one of the most effective ways to reduce your learning curve and focus your mental energies is to understand what "successful" people do in the field, and, equally important, understand what not to do.

With this philosophy in mind, we will take a step up in this chapter and look at projects as a whole and not just the project manager position. We will review the leading causes of "troubled" projects, and we'll discuss the common principles, techniques, and tools underlying most successful projects. With this foundation in place, you will better understand the purpose and the value of the fundamentals covered in the rest of this book, and as a result, be much better positioned for success on your project management assignments.

What Exactly Is a "Successful" Project?

You would think it would be relatively straightforward to describe the attributes of a successful project. Well, let's just say this endeavor has kept more than a few "spin doctors," "politicians," and "history revisionists" employed throughout organizations across our great land. Why is this the case? There are several reasons for this.

- There is a lack of universal harmony of what comprises project success metrics. It seems that every project management educational source and organizational process maturity standard has a slightly different definition of project success.
- For many projects, the acceptance and success criteria are never established or agreed to by all key stakeholders.
- In many cases, an organization may define a project as successful even when some of the textbook criteria for project success (such as schedule, cost, and client expectations) are not completely met. This is often the case if the project achieved strategic business or organizational objectives.
- In other cases, a "cancelled" project may be a "successful" project if there was a plan for one or more "go/no-go" decision points.

From a utopian, academic standpoint, the "ultimate" successful project would be defined as a project that:

- **Delivered as promised**—Project produced all the stated deliverables.
- **Completed on-time**—Project completed within the approved schedule.
- **Completed within budget**—Project completed under the approved budget.
- **Delivered quality**—Project deliverables met all functional, performance, and quality specifications.
- **Achieved original purpose**—The project achieved its original goals, objectives, and purpose.
- **Met all stakeholder expectations**—The complete expectations of each key stakeholder were met, including all client acceptance criteria, and each key stakeholder accepts the project results without reservation.

tip

An excellent technique is to identify, document, review, and approve any criteria that will be used to measure the success of the project during the project definition and planning processes.

- **Maintains "win-win" relationships**—The needs of the project are met with a "people focus" and do not require sacrificing the needs of individual team members or vendors. Participants on successful projects should be enthusiastic when the project is complete and eager to repeat a similar experience.

Learning from Troubled Projects

Before we review the common traits of many successful projects, there's a lot to be learned from "less than successful" projects. From my experience, the reasons for project troubles can be generally classified in two groups: organizational-level issues and project-level issues.

One of the key differences in the two groups is the level of control that the project manager has over these factors. For project-level issues, the project manager has tremendous influence on these matters. In most cases, the project manager can either avoid the issue or take action to resolve it if it does occur. For organizational-level issues, the project manager cannot generally fix the problem, but the project manager can certainly have influence on them by asking the right questions, anticipating the associated risks and issues, focusing extra efforts to compensate for the issue, and developing contingency plans to minimize the impact on the project.

Also, please note that these issues are not exclusive. In most cases, there is overlap, and if you have one of these factors present in a project, you will generally have others. Table 3.1 summarizes these issues, gives specific examples of each, and notes what type of issue it is (organizational, project, or both).

Table 3.1 Common Reasons for Troubled Projects

Reason	Example(s)	Type	Key Learning Point
Project not aligned	Project not aligned with business unit or organizational goals; Project not aligned with other projects	Org.	Verify alignment before project kicks off
Lack of management support	Insufficient funding; Insufficient resources; Issues not resolved; Senior mgmt performance criteria not aligned with project success criteria	Org.	Understand project impact of organizational structure; Ensure proper senior mgmt involvement in project organization; Advocate PMO and Steering Committee structures

Table 3.1 (continued)

Reason	Example(s)	Type	Key Learning Point
Lack of stakeholder "buy-in"	Purpose and goals not clear; "Trust" relationship not established; Inadequate communications; Mismatched expectations; All stakeholders not involved	Both	Gain acceptance of project purpose, goals, and success criteria up front; Ensure all stakeholders are identified and consulted; Constantly communicate and validate understanding
Inadequate project sponsor	Inactive, unengaged sponsor; Lack of leadership; Ethical issues; Not handling organizational issues; Not supportive of project management process	Org.	Educate the sponsor on their roles and responsibilities; Gain formal authorization of project and the project manager position; Understand sponsor's motives and incentives
Too many project sponsors	Conflicting project goals; Lack of ownership; Political battles	Org.	Relates to the need for proper project alignment and clear roles and responsibilities
Lack of clarity on roles and responsi-bilities	Inefficient work efforts; Missed deadlines; Lower team morale; Delayed issue resolution	Both	Use *Responsibility Matrix* to clarify all roles and responsibilities; Review roles and responsi-bilities with each individual; Validate expectations in advance
Poor communi-cation	Inconsistent, incomplete, or nonexistent status information on key project metrics; Inadequate tracking and monitoring of project progress; Not listening to stakeholder concerns or feedback; Not using proper mediums for certain project communications; Messages are not clear or occur too frequently	Project	Develop a project Communications Plan that is acceptable to all stakeholders; Establish tracking and monitoring mechanisms during planning; Constantly seek questions and feedback; Understand each stake holder's perspective; Clearly set context of each message
Price wars	Due to budget reduction measures or market pressures, management agrees to perform project at or below estimated costs	Org.	Develop complete, detailed project budgets; Communicate associated risks; Improve negotiating skills

Table 3.1 (continued)

Reason	Example(s)	Type	Key Learning Point
Resource conflicts	Lack of dedicated team members; Key resources not available when scheduled	Org.	Develop project Resource Plan; Gain commitments from Resource Managers; Encourage centralized organizational structure for resource planning/deployment
Inadequate project manager	Lack of leadership; Inexperienced or untrained project manager; Ineffective project manager	Both	Organizational commitment to PM education; Use of PM mentorship programs
Under-estimate change impact	Not understanding the complete effects on both and people existing processes that the "change" introduced by the project will have; Not properly preparing or planning for the "change"	Org.	Use project sponsor and business process owners to champion the new process; Involve additional stakeholders to understand their needs and to solicit their support; Plan for the necessary communications and training (change management plan); Plan for the "disruptive" deployment period; Utilize pilot approaches to minimize impact
Inadequate planning	Management does not require or allow time for proper planning; Incomplete scope or deliverables list; Incomplete "work" identification; Lack of detailed schedule; Inadequate risk identification; Assumptions not documented; Lack of schedule and budget contingency	Both	Educate senior mgmt on the value of proper planning; Use standard methodology for project planning; Gain formal acceptance of Project Plan before proceeding; Develop realistic project schedule and budget, as well as tools and processes to keep updated; Identify and document project risks and mitigation strategies

Table 3.1 (continued)

Reason	Example(s)	Type	Key Learning Point
Lack of change control management	Scope of work increases without proper schedule, budget, or resource adjustments; Changes occur to deliverables, schedule, or budget without proper notification and approval	Project	Utilize formal change control procedures to properly assess and communicate any change to the scope, schedule, budget, and targeted project deliverable
Lack of completion criteria	Missed stakeholder expectations; Increased costs or missed deadlines due to re-work; Lack of smooth transition from one phase to another	Both	Ensure success criteria is established during planning phase; Define user acceptance criteria for project deliverables; Define exit criteria for project phases
Inadequate progress tracking	Inability to measure project status and probability for success; Inability to review project at key points to make go/no-go decisions	Both	Establish and execute periodic status meetings and reporting (weekly in most cases); Review project at scheduled intervals against established criteria to determine if project should progress into next phase
Unforeseen technical difficulties	Effort spent resolving technical issues drive missed schedules and increased costs; Unproven technology does not meet user expectations	Project	Structure project to deal with high risk technical challenges early in the project; Prove the technology before making additional investment; Leverage technical expertise to support team capabilities

Learning from Successful Projects

After reviewing what makes a project successful and the common ills that befall many troubled projects, you likely have a good sense of the qualities and traits shared by most successful projects. While no two projects are ever the same, and every project has its own

caution

A good project manager can still end up managing a "troubled" project. Sometimes, your best project management work may be in minimizing the damage from a "troubled" project.

unique set of challenges, there is a common core of principles that successful projects share. By understanding these, a new project manager can better prioritize and better focus his/her project management efforts. These qualities are generally true about successful projects:

- Project is aligned with organizational goals.
- Project has effective management support.
- Project has effective leadership.
- All key stakeholders are in agreement on the purpose, goals, and objectives of the project.
- All key stakeholders share a common vision on the project results.
- All key stakeholders share *realistic* expectations for the project results.
- The project results meet the expectations of the key stakeholders.
- Stakeholder expectations are constantly managed and validated throughout the project.
- There is an investment made in proper planning.
- The project scope, approach, and deliverables are clearly defined and agreed upon during planning.
- Each stakeholder and team member's role(s) and responsibilities are clearly communicated and understood.
- A high priority is placed on accurate and complete work effort estimates.
- A realistic schedule is developed and agreed upon.
- The project team has a strong results-focus and customer-orientation.
- Project communications are consistent, effective, and focused on "understanding."
- Project progress is measured consistently from the current baseline.
- Project issues and subsequent action items are aggressively pursued.
- There is a strong sense of collaboration and teamwork.
- Expectations and changes surrounding scope, quality, schedule, and cost are closely managed.

- Project resources are skilled and available when needed.
- Project team proactively identifies risk and determines mitigation strategies to reduce project exposure.
- Project team anticipates and overcomes obstacles to ensure project meets objectives.

Essential Project Manager Toolkit

While there are many facets of project management and many lessons to be learned from both troubled projects and successful projects, there is an essential set of tangible tools that any project manager needs to have to best manage any project. Table 3.2 lists these essential tools and why they are important.

The important principles to remember regarding project management tools are as follows:

- Any planning document needs to be reviewed and agreed to by appropriate project stakeholders and team members.
- Separate documents are not always needed. Smaller projects might combine relevant information (especially "plan" documents) into a single "grouped" document.
- The essential tools represent the key information and thought processes that are needed to effectively manage the project.

Table 3.2 Essential Project Manager Tools

Tool	Description	Value	Notes
Project Charter	Authorizes project and the project manager	Provides official notice to the organization	May not always be a formal document; At a minimum, get an email notification
Project Definition Document	Defines project purpose, objectives, success criteria, and scope statement	Key for managing expectations, controlling scope, and completing other planning efforts	Core tool
Requirements Document	Defines the specifications for product/output of the project	Key for managing expectations and controlling scope	Core tool

Table 3.2 (continued)

Tool	Description	Value	Notes
Project Schedule	Shows all work efforts, properly estimated, with logical dependencies, assigned to responsible resources scheduled against a calendar	Key for directing all project team work efforts; Key for managing expectations; Allows for impact and what-if simulations when things change	Core tool
Status Reports	Periodic reviews of actual performance versus expected performance	Provides essential information to stakeholders; Allows for timely identification of performance variances	See Chapter 10, "Controlling a Project," and Chapter 17, "Managing Project Communications," for more details
Milestone Chart	A summary of the detailed project schedule showing progress against key milestone	Allows stakeholders to see high level project progress on one page	Detailed schedule roll-ups can be difficult to read and interpret; Incorporate into Status Report
Project Organization Chart	Shows all project stakeholders and the working relationships among them	Allows team members to get a better understanding of project roles and organizational dynamics	On smaller projects, may be combined with project plan or project definition document
Responsibility Matrix	Defines all project roles and indicates what responsibilities each role has	Key for managing expectations; Establishes accountability	On smaller projects, may be combined with project plan or project definition document
Communication Plan	Defines the how, what, when, and who regarding the flow of project information to stakeholders	Key for managing expectations; Establishes buy-in	On smaller projects, may be combined with project plan or project definition document

Table 3.2 (continued)

Tool	Description	Value	Notes
Quality Management Plan	Defines the approaches and methods that will be utilized to manage the quality levels of project processes and results	Key for managing expectations regarding quality, performance, and regulatory compliance matters; Impacts work efforts and project schedule Establishes accountability	On smaller projects, may be combined with project plan or project definition document
Staffing Management Plan	Lists how project resources will be acquired, when they are needed, how much they are needed, and how long they will be needed	Key for building schedule; Key for properly managing resources	May also include role profiles, rates, training needs; On smaller projects, may be combined with project plan or project schedule
Risk Response Plan	Lists each identified risk and the planned response strategy for each	Communicates potential issues in advance; Proactive measures help reduce impact to project	On smaller projects, may be combined with project plan or project definition document
Project Plan	Formal, approved document that is used to manage project execution	Includes all other supplemental planning documents; Key output of project planning	On smaller projects, may be combined with project definition document
Deliverable Summary	Defines and lists all deliverables to be produced by the project	Key to managing expectations; Ensures proper visibility, tracking, and reporting of targeted deliverables	May be combined with status reports

Table 3.2 (continued)

Tool	Description	Value	Notes
Project Log	Captures essential information for each project risk, issue, action item, and change request	Ensures proper visibility, tracking, and reporting of items impacting the project	Core tool
Change Request Form	Captures essential information for any requested change that impacts scope, schedule, or budget	Allows change item to be properly assessed and communicated before action is taken	Core tool
Project Notebook	Used by project manager to maintain official record of important project documents and deliverables	Part of managing project information	Electronic and/or hardcopy versions

The Absolute Minimum

At this point, you should have a solid understanding of the following:

- What defines a successful project and why it is not always easy to measure
- The common reasons why projects get in trouble and what you can do to avoid them
- The key principles that serve as the foundation for most successful projects
- The essential project management tools and why they are important

The map in Figure 3.1 summarizes the main points we reviewed in this chapter.

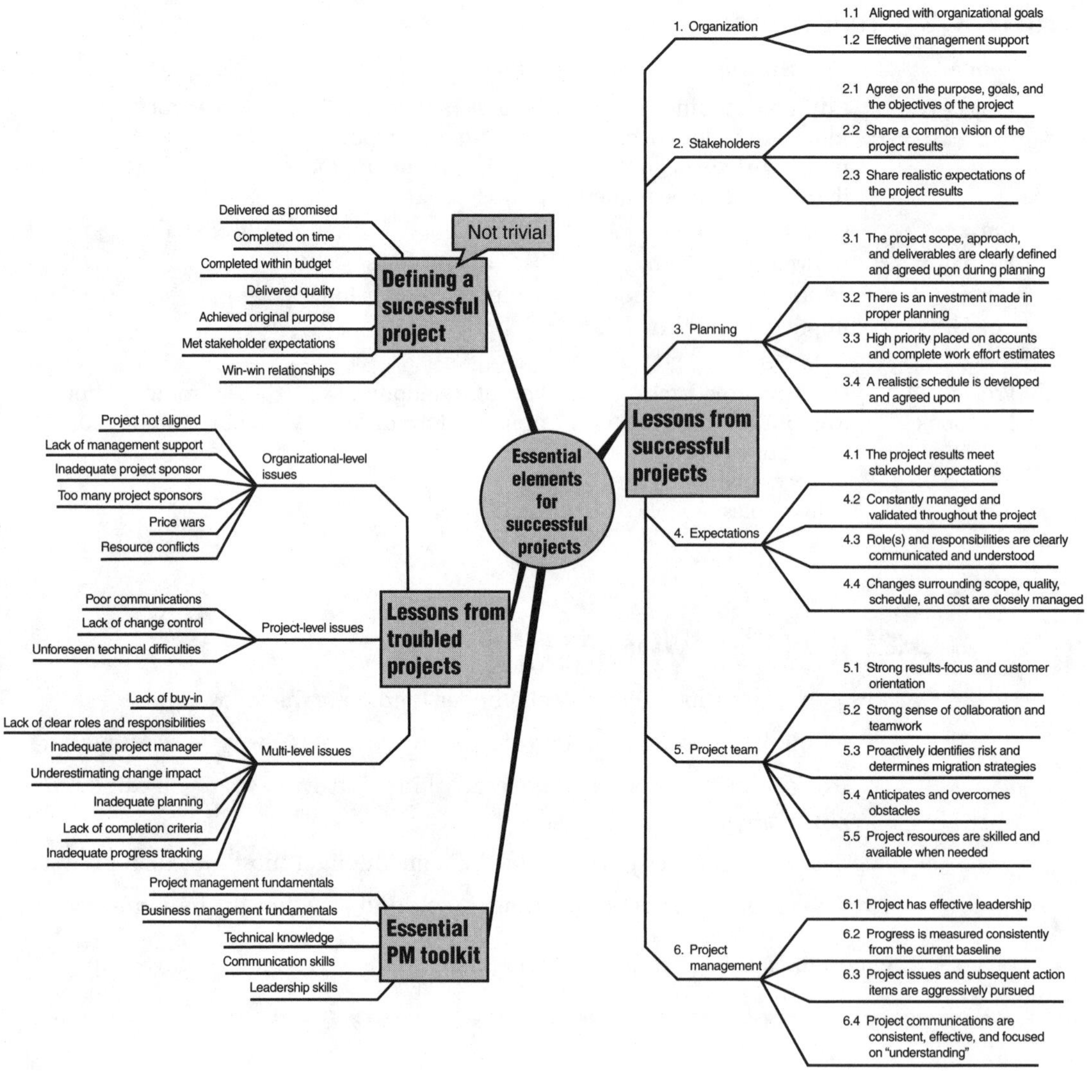

FIGURE 3.1

Essential elements for any successful project overview.

PART II

PROJECT PLANNING

IN THIS CHAPTER

- Understand the importance of defining a project correctly
- Learn what questions must be answered to properly define a project
- Understand how defining a project relates to planning a project
- Review the essential elements for a Project Definition document
- Learn how to determine whether a project has been properly defined

4

DEFINING A PROJECT

The journey begins...

The first stop on our journey down Project Management Boulevard is also the most important, because it builds the foundation for all other project management activities and sets the stage for our eventual project success (or failure).

The irony of this is that depending on your organization and industry, you (the project manager) may be the primary agent in getting this done, or you may not be involved at all until after project definition is complete.

In either case, you need to know how to properly define a project and how to evaluate if a project definition performed by others is complete before starting any detailed project planning efforts.

With all this in mind, we will review the critical importance this step plays, the key questions that must be answered and agreed upon, the "must-have" elements of your Project Definition document, and the success criteria for the project definition process.

Setting the Stage for Success

Pick your cliché of choice here: "getting everyone on the same page," "singing from the same songbook," "dancing to the same beat," "pointed in the same direction," and "painting the picture." They all apply, and they all communicate the importance of getting the key project participants to agree on the answers to these seven basic project definition questions:

1. Why are we doing this? (Purpose)
2. What organizational level goal(s) does this project support? (Goals and Objectives)
3. How does this project fit with the other projects that are going on? (Scope, Project Context, Project Dependencies)
4. What is the expected benefit from this project? (Expected Benefits, Business Case, Value, Success Criteria)
5. What are we going to do? (Scope)
6. Who is impacted by this and who must be involved? (Stakeholders)
7. How will we know when we are done or whether the project was successful? (Success Criteria)

Gaining consensus on these questions is paramount to managing the organizational level factors that get projects in trouble (such as alignment with organization and management support) and to controlling key project level factors that impact project success: stakeholder expectations and scope management.

How Does Defining a Project Relate to Project Planning?

Many people think of "defining a project" as part of the project planning process, and they are correct. It is the first step. However, it is important to make the distinction for several reasons:

- Logistically, before you develop a detailed and complete project plan, you need to know the parameters and boundaries for the project.
- Politically, you need to know the key stakeholders are all in agreement with the project mission (project purpose, goals, objectives, and success criteria) before proceeding forward.

As with all project management processes, the time and rigor invested should be consistent with the size and risk level of the project.

As a general guideline, 20% of the total project duration should be invested in definition and planning activities.

- Practically, the work to properly define a project is often not trivial. In fact, many process-focused and disciplined organizations handle "project definitions" as separate projects. Common examples include business case development projects, cost-benefit analysis projects, selection projects, and assessment projects.
- Historically, people have learned that detailed project planning and general project management are inefficient, and difficult at best, if project definition is not performed.
- Financially, effective execution of the project definition process enables the organization to leverage portfolio project management processes. This allows the organization to better invest their limited resources into initiatives that offer the greatest return.

PORTFOLIO PROJECT MANAGEMENT

Portfolio project management is a management practice that brings rigor and diligence to the project definition process. It is a management practice that allows executives to make better decisions regarding which projects to fund, gives them visibility to all targeted enterprise projects throughout the project lifecycle, and applies a consistent set of performance metrics and criteria to better compare project performance. It is a management practice that attempts to bring an end to projects that are not organizationally aligned, not prioritized, not resourced properly, and not monitored closely. Some of the key benefits of this approach to an organization include

- Requires each potential project to be fully defined up front.
- Engages the executives in the project selection and prioritization process, using a consistent, objective approach.
- Ensures that individual work efforts are prioritized and focused on most important projects.
- Maintains executive visibility on targeted projects. This helps maintain organizational alignment.
- Allows executives to identify "troubled" projects earlier. This provides them more options, and it allows them to re-allocate valuable resources much quicker.

caution

There are many different names for the Project Definition document. Some of the most common alternative names are Project Brief, Project Charter, Project Initiation, Scope Statement, and Statement of Work.

We are using Project Definition, because this term best describes the purpose of the document.

Project Definition Document

We've referred to "gaining consensus" and "getting agreement" on the answers to the important project defining questions several times. How do you do this? You write them down and get everyone to formally sign off on this document. We will refer to this document as the *Project Definition* document. In this section, we will review both the "must-have" elements and "good to have" elements of the Project Definition document.

tip

Whenever you define what is "in scope", it's a good idea to note what related work is "out of scope." This helps clarify understanding and expectations regarding project scope. As a rule, any work item related to your defined scope that someone could assume is included, but is not, should be listed as "out-of-scope."

Required Elements

First, let's review the must-have informational elements that should be included in your Project Definition document.

- **Purpose**—This section should answer the "Why?" question and clearly communicate the expected business value. It should reference the organizational objective being supported, the business problem being solved, and its relative priority level.
- **Goals and Objectives**—This section is derived from the Purpose and communicates the targeted outcomes for the project. It should answer the "What are you going to accomplish?" question.
- **Success Criteria**—Closely related to Goals and Objectives, this section should list the measurable, verifiable results that will determine the success level of this project. This section is often referred to as Critical Success Factors.
- **Project Context**—Documents how this project relates to other projects within the product program and within the organization as a whole. This section should also describe how the project fits within the organization and business process flow.
- **Project Dependencies**—Closely related to Project Context, this section clearly documents any dependencies that could impact the results or success factors of this project.
- **Scope Specifications**—Clearly designates the organizational, process, systems, and functional specification boundaries for the project. Should be high-level breakdown of the Goals and Objectives.
- **Out-of-Scope Specifications**—To better communicate what is considered to be "in scope," it is recommended that you clearly indicate the high level work items that are related (or associated) to this initiative, but that are not part of this project.

- **Assumptions**—This section clearly communicates the underlying basis or things to be considered true in regards to any other aspect of this document. In most cases, the Scope, Out-of-Scope, Assumptions, and Constraints sections combine to clearly define what work will be performed by this project.
- **Constraints**—This section lists any business event, schedule, budgetary, resource, or technical factor that will limit the options available to the project.
- **Risks**—This section lists any uncertain event or condition (risk) that, if it occurs, could have a negative impact on one or more project success criterion (schedule, budget, quality, and so on). For each risk, it is good to list the related causes, the perceived negative impacts, the likelihood it will occur, and the planned response strategy and action items. See Chapter 14, "Managing Project Risks," for more details.
- **Stakeholders**—This section lists all the individuals, business units, and organizations involved in the project, the role(s) each is expected to play, and an indication of how they relate to one another. A Project Organization chart and a Stakeholder-Role Description Table is highly recommended here.
- **Recommended Project Approach**—To better describe the intent of the initiative, this section highlights the recommended approach to getting the work of the project done and why it was selected over any other options. This section should note any key strategies, methodologies, and technologies to be used.

To expedite the process of getting agreement on the Project Definition document, walk through an initial draft that you develop with the stakeholder group rather than starting with a blank slate.

The process of project definition and project planning is a process of iterative refinement (or what PMI refers to as *progressive elaboration*), so your draft will help facilitate the discussions, negotiations, and modifications that need to occur amongst the stakeholders.

Additional Elements to Consider

These are informational elements that may not always apply, but if appropriate, are recommended additions to Project Definition document.

- **Alternative Project Approaches**—This section lists the approach details for any alternatives that were considered.
- **Organizational Change Issues**—Because most projects result in a change to the status quo, and the most common oversight in projects is not

adequately realizing, planning, and preparing for the "change" impact to current customers, business processes, and personnel, it is highly recommended that this area be a focus from the start of the project.

caution

The Project Definition document is a "living" document and should be updated to reflect the evolving circumstances, issues, and needs surrounding the project.

Changes are okay. The changes just need to be announced, reviewed, and approved by the relevant stakeholders.

- **Policies and Standards**—Given the priority that standardization, compliance, process improvement, security, and quality have in most organizations, it is highly recommended that any policy, regulation, or standard that will be applied to the project or the results of the project be identified from the start of the project.
- **Preliminary Cost, Schedule, and Resource Estimates**—Generally, there is some preliminary "ballpark" expectation for the cost, timing, and resource needs of this project. In many cases, these will be noted as either project objectives or as project constraints. The most valuable information here is not necessarily the date or the dollar amount, but an explanation for what is driving the figures presented.
- **References to Supporting Documents**—For any situation, where the results of a preliminary or related project served to define the need or details for this project, always include a reference to those supporting documents. Common examples would be a Business Case, Cost-Benefit Analysis, Assessment Results, Requirements Document, and Business Process Engineering Studies.
- **Visual Scope Summary**—For most projects, a visual summary of the project scope can be an invaluable tool for communicating the objectives, boundaries, and "change" elements of the project. It can help validate the definition of the project, identify potential risks, and greatly improve the common understanding of the project stakeholders. Especially for any project that is introducing significant change, the effort to create this visual summary is one of the best investments you'll make.

tip

Use a visual project scope summary to gain a clearer picture of project purpose, context, goals, and change impact amongst key stakeholders.

The creation of a visual scope summary definitely falls into the "art" part of project management—there is not a single way to do this. The specific tool/medium used can vary depending on skill set and tools available. The specific approach depends on the nature of the project. For product and construction projects, a prototype or visual drawing of the target can be used. For projects impacting business processes, a variant of a flow diagram (process, data, system) showing current state and proposed future state can be very effective. There is no right answer—you just need to be effective.

Project Definition Checklist

Here's a checklist that can help you to determine whether your project is defined properly and whether you are ready to proceed to the next iteration of detailed planning. If you find that your project is not properly defined, you have the following options available:

- Resolve any gaps with appropriate stakeholders before moving on to the next phase.
- If the project has already been defined, work to resolve these gaps during the detail planning phase.
- If gaps cannot be resolved, then handle as project risks or issues (whichever is appropriate for the specific gap).

tip

For anyone who has not attended a Goal Setting 101 course, let's do a quick review of SMART goals.

Actually, I've seen two different definitions of SMART goals, and they both apply:

- Definition #1—SMART goals are **S**pecific, **M**easurable, **A**chievable, **R**ewarding, and **T**ime-based.
- Definition #2—SMART goals are **S**pecific, **M**easurable, **A**greed-To, **R**ealistic, and **T**ime-based.

Perhaps, the acronym should be SMAARRT. For projects, the second definition is more important due to the "Agreed-To" element.

General

- Is it clear why this is project is being undertaken?
- Is there a clear picture of the desired results of this project?
- Is there a clear picture of how this project fits within the organizational landscape?
- Is there a gap between available and needed funds?
- Have the success factors been identified? Are they complete? Are they SMART?
- Have any future state performance targets been defined as success factors? Are they SMART?

- Is the gap between the current state and the desired future state clearly documented and understood?
- Has the expected "change impact" on existing business processes, customers, systems and staff been clearly documented?
- Do you understand who is funding the project initiative?

Scope

- Does project scope indicate boundaries among impacted processes, systems, and organizations?
- Is project scope defined clearly enough to show when scope creep is occurring?
- Have any external process or system interfaces that will be impacted by this project been identified?
- Has the process workflow between business units or business functions been properly considered?
- Have the organizational and geographic boundaries been clearly defined?
- Does project scope include related items that are out-of-scope?
- Does project scope include any other organizational or technology-based initiative that is needed to fully support the project objective?
- If project scope includes any requirements, have the requirements been properly validated?
- Have any and all project constraints been identified?
- Have any and all project assumptions been identified?
- Are there any known policies, regulations, or standards that will apply to this project (such as procurement, quality, security, regulatory compliance, and so on)?

Stakeholders

- Has the project sponsor been identified and engaged?
- Is each impacted business unit and business process step represented on the project team?
- Is each customer group represented on the project team?

tip

Use a *Project Organization Chart* to effectively summarize the project team members and the key stakeholders (see Chapter 5).

- Are all stakeholders identified in a project organization chart?
- Are the reporting relationships indicated in the project organization chart?
- Are project roles described and assigned to each stakeholder?
- Have we identified which stakeholders will form the core management steering committee?
- Have we identified which stakeholders will need to review and approve any requested changes to the project definition?

Project Approach

- Does the recommended approach explain why it was selected over the alternatives?
- Are the proposed technologies, strategies, and methodologies documented?

> **caution**
>
> As with all project documents, make sure you have a way to control changes to the Project Definition document and that you have proper backups of it.
>
> Your Configuration Management Plan (discussed in Chapter 12, "Managing Project Deliverables") will document this.

Other

- Are the project definition elements documented?
- Is the Project Definition document under configuration management (version control)?
- Have high level risks and planned responses been identified?
- Have preliminary timeline and budget been stated? Are the supporting reasons and assumptions documented?

Acceptance

- Have all stakeholders reviewed, agreed upon, and approved the Project Definition document?
- Has the project and the project manager been officially authorized?

THE ABSOLUTE MINIMUM

At this point, you should have a solid understanding of the following:

- A properly defined project greatly increases the odds for project success.
- The project and the project manager position should be officially announced and formally authorized to proceed.
- The primary project management tool for defining a project is the Project Definition document.
- The key skills used by the project manager when defining a project are facilitation, interviewing, negotiation, and general interpersonal skills.
- The Project Definition document should clearly communicate why the project is being undertaken, how it fits within the organization, what it will accomplish, the boundaries for the project work, who will be involved, and how project success will be measured.
- Two effective visual tools for communicating the definition of a project are the Project Overview Map and the Project Organization Chart.
- The Project Definition document is a living document throughout the project. However, any changes to the document must be approved by the same set of original stakeholders.
- All stakeholders in the project must be identified.
- All major stakeholders must approve the Project Definition document.

The map in Figure 4.1 summarizes the main points we reviewed in this chapter.

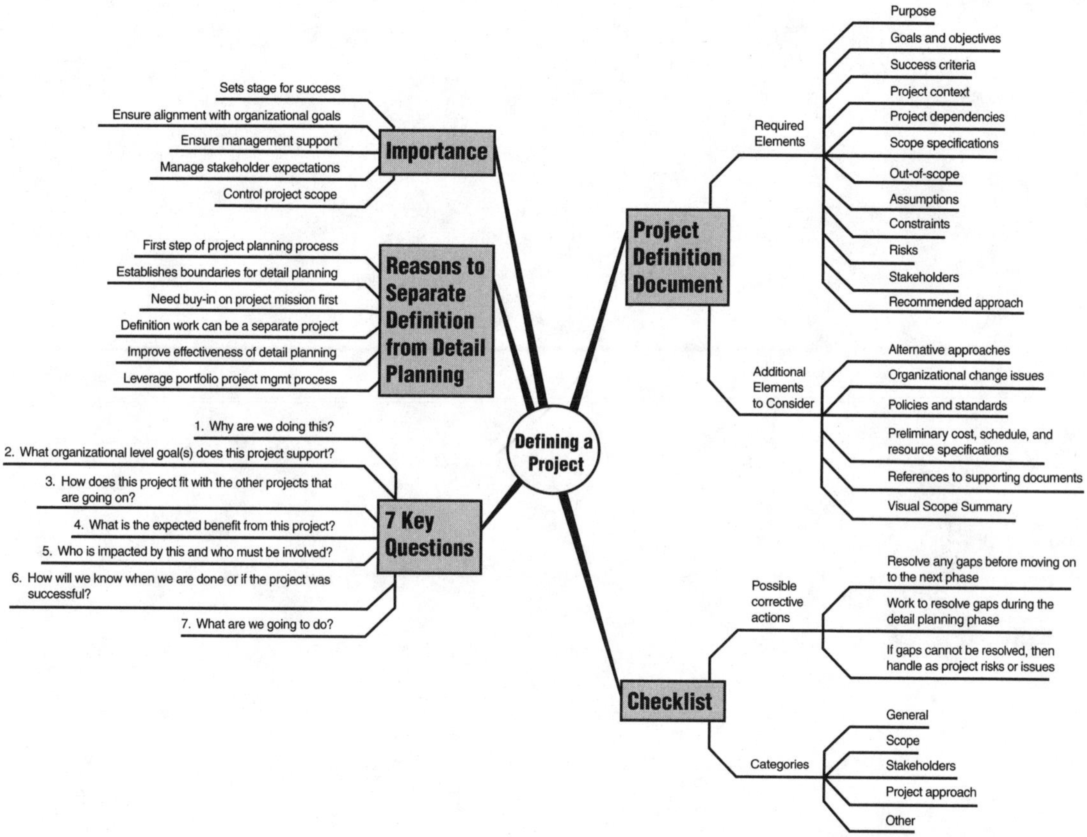

FIGURE 4.1

Defining a project overview.

In This Chapter

- Understand the key principles of effective project planning
- Learn the important questions that project planning should answer
- Understand that a project plan is not a Microsoft Project file
- Review the essential elements for a project plan
- Learn how to develop a project plan
- Learn how to avoid the common project planning mistakes

5

Planning a Project

The journey continues…

As is true with defining a project, project planning is essential for project success. In defining a project, we ensure that we agree on *what* we will do and who will be involved. In planning a project, we focus on *how* the work will be done. This involves both how the deliverables will be developed and how the project will be managed. Thus, project planning involves the traditional areas of work tasks, resources, schedule, and costs, and it also sets the stage for managing project changes, project communications, project quality, project risks, project procurement activities, and the project team. Each of these factors directly impact stakeholder expectations and our ability to successfully control and execute the project.

Unfortunately, there are many misconceptions about project planning, and often it is performed incompletely or incorrectly.

With this in mind, we will review the key principles of project planning, how to properly plan a project, the key planning questions that must be answered and agreed upon, the "must-have" elements of your Project Plan document, and the success criteria for the project planning process.

A planning technique that is often used to deal with the "realities" of planning project work is called *rolling wave planning*. Rolling wave planning is a technique that plans work *details only* for the *next* project phase. The planning for the subsequent phases is kept at a high level. As part of the closing process and review of the current phase, the work details for the next phase are then planned out.

Key Project Planning Principles

While most reasonable people will, at least, acknowledge there is value to "planning" at a logical level, many of those same people are less than "emotionally committed" to the practice. Why is this? Generally, it is because the "project planning" they have previously witnessed has violated one or more of the following key project planning principles.

- **Purpose**—The purpose of project planning is to develop a plan that enables the project to be executed and controlled, as shown in Figure 5.1.

FIGURE 5.1

Highlights the interactions between the planning, executing, and controlling project management processes.

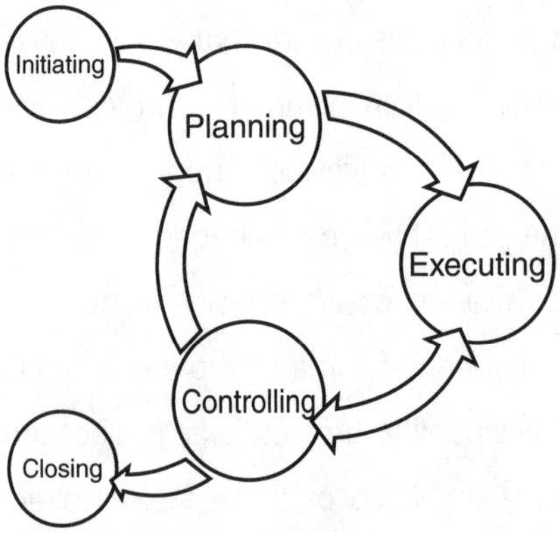

- **Multiple passes required**—Project planning is not a one-time activity performed at the beginning of a project. For starters, it generally takes several iterations to get to a comprehensive plan given the multitude of inputs that must be integrated and the number of stakeholders that need to agree on the plan. In addition, as things happen and we learn more, plans will need to be adjusted and details ironed out as the project moves along.

- **A project plan is NOT a Microsoft Project file**—Before we go any further, let's make sure we are clear on a few key terms. A project plan is not a project schedule or a Work Breakdown Structure (WBS). A project plan is an all-encompassing document used as the basis for controlling and executing a project.
- **Give me one**—The planning exercise and the planning team must have control over one of the traditional project success factors (scope, time, cost, or performance). Senior management can set all but one of these factors—just not all of them.
- **"Proactive" project management**—Effective planning enables a "proactive" project management approach. Before the execution of the project gets underway, we ask the questions and determine the approaches we will take to manage the project and stakeholder expectations regarding project communications, stakeholder responsibilities, quality management, risks, responses to specific performance variances, procurement management, and project team management.
- **Stay down from the mountain"**—Project planning is not the time for the top-down, Mount Olympus approach to management. Project planning is the time for questions, facilitation, interaction, and feedback.

  Specifically, you need to conduct a *stakeholder analysis* on all your management and customer stakeholders to validate the project definition elements, understand their expectations and communication needs, and to review procedures for dealing with critical issues, risks, change requests, and performance variances.

note

A project plan is an all-encompassing document that is used as the basis for controlling and executing a project.

caution

A Microsoft Project file (or anything else resembling a project schedule, timeline, or WBS) is not a project plan.

A project plan generally references other documents and supplemental plans, including a WBS and project schedule.

tip

Change control, communications, risk, and quality project management are excellent examples of *proactive* project management.

The team approach to project planning greatly increases its acceptance and commitment level to the project plan.

In addition, the team members who will be *doing* the work should be heavily involved in *defining* and *estimating* the details of the work to be performed. We address this further in Chapter 6, "Developing the Work Breakdown Structure" and Chapter 7, "Estimating the Work." This approach leads to a better definition of the work required and a higher commitment level toward scheduled work assignments.

Important Questions Project Planning Should Answer

Think of project planning as a process of "asking questions" and working with your team to "get the answers." Although the process of defining a project answers some key fundamental questions to get us started, such as

- Why are we doing this project?
- What is the project supposed to accomplish?
- Who are the key stakeholders? The sponsor? The customers?

It is the process of "detail planning" a project that allows us to answer the questions we need addressed to implement and manage the project. These important questions focus on both the work to produce the targeted deliverables and on the work to manage the project. Some of these key questions include the following:

- How exactly will the deliverables be produced?
- What work tasks must be performed to produce the deliverables?
- Who will do the work?
- What other resources (facilities, tools) will we need to do the work?
- Where will the work occur?
- How long will it take to do the work?
- When will the work be done?
- How much will this project cost?
- What skills, skill levels, and experience are needed for each role? When do I need them?
- When do I need each resource? How do I get resources?
- Who is responsible and accountable for what?
- How will changes be controlled?

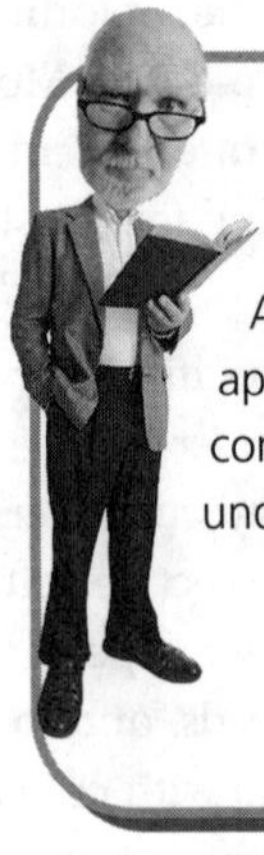

tip

Always get sign-off from appropriate stakeholders to confirm agreement and understanding.

- How do I ensure acceptable quality in deliverables and in the process?
- How will I keep stakeholders informed, get their feedback, and what mediums are best?
- How will I track issues? How will critical issues be escalated?
- How do we handle variances? What is the threshold for senior management? What communication needs to occur?
- What risks exist? What are our response strategies?
- How will version control be conducted?
- How will project information be maintained and secured?
- How will I manage the project team? What training needs exist? How will their performance be evaluated? How will I orient any new team member?
- If we are leveraging external resources (vendors, suppliers), how do we manage their performance?
- How will project performance be measured and reported?
- And ultimately, do I have a plan that will allow me to execute and control this project?

As we determine these answers, we capture them in the project plan. We can then review the project plan with our key stakeholders to ensure we have agreement and understanding. Next, let's step through a typical project plan, review what each section is for, and determine how we go about getting this information.

tip

As you visit with stakeholders during detail planning, make sure to validate their project definition understanding and expectation.

Re-confirm that the business case for the project is still valid after the detailed project planning exercise is complete.

Building a Project Plan

The first step in building a project plan is to validate the elements of the project definition document. Depending on the length of time between acceptance of the project definition and the start of detail planning, you may need to confirm that there have been no changes in the purpose, objectives, success criteria, and scope of the project with your key stakeholders.

- **Validate project definition**—This section should reference the project definition document and includes all required elements of a project definition document. The key task here is to revalidate the business case for the project. This is especially important if there has been a time lag between project definition and detail project planning, or if the planning exercise results in time and cost estimates significantly greater than originally estimated during project definition.

tip

To simplify the review process and to minimize future document modifications, capture any information that is shared, needs to be reviewed separately, or is likely to be updated frequently in its own document. Common examples are assumptions, WBS, communications plan, project schedule, requirements, project organization chart, and responsibility matrix.

- **Determine what needs to be done**—This section should provide any additional details regarding the project approach (how this will be done), the targeted deliverables that will be produced, and all the work that is required to complete the project. This process is explained in greater detail in Chapter 6.

  This section normally refers to a list of deliverables and to the WBS.

- **Determine acceptance criteria**—This information can be part of other components, such as deliverables list, WBS, project approach, or quality management plan, and may not be its own section. However, to validate that all required work has been identified and to improve the quality of work estimates, it is best to clearly document (somewhere in the project plan) what the acceptance criteria is for each deliverable and for each project phase.

- **Determine resource needs**—Based upon the tasks and activities that need to be performed, determine the type and quantity of resources needed. Resources include people (roles), facilities, and tools. These resource needs should be determined when developing the WBS with the team members who will be doing the work.

  To assist the acquisition and management of these resources, all resource needs should be documented (resource management plan). For people resources, document the role description and the prerequisite skills, skill levels, and experience.

  As part of the scheduling process, the timing of resource needs should be noted and finalized in the resource management plan. A sample resource management plan is illustrated in Figure 5.2.

- **Acquire resources**—After the resource needs are documented, you can now begin the process of acquiring those resources. The key questions to be answered here are

  - Will I be able to get the "quality" of resource requested?
  - Will I be able to get this resource in-house or will I need to obtain it from an external supplier/vendor?

- Will the resource be available when needed?
- How will this impact my cost estimates and budget?

FIGURE 5.2
Basic example of a resource management plan.

Role	Team Member	Training Needs	Projected Start Date	Projected Roll-off Date	Percent Allocation
Technical Leader	B Gates	• Advanced Enterprise Web Development	6/1/2007	10/30/2007	80%
Business Process Leader	S Jones	• Process Modeling • Power PowerPoint User	6/1/2007	10/30/2007	100%
Lead Developer	L Gregory	• Advanced Enterprise Web Development	6/15/2007	10/30/2007	100%
Lead Analyst	E Michael	• Rational Test Studio	6/1/2007	10/30/2007	100%
Test Manager	Q Victoria	• Advanced Load Testing	6/15/2007	10/30/2007	100%
Developer	R Alexander	• Accelerated OO Development	7/15/2007	9/30/2007	100%

- **Estimate the work**—After we know what all the work activities are, and we know what level of resource will be doing the work, we can now estimate the effort and duration for each activity. Due to the critical importance and difficulty of this step, we review this in greater detail in Chapter 7.
- **Develop the schedule**—Now that we understand the required resources and estimated effort for each work task, we are now in position to identify the relationships between these tasks and build a schedule to complete the work. Due to the critical importance and common errors in this step, we review this in greater detail in Chapter 8, "Developing the Project Schedule."

  At a minimum, schedule information should be available in at least one

The responsibility matrix is often referred to as a RACI ("Ray-Cee") matrix or RASIC ("Ray-Sick") matrix. The acronyms represent each level of potential responsibility.

R—Responsible	R—Responsible
A—Accountable	A—Approve
C—Consulted	S—Support
I—Informed	I—Informed
	C—Consulted

summary form (such as a milestone summary listed in Figure 5.3) and always available in complete detail.

FIGURE 5.3

Example of a milestone schedule summary that tracks any approved schedule variances.

Project Milestone	Original Est. Completion Date	Revised Est. Completion Date 06/15/07	Variance
Plan Phase Toll-Gate	Apr 30, 2007	-	-
Design Phase Toll-Gate	Jun 15, 2007	Jun 22, 2007	1 week
Iteration 1 Development Complete	July 15, 2007	July 22, 2007	1 week
Iteration 2 Development Complete	Aug 15, 2007	Aug 29, 2007	2 weeks
Iteration 3 Development Complete	Sep 15, 2007	Sep 30, 2007	2 weeks
Stress Testing Complete	Sep 30, 2007	Oct 15, 2007	2 weeks
User Acceptance Testing Complete	Oct 30, 2007	Nov 15, 2007	2 weeks
Deploy Phase Toll-Gate	Nov 7, 2007	Nov 22, 2007	2 weeks
Pilot Site Implementation	Nov 17, 2007	Nov 29, 2007	2 weeks
Pilot Implementation Review	Dec 15, 2007	Jan 15, 2008	4 weeks
Close Phase Toll-Gate	Dec 22, 2007	Jan 22, 2008	4 weeks

- **Update roles and responsibilities**—This step has two parts.

  First, if any new role has been identified, then update the *stakeholder-role description* table (first mentioned in the project definition document) with the name of the required role and the specific responsibilities that role has. Once specific individuals are assigned to roles, the project role responsibility chart can be updated to reflect role assignments. An example of a partial project role responsibility chart is presented in Figure 5.4.

  Second, for each significant work package listed in the WBS, map the responsibility level that each role has regarding that item. This mapping is routinely captured in a responsibility assignment matrix. An example of a partial project responsibility assignment matrix is presented in Figure 5.5.

  This summary map is a powerful tool to help stakeholders clearly understand their roles and what is expected of them.

tip

To help identify relevant stakeholders, make sure to understand the complete business workflow process(es) and how each person involved is impacted by your project objectives.

FIGURE 5.4
A partial role responsibility chart for a software development project.

Project Role	Project Responsibilities	Assigned Team Member
Project Sponsor	* Responsible for championing the project and communicating all aspects of the project to other senior management stakeholders. * Has ultimate authority over and is responsible for the project and/or the program. * Approves changes to the scope and provides the applicable funds for those changes.	T. Terrific
Project Manager	* Provides direction and oversight to the initiative * Works with stakeholders to ensure that expectations are met * Develop and manage project plan * Design and execution of a project communications plan * Measure, evaluate, and report progress against the project plan * Provide project status reports * Coordinate and manage activities of project personnel * Resolve project issues * Conduct scheduled project status meetings * Establish documentation and procedural standards for the project * Perform quality review of deliverable documents * Maintain project communication with the Client Project Manager * Review and administer Project Change Control Procedures.	M. Yost
Technical Leader	* Provide technical leadership on the design of application architecture * Lead resolution of any application development issues * Facilitates technical design sessions * Provides quality assurance to technical deliverables	B. Gates
Quality Assurance Manager	* Provides quality assurance to the overall project processes, procedures, and deliverables. * Works with the Project Leadership to ensure project expectations are met	N. Reed
Business Process Leaders	* Provide business competence to the project team * Participate in information gathering sessions * Provide pertinent strategic business documentation and information * Assist in the identification of business critical processes * Validate viability of recommendations * Serve as primary user acceptance testers	S. Jones G. Griffey

FIGURE 5.5

A partial RASIC responsibility matrix.

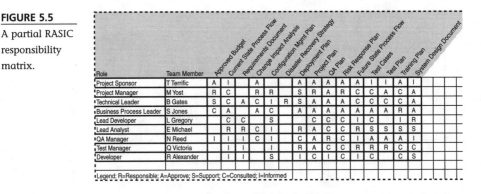

Role	Team Member	Approved Budget	Current State Process Flow	Requirements Document	Change Impact Analysis	Configuration Mgmt Plan	Disaster Recovery Strategy	Deployment Plan	Project Plan	QA Plan	Risk Response Plan	Future State Process Flow	Test Cases	Test Plan	Training Plan	System Design Document
Project Sponsor	T Terrific	A	I		A			A	A	A	A	A	I	I	A	I
Project Manager	M Yost	R	C		R	R		S	R	A	R	C	C	A	C	A
Technical Leader	B Gates	S	C	A	C	I	R	S	A	A	A	C	C	C	C	A
Business Process Leader	S Jones	C	A		A	C		A	A	A	A	A	A	A	R	A
Lead Developer	L Gregory		C	C		S			C	C	C	I	C		I	R
Lead Analyst	E Michael		R	R	C	I		R	A	C	C	R	S	S	S	S
QA Manager	N Reed	I	I	I	C	I		C	A	R	C	I	A	A	A	I
Test Manager	Q Victoria		I	I		I		R	A	C	C	R	R	R	C	C
Developer	R Alexander		I	I		S		I	C	I	C	I	C		C	S

Legend: R=Responsible; A=Approve; S=Support; C=Consulted; I=Informed

- **Update project organization**—Also previously mentioned in the project definition document, this section lists all the individuals, business units, and organizations involved in the project, the role(s) each is expected to play, and an indication of how they relate to one another. A project organization chart as shown in Figure 5.6 is highly recommended here.

FIGURE 5.6

A project organization chart for an outsourced software development initiative.

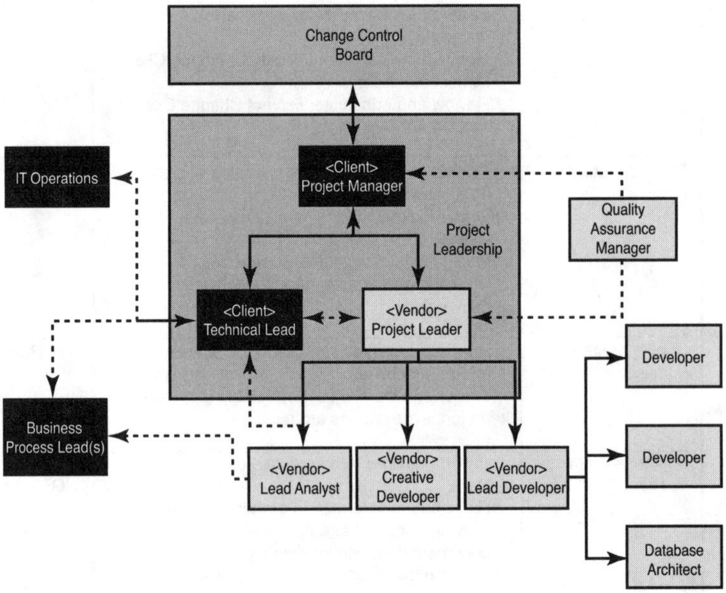

- **Determine project costs and budget**—Now that we have our resource needs and a preliminary schedule, we can tabulate estimated project costs and a phased project budget. We will discuss this in greater detail in Chapter 9, "Determining the Project Budget."

- **Determine project control system**—Specifically, we need to get agreement on how the performance of the project will be measured, how often, and how it will be reported. In addition, we need to determine how performance variances should be managed. Frequently, this information is documented in either the project plan itself, the project communications plan, and in the quality management plan. We will discuss this in greater detail in Chapter 10, "Controlling a Project."
- **Plan for change**—All plans are subject to change. The difference with successful projects is that they anticipate the changes and establish procedures in advance to review, assess, and manage any request or any factor that impacts the key performance factors (scope, quality, time, and cost). These procedures help to ensure that the right people are involved in the process and that the right people are informed of any "change" decision. We will discuss this in greater detail in Chapter 11, "Managing Project Changes."
- **Plan for project information**—There are two primary objectives of this step:
  - Where will the project repository be located? Who can access it? Who controls it?
  - How will changes to project deliverables be managed and controlled?

  This information is frequently maintained in a configuration management plan. We will discuss this in greater detail in Chapter 12, "Managing Project Deliverables."
- **Plan for issues**—All projects have issues and action that must be taken to resolve them. The difference on successful projects is that they establish a process in advance to closely track these issues and establish a procedure in advance to escalate any critical issue to the appropriate management stakeholders. We will discuss this in greater detail in Chapter 13, "Managing Project Issues."
- **Plan for quality**—Another proactive management approach to determine the quality standards and policies that project deliverables and processes must meet. For planning, the significance is that additional roles, work activities, and costs will likely impact the project schedule and the project budget. We will discuss this in greater detail in Chapter 15, "Managing Project Quality."

> The risk management process can impact the project plan throughout the project because it is a continuous, proactive project management activity.

- **Plan for communications**—A proactive management approach to determine the information and communication needs of each project stakeholder. These needs should be determined as part of the stakeholder analysis. The work efforts associated with delivering project communications should be accounted for in both the WBS and the project schedule. We will discuss this in greater detail in Chapter 17, "Managing Project Communications," and in Chapter 18, "Managing Expectations."
- **Plan for team management**—While we have already taken key steps to lay the groundwork for an effective project team by involving them in the "planning" process, establishing clear role descriptions, and scheduling clear assignments, there are additional steps to consider too, including training needs and performance evaluation. We will discuss this in greater detail in Chapter 19, "Keys to Better Project Team Performance."
- **Plan for procurements**—This step is closely linked to resource planning. If resources will need to be obtained externally, then the work to manage the procurement process must be planned and added to the WBS, project schedule, and project budget. We will discuss this in greater detail in Chapter 21, "Managing Vendors."

caution

The project plan document and its components are "living" documents and can be updated to reflect the evolving circumstances, issues, and needs surrounding the project.

Changes are okay. The changes just need to be announced, reviewed and approved by the relevant stakeholders.

The formality and detail of each Project Plan section or supplemental plan will vary depending on project need, project size, industry, and organizational culture.

Summary of Supplemental Project Plan Components

In the previous section, we introduced several new planning components, in addition to the core work plan, budget, and control elements you expect and made reference to the impact that several of them have on the overall project planning effort. To help summarize and organize this information, see Table 5.1.

Table 5.1 Summary of Supplemental Project Plan Components

Project Plan Component	Purpose	Key Elements/ Notes	Impact on Project Planning
Change Control Plan	Describes how the project success factors (scope, cost, schedule, quality) will be managed and how changes will be integrated.	Can include assessment of expected stability of project scope.	Proactive approach; manage expectations.
Communications Plan	Describes how the information and communication needs of project stakeholders will be met.	Often documented and presented in tabular form.	Communications management plan details must be added to WBS and project schedule.
Configuration Management Plan	Describes how changes to project deliverables and work products will be controlled and managed.	Should include both technical work products and project documentation.	Proactive approach; manage expectations.
Procurement Management Plan	Describes how the procurement process will be managed.	Contract types Roles of project team and procurement department.	Remaining procurement management tasks must be added to project schedule. Constraints of scheduling procurement activities with third-party vendors may impact the project schedule.
Quality Management Plan	Describes the project quality system.	Should address both project work products and the project processes.	Cost and schedule adjustments may be needed to meet quality standards. Quality assurance and quality control activities must be staffed and added to the project schedule.
Responsibility Matrix	Lists the project roles and responsibilities. Cross-references roles with assigned resources.	RACI matrix.	Ensure all required resources are accounted for.

Table 5.1 (Continued)

Project Plan Component	Purpose	Key Elements/ Notes	Impact on Project Planning
Resource Management Plan	Indicates when project resources are needed on the project (start and end dates).	Impact if resource cannot meet all skill requirements. Impact if resource must be acquired at rates higher than estimated.	Cost baseline, work estimates, and project schedule are in flux until the final resources are acquired.
Risk Management Plan	Describes how the risk management process will be structured and performed.	Describes the process to be used.	Ensure risk management tasks are added to WBS and project schedule.
Risk Response Plan	Describes the response strategies for identified risks.	Risk Log. Details action steps to be taken if risk event occurs.	Risk response strategies may entail the allocation of additional resources, tasks, time, and costs. Budget reserves, contingency plans.
Variance Management	Describes how performance (cost, schedule) variances will be managed.	Documents planned responses to different variance levels.	Proactive approach; manage expectations.

To assist the review and acceptance process of the project plan, consider the following:

1. Distribute project plan and components to reviewers in advance of the official review meeting.
2. Prepare a summary presentation of the project plan.
3. Encourage open, honest feedback.
4. Seek understanding and "buy-in" first; then and only then, ask for the acceptance sign-off.

Project Plan Checklist

Here's a quick checklist that can help you to determine whether your project is planned properly and whether you are ready to proceed to execute your project.

- Have you answered all the questions in the section, "Important Questions Project Planning Should Answer?"
- Have you reviewed your WBS, work effort estimates, project schedule, and project budget against their respective checklists?
- Has the project plan been reviewed and approved?
- Was the project plan signed off in a review meeting? In-person?

The Absolute Minimum

At this point, you should have a solid understanding of the following:

- Project definition is focused on *what* the project will do. Project planning is focused on *how* the project will get it done.
- A project plan is all-encompassing document that provides the basis for project execution and control, and it is not a Microsoft Project file.
- The project plan document should clearly communicate what work will be performed, who will do it, when they will do it, who is responsible for what, and how the project will be managed, monitored, and controlled.
- The project plan document and its components are living documents throughout the project. However, any change to the document must be approved by the same set of original stakeholders.
- The key skills used by the project manager when planning a project are facilitation, analytical, organizational, negotiation, and general interpersonal and leadership skills.
- All major stakeholders must approve the project plan document, preferably in person.
- A sign-off does not have to be a physical document signature. It can also be an email or a verbal acceptance (if it is documented in meeting minutes). However, the risk of misunderstandings is usually increased.

The map in Figure 5.7 summarizes the main points we reviewed in this chapter.

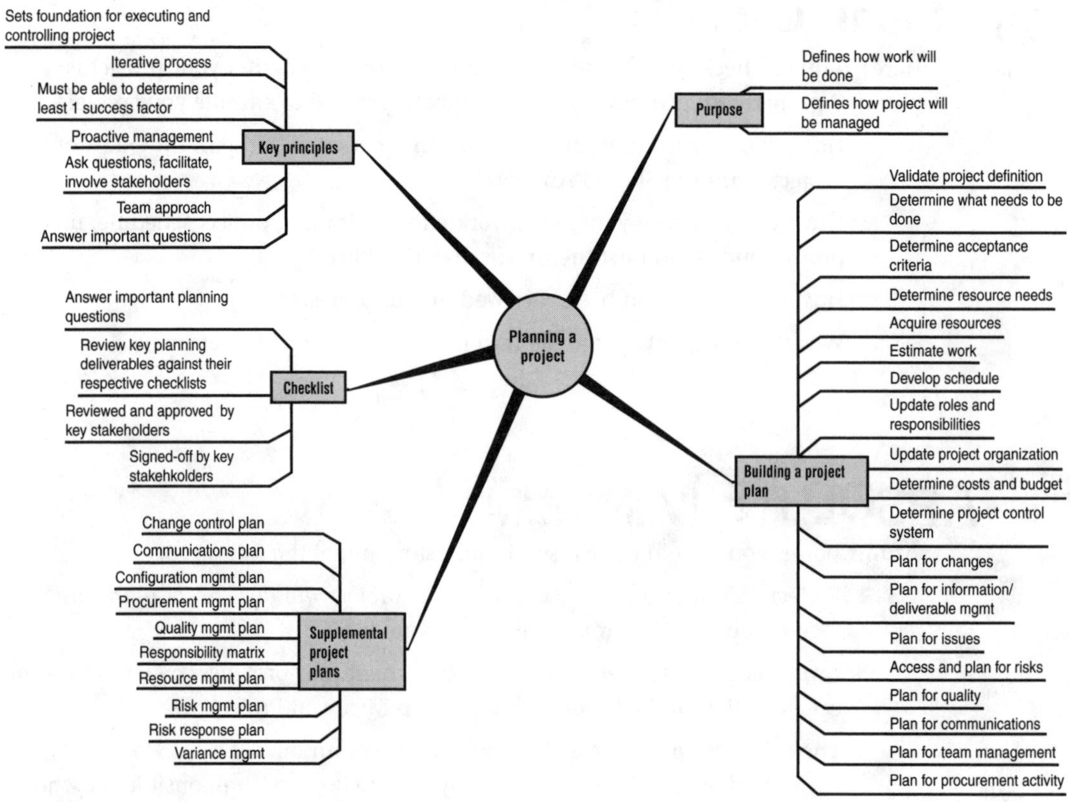
Planning a project
Key principles
Sets foundation for executing and controlling project
Iterative process
Must be able to determine at least 1 success factor
Proactive management
Ask questions, facilitate, involve stakeholders
Team approach
Answer important questions
Purpose
Defines how work will be done
Defines how project will be managed
Checklist
Answer important planning questions
Review key planning deliverables against their respective checklists
Reviewed and approved by key stakeholders
Signed-off by key stakehkolders
Supplemental project plans
Change control plan
Communications plan
Configuration mgmt plan
Procurement mgmt plan
Quality mgmt plan
Responsibility matrix
Resource mgmt plan
Risk mgmt plan
Risk response plan
Variance mgmt
Building a project plan
Validate project definition
Determine what needs to be done
Determine acceptance criteria
Determine resource needs
Acquire resources
Estimate work
Develop schedule
Update roles and responsibilities
Update project organization
Determine costs and budget
Determine project control system
Plan for changes
Plan for information/ deliverable mgmt
Plan for issues
Access and plan for risks
Plan for quality
Plan for communications
Plan for team management
Plan for procurement activity

FIGURE 5.7

Planning a project overview.

IN THIS CHAPTER

- Clarify what a work breakdown structure (WBS) is, and is not
- Understand why the WBS is considered the most important tool of the project manager
- Learn what makes an effective WBS
- Learn how to avoid the common mistakes when developing a WBS

6

DEVELOPING THE WORK BREAKDOWN STRUCTURE

If you were to ask anyone off the street what they think of when they hear "project management," you are likely to hear "planning." And if you further ask them what they mean by "planning," you are likely to hear "schedule" or "work plan." Yes, even to the uninitiated, people know that project managers "plan" and develop "work schedules," if they do nothing else.

Yet, the process of understanding all the work that needs to be done and building a realistic project schedule continues to be the Achilles' heel of project management.

In this chapter, we begin our close review of the schedule development process by understanding the power and the purpose of the work breakdown structure (WBS). By performing this step correctly, we will do a much better job at the other detail project planning activities such as identifying resources, identifying risks, getting better estimates, building a realistic schedule, and developing an accurate project budget. In addition, a solid WBS allows us to better manage stakeholder expectations and the critical success factors throughout the project life cycle.

As part of this review, we will clarify exactly what a WBS is (and is not), we will understand why the WBS is crucial to our other project management activities, and we will learn how to develop an effective WBS and avoid the common miscues in this arena.

What Is a WBS Exactly?

As I mentioned in Chapter 1, "Project Management Overview," project management is not "brain surgery" and does not require advanced logic and reasoning skills to achieve winning results (I'm a great example of this). In most cases, the disciplines and terms used in project management are very common sense and obvious in nature. A WBS is a classic case. As the terms defining the acronym indicate, a WBS is logical breakdown (decomposition) and representation (hierarchical structure) of the "work" required by the project.

A WBS can take one of two forms: graphical or outline. See Figures 6.1 and 6.2 for examples of each.

Both types have their place in your toolbox. The graphical form is best for communicating the top 3–5 levels of work activity to senior management or customer stakeholders. The outline form is best for capturing the details needed for cost and schedule development.

A WBS shows the work and any interim deliverables that will be required to produce the major project deliverables identified in the project definition process. In most cases, the WBS reflects the components that make up the final deliverables and the approach (methodology) used to develop, integrate, and validate them. In short, the WBS is an organized task list.

By simply doing this, we create an organized picture that allows us to see, and more importantly, allows our stakeholders to see, all the work required to accomplish the project objectives. You can begin to see the power of the WBS in managing expectations.

WBS is a logical, hierarchical, organized task list developed with the team.

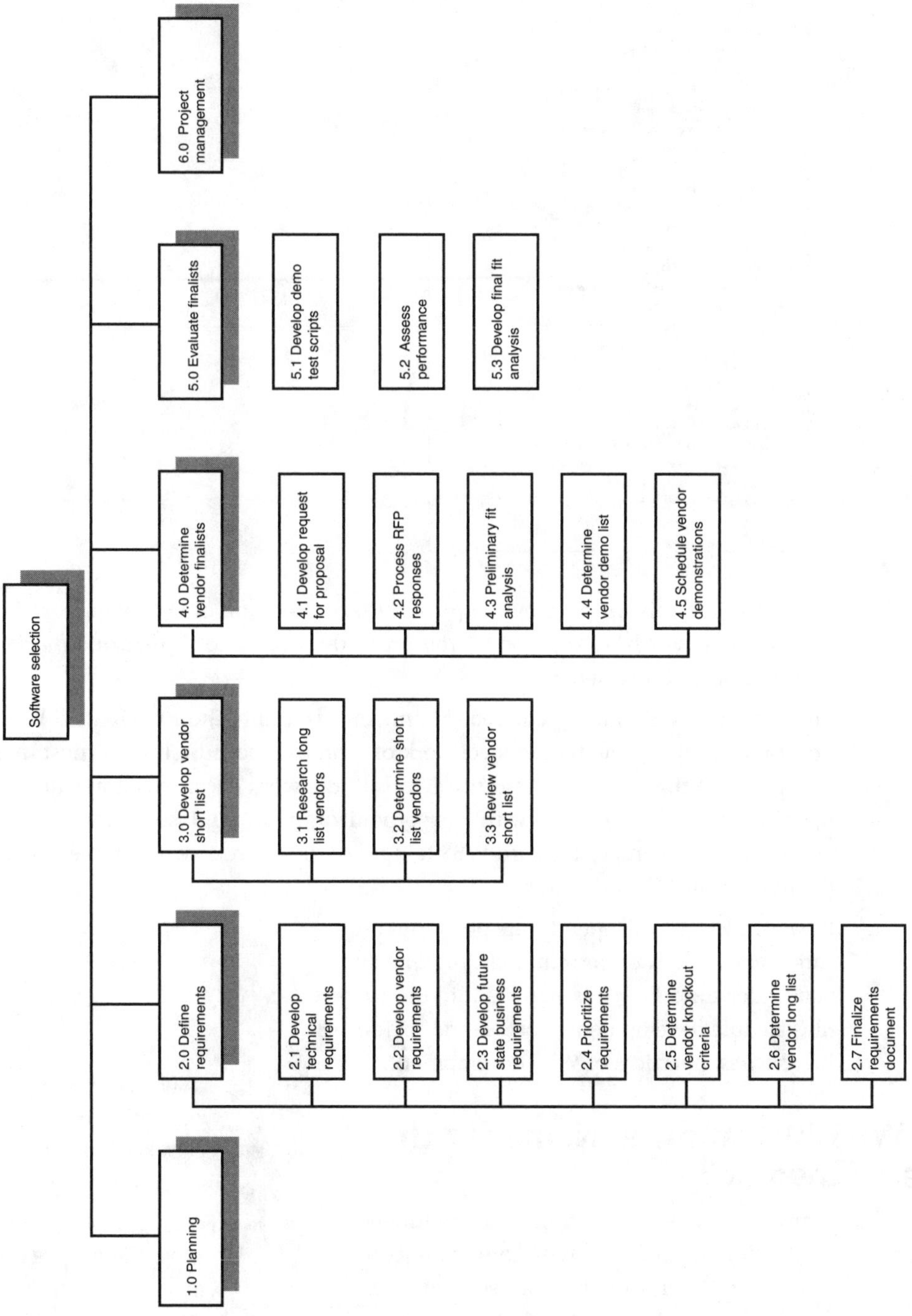

FIGURE 6.1
Partial graphical WBS for a software selection project.

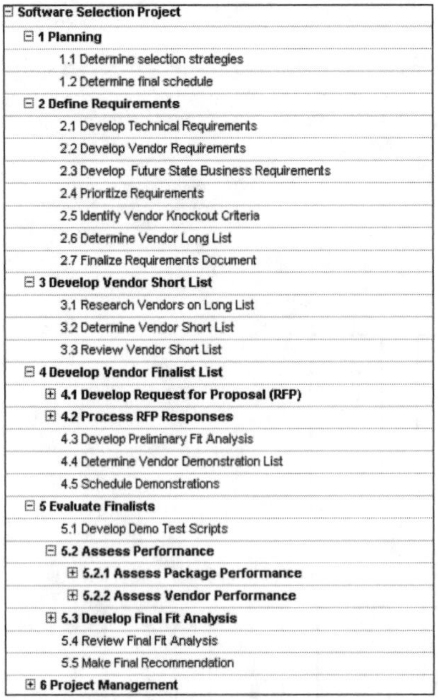

- **Software Selection Project**
  - **1 Planning**
    - 1.1 Determine selection strategies
    - 1.2 Determine final schedule
  - **2 Define Requirements**
    - 2.1 Develop Technical Requirements
    - 2.2 Develop Vendor Requirements
    - 2.3 Develop Future State Business Requirements
    - 2.4 Prioritize Requirements
    - 2.5 Identify Vendor Knockout Criteria
    - 2.6 Determine Vendor Long List
    - 2.7 Finalize Requirements Document
  - **3 Develop Vendor Short List**
    - 3.1 Research Vendors on Long List
    - 3.2 Determine Vendor Short List
    - 3.3 Review Vendor Short List
  - **4 Develop Vendor Finalist List**
    - **4.1 Develop Request for Proposal (RFP)**
    - **4.2 Process RFP Responses**
    - 4.3 Develop Preliminary Fit Analysis
    - 4.4 Determine Vendor Demonstration List
    - 4.5 Schedule Demonstrations
  - **5 Evaluate Finalists**
    - 5.1 Develop Demo Test Scripts
    - **5.2 Assess Performance**
      - **5.2.1 Assess Package Performance**
      - **5.2.2 Assess Vendor Performance**
    - **5.3 Develop Final Fit Analysis**
    - 5.4 Review Final Fit Analysis
    - 5.5 Make Final Recommendation
  - **6 Project Management**

FIGURE 6.2
Partial outline WBS for a software selection project.

Also, by doing this, we employ the primary secret weapon of managing large, complex projects, which is "You don't!" You break the work into chunks and manage many smaller components.

I'm not going to spend a great deal of time on explaining how to create a WBS and how to break down the higher level work of a project, because I think most analytical people do this naturally, and the details of the work decomposition will depend upon the specifics associated with your organization and industry. In fact, many organizations leverage standard WBS templates to ensure any new project includes the recommended work items.

However, what I will spend time on is making sure you are clear on terminology, making sure you understand how this step fits into the overall schedule development process, and reviewing the best practices of WBS development.

tip

Always clarify terms with your project team and project stakeholders in any communication.

For an official repository of project terms, the use of a project glossary document can be helpful.

Isn't WBS Just Another Name for the Project Schedule?

Many industries and organizations routinely use the following terms in an interchangeable fashion: WBS, project plan, project schedule, and work plan. As you know by now, these terms do represent different project management elements and should not be used interchangeably. However, as with all “less than ideal” practices, there are reasons they develop. Understanding the reasons is always helpful, and in this case, can provide additional insights as to why projects can get into a “troubled” state.

When you think about the process for developing a schedule (see Figure 6.3), determining the work (detail tasks) that is required is the first step.

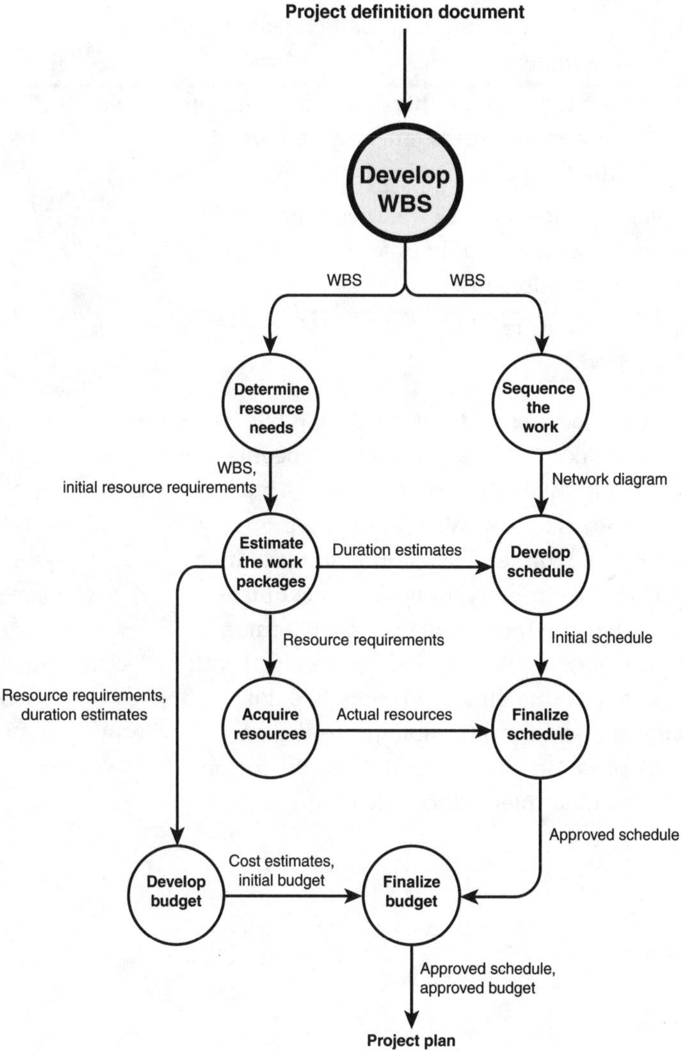

FIGURE 6.3
The role of the WBS in the development of the project schedule.

Once you have identified the work tasks, you can then determine what resources are required for each task, how much effort each task will take (process details discussed in Chapter 7, "Estimating the Work"), and what logical dependencies exist between the tasks (these details are covered in Chapter 8, "Developing the Project Schedule"). At this point, you can begin to construct the first of several iterations of a project schedule.

Sounds logical enough—so, where's the problem?

In general, the problems lie with the use and application of project scheduling software such as Microsoft Project. Here's a common scenario:

- Joe Manager is told to go build a work plan for the project.
- Joe Manager goes to his desk and opens up MS Project and starts entering and organizing the tasks that need to be performed.
- Joe Manager enters estimated durations and start and end dates for some of the key or most visible tasks.
- Joe presents results to his supervisor for review.

So, what did Joe present to his boss? A WBS? It does have work tasks listed. A project schedule? It was created in MS Project. A work plan? That's what his boss asked for. Well, what you probably have here is a high level WBS and an initial milestone schedule summary, at best. This example illustrates how an inadequate project planning and schedule development process combined with inadequate training on the project scheduling software can lead to "terminology" confusion. Table 6.1 summarizes these terms and the factors that lead to their interchangeable use.

Avoid judging a current work practice or process or the people involved before you understand *why* it is done this way or *how* it evolved to the current point.

This approach keeps you results-focused, improves your ability to develop solution alternatives, increases your effectiveness in leading change, and enhances your relationships with all stakeholders.

Table 6.1 Terms Used for Planning Project Work

Term	Description	Key Factors	Notes
Project Plan	All-encompassing planning document used as basis for execution and control.	Often incorrectly used to describe project schedule or work plan.	Common tendency to think of project "scheduling" software as project "management" software.
Project Schedule	Shows when the work will be done and by whom. Drives project execution.	Many "schedules" are more like task lists (WBS), because the task dependencies and resource assignments are not properly captured.	Inadequate training on project scheduling software. Inadequate schedule development and review process.
Work Plan	A generic term used to refer either of the other three.	Usually refers to project schedule.	Need to clarify terms up-front.
WBS	Work Breakdown Structure Hierarchical representation of work to be performed.	WBS often created with project scheduling software (MS Project) WBS templates often created and saved with project scheduling software (MS Project).	Use of project scheduling software is acceptable as long as the proper process is followed.

Key Differences Between the WBS and the Project Schedule

The key differences between the WBS and the project schedule include the following:

- **Task dependencies**—WBS does not show them; a project schedule does.
- **Scheduled tasks**—WBS does not show when tasks occur; a project schedule shows start and end dates for each task.
- **Task assignments**—WBS does not show who is assigned to an individual task; a project schedule does.

Different Types of Breakdown Structures

Another factor that can impact understanding of the WBS term and concept is that many industries utilize other breakdown structures and related acronyms that can confuse this subject. Therefore, to better understand what is meant by a WBS, you should be familiar with these other types of breakdown structures, as listed in Table 6.2, and how they are different from a WBS.

Table 6.2 Different Types of Breakdown Structures

Acronym	Description	Notes
CWBS	Contractual WBS	Defines the level of reporting between the seller and buyer. The CWBS is not as detailed as the WBS used to manage the actual work.
OBS	Organizational Breakdown Structure	Maps work components to organizational units.
RBS	Resource Breakdown Structure	Maps work components to individuals.
BOM	Bill of Materials	Describes the physical components needed for the project.
PBS	Project Breakdown Structure	The PBS is actually the same as the WBS. This term is only used in areas where the term WBS is incorrectly used to refer to a BOM.

Why Is the WBS Important?

The Project Management Institute (PMI) considers the WBS the most important tool of the project manager. Why?

More than any other project management tool, the WBS provides the foundation for defining and organizing the work needed to fulfill the project objectives. Through the WBS, the work to produce the targeted deliverables is structured, assigned, scheduled, tracked, and reported. Through the WBS, the work of the project is effectively represented and communicated to all stakeholders. A well-done WBS accomplishes the following objectives for the project manager:

caution

Any work not defined in the WBS is considered to be outside the project scope.

- **Manage the Pieces**—It provides a mechanism to manage any project size or complexity. Through decomposition, you can manage the pieces (work packages) rather than the whole project.
- **Better Work Definition, Less Changes**—It enables identification of all necessary work for the project and only the necessary work. It also reduces the number of items that "slip through the cracks" as well as the "Oh, I didn't think of that!" moments.
- **Better Estimates, Better Planning**—It improves the accuracy of cost, duration, and resource estimates.
- **Better Control**—It defines a baseline for performance measurement and control.

- **Clear responsibilities**—It facilitates clear responsibility assignments at both an individual and organizational level.
- **Stakeholder buy-in on scope work effort**—It facilitates understanding and buy-in of the project scope, the project approach, the work effort involved, and alignment between scope and work from each stakeholder.
- **Tighter management integration**—It provides a mechanism to relate the work directly to schedule, budget, and resource allocation plans.
- **Better team performance**—It allows each team member to easily understand how his or her work fits into the overall project, how it impacts the work of other team members, and to stay focused on deliverables.
- **Risk factors are identified early**—Through decomposition of the work, a more complete and effective risk analysis can be performed during project planning.
- **Confidence increases**—When people see that the work of the project is structured, definable, and doable, their confidence level in the project increases.

tip

A well-done WBS can become a template for similar, future projects.

The Process of Building a WBS

Now that we understand what a WBS is and the importance it plays to our project, let's review the key techniques, guidelines, and principles in building an effective WBS.

In general, the process of breaking down work is something we do frequently and is a straightforward logical endeavor. However, there are frequently two common challenges in the WBS development process.

- Where do I start?
- Where do I stop?

Major deliverables should come from the project definition document and are likely second-level WBS elements.

There is no one way to organize a WBS. It should be organized in a manner that emphasizes the most important aspects and that best communicates the entire scope of the project to your stakeholders.

Getting Started

To start the work decomposition process, think about the following:

- Does a template WBS exist as part of our methodology or from a past project that I can use?
- What are the major deliverables?
- What is the project approach? The project lifecycle? The major project phases?
- Think through the entire project. What does the "end" look like?

To continue the work decomposition process, think about these questions:

- Can I break down this WBS element (deliverable) into sub-components?
- How exactly will the deliverables be produced? What processes and methods will be used?
- How do I ensure acceptable quality in deliverables and in the process?
- Can I make adequate costs and duration estimates from this level of detail?

Guidelines for Effective WBS

Here are a few "guidelines" regarding the development of the project WBS that you will want to keep in mind:

- *All* the work of the project is included in the WBS.
- The WBS should be "deliverable focused."
- All deliverables are explicit in the WBS.
- The WBS should be developed "with the team."
- The WBS is refined as the project progresses.
- The WBS is a top-down decomposition and is logical—the summary tasks go with lower-level tasks.
- The WBS should be organized in a manner that emphasizes the most important aspects of the project and that best communicates the entire scope of the project to your stakeholders.
- The lowest level of the WBS is the work package or activity level and is used for schedule and cost development. This is the level where effort and cost can be reliably estimated.
- Unique identifiers are assigned to each item in the WBS to allow for better management reporting of costs and resources.
- WBS elements should be consistent with organizational and accounting structures.

- The coding scheme should clearly represent a hierarchical structure.
- Review and refine the WBS until all key project stakeholders are satisfied.
- Each WBS element represents a single deliverable and should be an aggregation of lower-level WBS elements.
- Each WBS element has only one parent.
- Upper levels of the WBS represent major deliverables or project phases.
- The WBS should include project management tasks and activities.
- The WBS should include and isolate any work needed to integrate components/deliverables.
- The WBS should account for any subcontracted or externally committed deliverable.
- The WBS should represent all work needed to ensure completeness, correctness, and acceptance of deliverables.
- Depth of WBS depends on three key factors:
    - The amount of project risk.
    - The reporting requirements.
    - The balance of control versus costs.

The level of depth (granularity) for the work package level in a WBS (lowest levels) will vary. It depends on what level of detail the project manager needs for effective management and control of the project.

In a program, or on large projects, the work package level may represent efforts in the hundreds of hours. In these cases, it is expected that the teams assigned to these work packages (or subprojects) will define the detail activities and tasks needed to complete the work package. From a practical standpoint, these teams should develop their own WBS that can then be rolled-up into the master WBS.

WBS should always be defined at least one level lower than what is required for management reporting purposes. This allows you to better identify the source of any issues or variances.

In general, the more detail in the WBS, the more accurate the work estimates and the better level of control. However, there is a balance. Too much detail and you will incur excessive costs performing data collection, tracking, and reporting. Too little detail and you incur higher risks and be unable to effectively manage.

caution

Most troubled projects have WBS elements that are too large. If each lower-level element should be completed within the standard reporting period (every week or every two weeks), it is much easier to track actual progress and to take any corrective actions.

Knowing When to Stop

The other aspect of WBS development that creates frequent uncertainty is knowing when to stop. To determine if you have enough detail in your WBS, review these questions for each lower-level item:

- Can each lower-level item be estimated, scheduled, budgeted, and assigned to a responsible party?
- Do I need more detail to make it easier to estimate effort, assign work, track costs, or measure progress?

  You will read about common rules of thumb for the proper size of work packages. The most common rules are 8/80 and 4/40, which means no task should be less than 8 hours or more than 80 hours, or in the case of 4/40, it would less than 4 hours or more than 40 hours.
- In addition, consider further decomposition of the lower-level item, if any of the following are true:
  - The work cannot be completed within the standard reporting period for the project.
  - There are specific risks associated with a smaller portion of the work element.
  - More than one individual or group is responsible.
  - More than one deliverable is included.
  - More than one work process is included.
  - There is time gap involved.
  - The resource requirements for the work element are not consistent.

> These are solid guidelines…not rules.
>
> The most important thing to remember is to size the work package to the level you need for effective management and control. Again, setting the maximum size to correspond to your reporting period is an excellent idea.

The importance of the WBS cannot be over-emphasized. Since the correctness and completeness of the WBS has a direct impact on how well we determine our resource needs, estimate the work efforts, and properly sequence the work, it is the foundation that drives our schedule and most of our planning efforts.

THE ABSOLUTE MINIMUM

At this point, you should have a solid understanding of the following:

- A WBS is a logical breakdown of all the work to be performed by the project.
- A WBS is neither the project schedule nor the project plan.
- The WBS should be developed with the project team.
- The WBS is a vital tool to the project manager.
- Avoid judging a current work process or the people involved before you understand *why* it is done this way or *how* it evolved to the current point.
- How to evaluate a WBS.
- How to avoid the common challenges and issues with WBS development.
- The WBS is the foundation for developing a realistic schedule, determining project resource needs, and figuring an accurate project budget.
- The work packages included in the WBS should be detailed enough to support effective management and control.
- The maximum size of a WBS work package should correspond to the standard reporting period for the project.

The map in Figure 6.4 summarizes the main points we reviewed in this chapter.

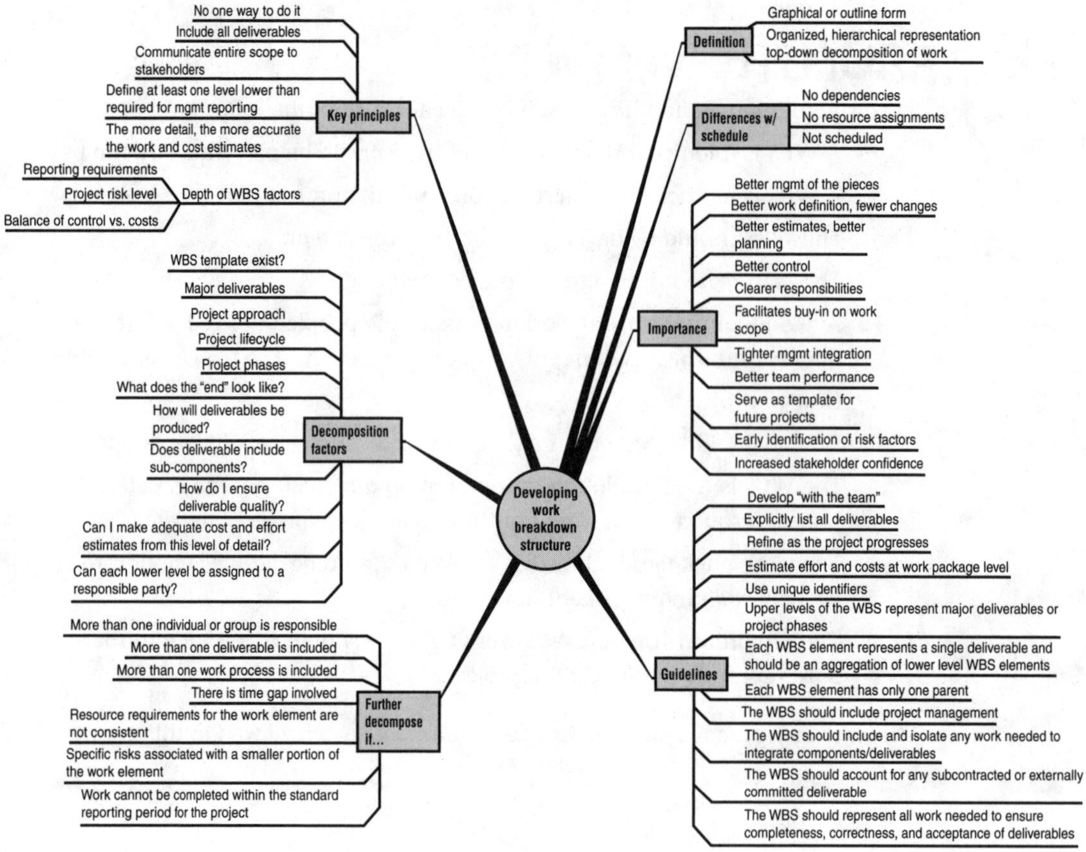

FIGURE 6.4

Developing a work breakdown structure overview.

In This Chapter

- Understand the importance that estimating plays in the success of a project
- Understand how estimating is used to manage project risk
- Review the common reasons for poor estimates and how to avoid them
- Review the key estimating techniques and methods
- Understand the power of bottom-up estimating
- Learn how to properly ask for an estimate
- Understand how to deal with uncertainty
- Learn the best estimating practices of successful projects

7

Estimating the Work

Estimating. Nothing else symbolizes the challenges of project management better. Negotiate with senior management and customers to prevent "ball park" estimates from becoming your targets; team with subject matter experts (SMEs) and knowledge workers to develop accurate estimates for work that has never been done before in these conditions, with these tools, by these people; assess your risks; educate stakeholders on the estimating process; and continuously manage the time-cost-quality equilibrium. Plus, you likely must do all of this in an organization that has not made the investment to improve estimating accuracy. Is it any wonder we love this job? For most people and most organizations, you would need a U-Haul truck to carry all the baggage that comes along for the ride when estimating is discussed. The baggage accumulates from political battles, misunderstandings, a sense of no control, and past troubled projects. As a result, there are complete educational courses and books in the marketplace that cover nothing but estimating—not to mention the many reputable therapists that can improve your emotional and spiritual well-being (just kidding; it's not that bad).

In this chapter, we will show you how to leave that U-Haul behind and take control of the estimating process. It can be done. First, we will review how estimating the work fits in with the overall schedule development process and how it is an integral part of how we manage risk on the project. Then, we will learn the key estimating techniques and methods and understand how to use them. And finally, we will discuss the common reasons for poor estimates and review the golden guidelines of estimating. This will allow you to improve your estimating accuracy and to get it right the first time.

Next Step in the Schedule Development Process

Before we get into the details of estimating, let's make sure we are clear on where estimating falls in the schedule development and planning process. If someone stopped you on the street and asked you for an "estimate," what is the minimum information that you would need? You would need to know what the estimate is for—what work is to be done. And you would need to know who is going to do it—what type of resources will be involved in performing the work. This is what we show in Figure 7.1. Estimating the work should occur after you have identified the work and after you have thought about what resources are needed for the project.

Accurate estimates build the foundation for a realistic schedule and an accurate project budget.

It sounds so simple, doesn't it? Then why is this so tough? Well, we will cover this in more detail later in this chapter, but these two basic prerequisites are where most estimating woes originate. There is often not a clear or complete understanding of the work to be performed by the person doing the estimate, and the relationship between the work estimate and the resource doing the work is not defined or communicated. In addition, there is the challenge of estimating work that has not been done before in exactly these conditions.

Yet, estimating the work effort is a cornerstone activity for planning the project. From these work estimates, we determine the project costs (see Chapter 9, "Determining the Project Budget"), develop the project schedule (Chapter 8, "Developing the Project Schedule"), and identify key project risks. This relationship is illustrated in Figure 7.2.

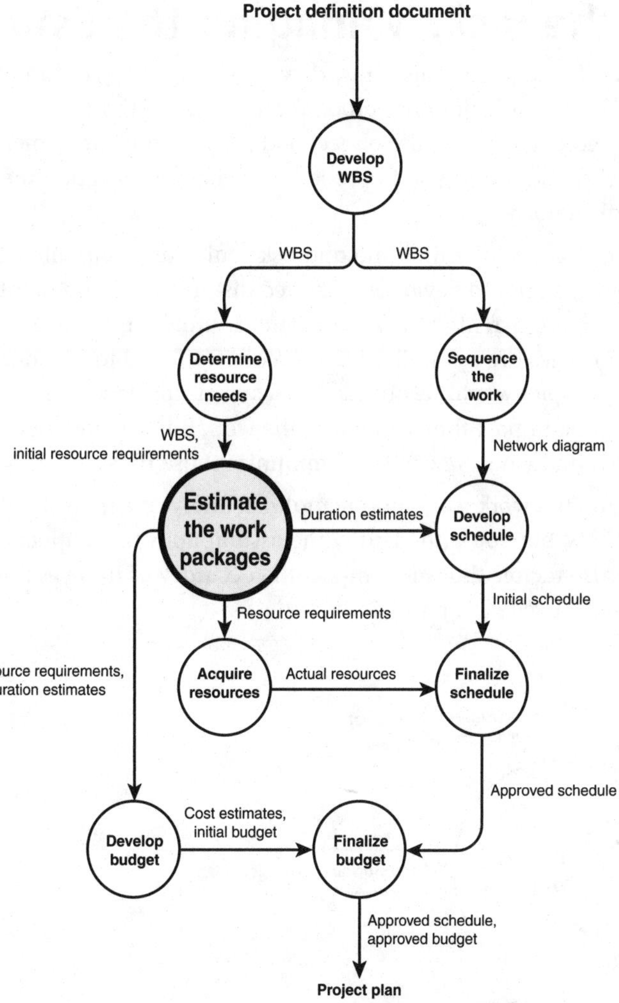

FIGURE 7.1
The step of estimating the work in the development of the project schedule.

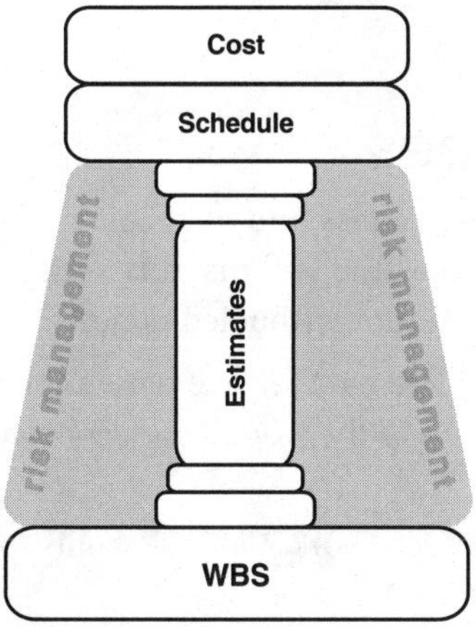

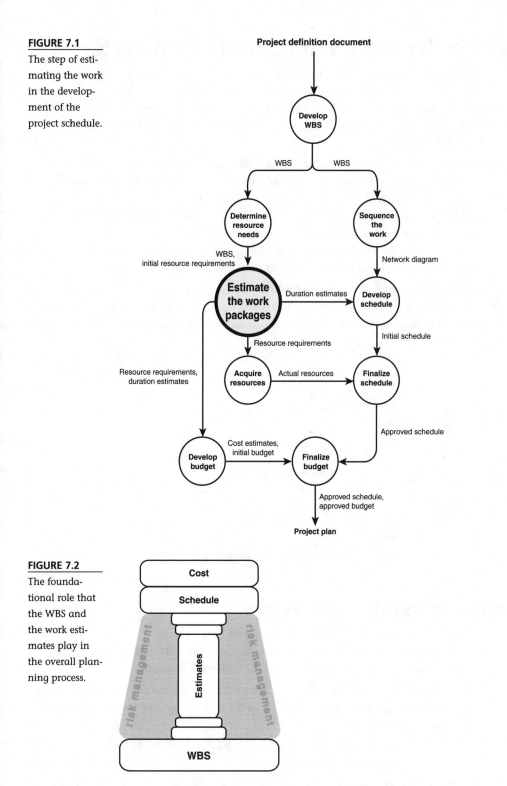

FIGURE 7.2
The foundational role that the WBS and the work estimates play in the overall planning process.

Managing the Risk, Managing the Estimates

There lies the key challenge. How do you manage the uncertainty that is naturally involved with the estimating process? Since these estimates form the foundation for the project schedule and the project budget, you must implement techniques and approaches that allow you to properly manage this risk and the expectations of your stakeholders.

While this subject of estimating and risk could easily slip into a review of statistics, probability, standard deviations, skewed distributions, and Monte Carlo analysis, we will not go there. In many real-world environments, these advanced concepts and techniques are not utilized to estimate work and to manage the associated risk, and these topics would be outside the scope of this book. Our focus will be understanding the impact that estimating the work has on our overall risk management approach and what we can do to minimize those risks.

Estimating the work is a fundamental risk analysis step. Not only do you estimate work efforts, but you also identify the assumptions that support the estimate and the key risk factors that may impact the accuracy of those estimates. These key outputs are depicted in Figure 7.3.

FIGURE 7.3

Estimates are key inputs for scheduling, budgeting, and risk management.

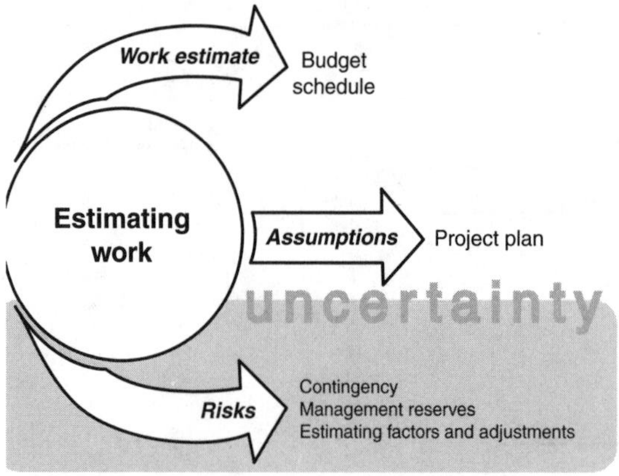

Reasons for Estimating Woes

Before we review the key estimating techniques and methods that we need to know to best plan our projects and manage our risk, let's first take a deeper look at the common reasons for estimating woes on many troubled projects:

- **Improper work definition**—The number one reason for inaccurate work estimates is inadequate definition of the work to be performed. This includes the following:
  - Estimates based on incomplete work. Work elements (packages) not accounted for in the WBS.

- Estimates based on lack of detail work breakdown.
- Estimates made without understanding the standards, quality levels, and completion criteria for the work package.

- **Wrong people estimating**—Another key reason for inaccurate work estimates is that the wrong people make the estimates. While it may be appropriate for management to make ballpark estimates during the early defining and planning stages, when firm commitments must be made, it is best to have the people who have experience doing the work make the estimates (or at least review and approve any proposed estimate made by someone else).
- **Poor communications**—This reason hits on the process of facilitating estimate development. This category includes such events as:
  - Not sharing all necessary information with the estimator.
  - Not verifying with the estimator what resource assumptions and other factors the estimates are based on.
  - Not capturing and communicating the estimate assumptions to all stakeholders.
- **Wrong technique used**—We will cover this in greater detail in the next section, but this category includes events such as:
  - Making firm budget commitments based on top-down or ballpark estimates rather than bottom-up estimates.
  - Not asking for an estimate range or multiple estimates.
  - Not leveraging the project team.
  - Not basing estimates on similar experiences.
- **Resource issues**—Related to the poor communications category, but this is a specific case where it's not really an estimate issue. This is when the person assigned to do the work is not producing at the targeted level or when there are performance quality issues with any of the materials, facilities, or tools. Without documented assumptions, these issues can appear as inaccurate estimates to stakeholders.
- **Lack of contingency**—In many cases, especially on projects involving new technologies and new processes, the identified risk factors are not properly accounted for in the work estimates. The uncertainty level in specific work estimates needs to be identified and carried forward into the project schedule and budget as part of the contingency buffer or management reserve.
- **Management decisions**—In many situations, senior management influence and decisions impact the estimating accuracy level. This category includes events such as:
  - Senior management making firm budget commitments based on initial, high level estimates and not accounting for accuracy ranges.

- Senior management not willing to invest time or resources to get detailed, bottom-up estimates.
- Estimators factoring their estimates for senior management expectations rather than the actual work effort.
- Management requesting that estimates be reduced to make the work meet the budget or schedule goals.
- Management decisions to bid or accept work for less than estimated cost.
- No use of management reserve to account for risk/uncertainty.

Powerful Estimating Techniques and Methods

There are several key estimating techniques you should know about. Table 7.1 lists these techniques and summarizes the key characteristics of each.

Table 7.1 Estimating Techniques

Estimating Technique	Key Characteristics	Notes
Analogous (top-down) estimating	Used in early planning phases and project selection. Utilizes historical information (actual duration periods from previous projects) to form estimates.	Reliable if WBS from previous projects mirror the WBS needed for this project.
Bottom-up estimating	Used to develop detailed estimates. Provides estimate for lowest level of the WBS (work package). Provides the most accuracy.	Best technique for identifying risk factors. Takes most time and money to develop.
Effort Distribution estimating	Uses project phase percentages to estimate. Example would be Initiation Phase—10% Plan Phase—10% Elaboration Phase—20% Construction Phase—40% Deploy Phase—20%	Used in organizations that use common methodology and/or that do similar projects. Can be used if enough information is known for one of the major project phases.
Heuristic estimating	Based on experiences. "Rule-of-thumb" estimating. Frequently used when no historical records are available.	Also known as Delphi technique and expert judgment.

Table 7.1 (continued)

Estimating Technique	Key Characteristics	Notes
Parametric estimating	Uses historical data and statistical relationships. Developed by identifying the number of work units and the duration/effort per work unit. Examples include Lines of code for software development. Square footage for construction. Number of sites for network migration.	Also known as Quantitative-based estimating. Can be used with other techniques and methods.
Phased estimating	Estimates the project phase by phase. Provides for a detailed, bottom-up estimate for the next phase and a higher level, top-down estimate for the other phases. Best technique to use on high-risk projects.	Incorporates "re-estimating" as part of the management approach. Best use of estimating resources. Excellent risk management tool.

For each estimating technique (approach), there are one or more methods that can be leveraged. Table 7.2 lists these methods and summarizes the key characteristics of each.

Table 7.2 Estimating Methods

Estimating Method	Key Characteristics	Notes
Expert judgment	Relies on subject matter expert (SME) in targeted work area.	Used most effectively with bottom-up estimating.
Historical information	Relies on actual durations from past projects. The three types are project files, commercial databases, and project team members.	Many organizations do not accurately capture this information. Recollection of project team. members is the least reliable source. Critical to improving estimate accuracy in an organization.
Weighted average (PERT)	Uses three estimates for each activity (weighted average): optimistic, most likely, pessimistic $E = (O + 4M + P) / 6$ Each estimate is captured for each activity.	Used mainly on large scale or high-risk projects. Excellent risk management technique. This technique is time-consuming. PERT = Program Evaluation and Review Technique.

Table 7.2 (continued)

Estimating Method	Key Characteristics	Notes
Risk Factors	Adjusting an original estimate based on one or more risk factors. Used in conjunction with other methods.	Common risk factors impacting effort estimates include: Complexity—technical, process Organizational change impact Requirements—volatility, quality Resources—skills, costs, etc.
Team (Consensus) estimating	Uses multiple SMEs to develop independent estimates. Facilitation meeting used to reconcile differences and develop consensus estimates.	Best for identifying assumptions and other risk factors. Avoids one person being accountable for estimate. Allows for multiple historical perspectives to be taken into account. Allows SMEs from different backgrounds to complement one another.

As with all other planning activities, work estimates are refined and improved as more is learned about the project. At a minimum, each project (or project phase) should be estimated three times. Each estimate provides a greater degree of accuracy. To better understand this concept and to better educate others in your organization, see the three levels of estimate accuracy recognized by PMI in Table 7.3.

Table 7.3 Estimate Accuracy Levels

Level	Accuracy Range	Generally Used During
Order of magnitude	–25% to +75%	Initiating (defining) phase
Budget	–10% to +25%	Planning phase
Definitive	–5% to +10%	Planning phase

Best Practices

Now that we have an overview of the estimating techniques and methods that are available to us, and we have a feel for the estimating mistakes that are commonly made, let's review the estimating best practices of successful organizations and projects.

- Estimating should be based on the work breakdown detailed in the WBS.
- Estimating should be performed (or approved) by the person doing the work.
- The work estimates for lower level WBS items should be less than the standard reporting period for the project (typically one or two weeks).

As discussed in Chapter 6, if the work estimate is not less than this, it is a good sign the task needs further decomposition.

- Estimating should be based on historical information and expert judgment.
- Estimates are influenced by the capabilities of the resources (human and materials) allocated to the activity.
- Estimates are influenced by the known project risks and should be adjusted accordingly to account for those risks.

tip

There are two primary reasons estimating should be performed (or approved) by the person doing the work: More accurate estimates and higher commitment levels to the project.

- All bases and assumptions used in estimating should be documented in the project plan.
- When asking an SME for an activity estimate, make sure to provide the following whenever possible:
    - Project definition document (context, approach, assumptions, constraints)
    - WBS
    - The applicable standards, quality levels, and completion criteria for the work package
- When asking an SME for an activity estimate, make sure to ask for the following at a minimum:
    - An estimate range (not just a single value)
    - Factors driving that range
    - Assumed resource level, skills and productivity
    - Assumed quality level and acceptable completion criteria
- Estimates should be given in specific time ranges.

I have no doubt that the use of buffers and historical information when developing work effort estimates is common, everyday practice in your "real-world" experience…or maybe not.

They represent a clear example of why leadership, negotiation, and communication skills are so important for project managers.

- For managing high-risk projects, the following estimating techniques are recommended:
    - Use of phased and bottom-up estimating techniques
    - Use of the average weight and team consensus estimating methods

- For high-risk projects where the organization lacks significant previous experience or process knowledge, consider outsourcing the planning phase to an outside firm as an assessment engagement.
- A project's time and cost estimates should be based on project needs and not dictated by senior management. The project manager should work with senior management to reconcile any differences.
- Reserve time (contingency, buffer) should be added to either the project schedule or to individual activity duration estimates to account for the level of risk and any uncertainty that exists.
- Historical information is vital to improving estimates. If you don't measure actual performance, you will not have the feedback to improve estimating accuracy.

Critical Chain management (scheduling) is an increasingly popular technique of estimating and scheduling work. We'll take a closer look at this approach in Chapter 25, "Intriguing Project Management Concepts and Topics."

The Absolute Minimum

At this point, you should have a solid understanding of the following:

- It takes time and money to develop accurate estimates.
- Any estimating technique will improve results if it is used consistently by leveraging lessons from the past.
- To get science in the process, estimates must be compared to actual performance.
- Multiple estimating techniques can be used together. The art is knowing when to use which technique and knowing how much accuracy is required for the business decision at hand.
- Many variables beyond the control of the project team, such as changing specs, team turnover, and failed technology, can invalidate original estimates.
- Project managers should never work independently when making estimates.
- Organizations must make a conscious effort to establish rigor and procedures to estimating to improve accuracy over time.
- All stakeholders are responsible for estimates.

The map in Figure 7.4 summarizes the main points we reviewed in this chapter.

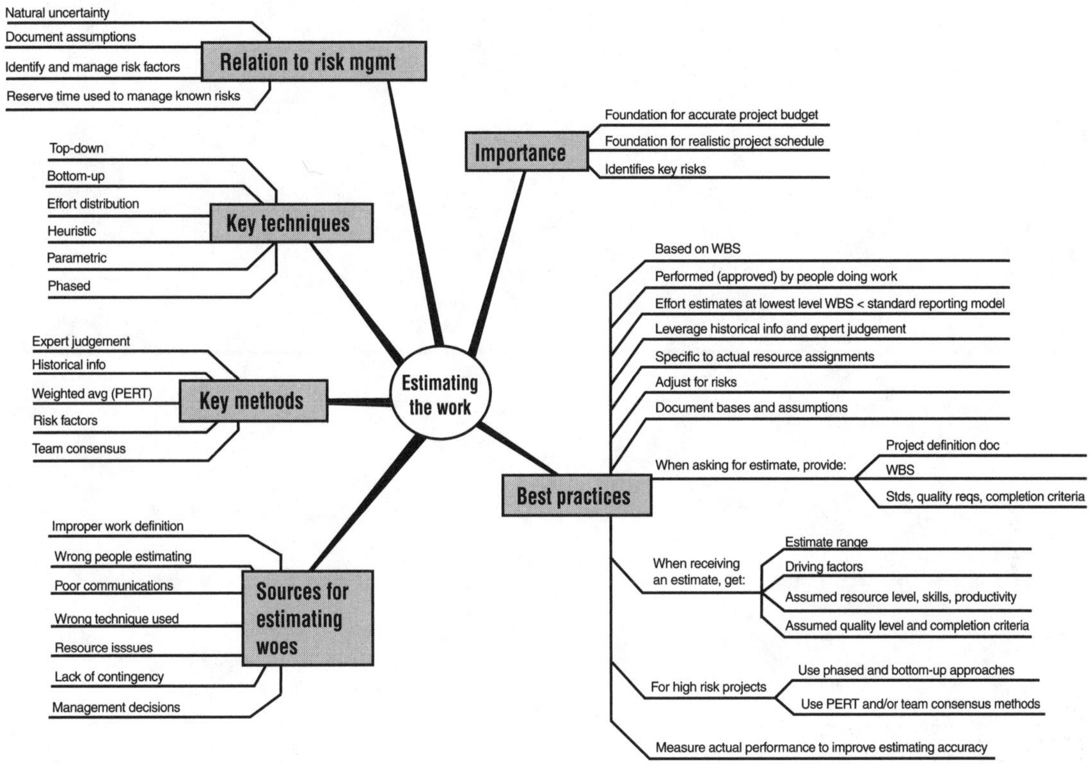

FIGURE 7.4

Estimating the work overview.

In This Chapter

- Understand why the project schedule is vital to a successful project
- Review the process for creating a realistic schedule
- Learn the characteristics of a good schedule
- Learn how to avoid the common mistakes that even experienced project managers can make when building a schedule
- Review the options for effectively presenting your schedule to others

8

Developing the Project Schedule

It's funny really. The one activity that the common person associates with project management is planning, and the main output from this planning effort is a schedule. Yet, it is a challenge to find a project manager who can develop one accurately. Although scheduling is one of the two primary technical aspects of project management, it is a common technical weakness of many project managers.

Why is this? Well, from my own experience, I can state at least four reasons: lack of time for proper planning, lack of education on the schedule development process, lack of training with the scheduling software, and a belief that a detailed schedule is not necessary. I believe this issue is one of the fundamental reasons why many organizations started project management offices (PMOs)—internal support and governance organizations to improve project performance. Unrealistic project schedules have an adverse impact on resource management and project investment decisions.

Of course, as a reader of this book, you will know the proper process for developing a schedule, you will understand the necessity of a detailed schedule, and you will have plenty of ammunition to use when negotiating for project planning time. Combined with proper knowledge of the scheduling software you are using, you will possess a key strength for successful project managers and be a key asset to your stakeholders. Given that, let's continue our review of the overall schedule development process.

In this chapter, we will emphasize the vital importance of the project schedule, step through the process for developing a realistic schedule, and highlight the areas where people often go astray. This will lead to a schedule that your stakeholders will believe and accept, and it will provide you with the foundation to properly execute and monitor the project.

The Impact of the Project Schedule

The project schedule is the tool that merges all the work tasks to be performed, their relationships, their estimated durations, and their assigned resources to a calendar. Examples of partial schedules are illustrated in Figures 8.1 and 8.2. For most, specialized scheduling software (such as Microsoft Project) is used to produce a project schedule. For those managers who use Microsoft Project, we discuss how to make better use of this tool in Chapter 23, "Making Better Use of Microsoft Project."

FIGURE 8.1

An example of a partial schedule displayed in table form.

Software Selection Project Schedule

ID	❶	Task Name	Work	Duration	Start	Finish	Predecessors	Resource Names
0		**Software Selection Project**	**1,112 hrs**	**46.5 days**	**Mon 1/12/04**	**Tue 3/16/04**		
1		**1 Planning**	**32 hrs**	**2 days**	**Mon 1/12/04**	**Tue 1/13/04**		
2		1.1 Determine selection strategies	24 hrs	8 hrs	Mon 1/12/04	Mon 1/12/04		Technology Advisor,Business Analyst,Project Leader
3		1.2 Determine final schedule	8 hrs	8 hrs	Tue 1/13/04	Tue 1/13/04	2	Project Leader
4		**2 Define Requirements**	**144 hrs**	**11 days**	**Wed 1/14/04**	**Wed 1/28/04**	1	
5		2.1 Develop Technical Requirements	24 hrs	24 hrs	Wed 1/14/04	Fri 1/16/04		Technology Advisor
6		2.2 Develop Vendor Requirements	16 hrs	8 hrs	Mon 1/19/04	Mon 1/19/04	5	Technology Advisor,Business Analyst
7		2.3 Develop Future State Business Requirements	16 hrs	16 hrs	Tue 1/20/04	Wed 1/21/04	6	Business Analyst
8		2.4 Prioritize Requirements	48 hrs	16 hrs	Thu 1/22/04	Fri 1/23/04	5,6,7	Technology Advisor,Business Analyst,Project Leader
9		2.5 Identify Vendor Knockout Criteria	12 hrs	4 hrs	Mon 1/26/04	Mon 1/26/04	8	Technology Advisor,Business Analyst,Project Leader
10		2.6 Determine Vendor Long List	12 hrs	4 hrs	Mon 1/26/04	Mon 1/26/04	9	Technology Advisor,Business Analyst,Project Leader
11		2.7 Finalize Requirements Document	16 hrs	16 hrs	Tue 1/27/04	Wed 1/28/04	10	Business Analyst
12		**3 Develop Vendor Short List**	**56 hrs**	**7 days**	**Tue 1/27/04**	**Wed 2/4/04**		
13		3.1 Research Vendors on Long List	40 hrs	5 days	Tue 1/27/04	Mon 2/2/04	10	Technology Advisor
14		3.2 Determine Vendor Short List	8 hrs	1 day	Tue 2/3/04	Tue 2/3/04	13	Technology Advisor
15		3.3 Review Vendor Short List	8 hrs	1 day	Wed 2/4/04	Wed 2/4/04	14	Technology Advisor
16		**4 Develop Vendor Finalist List**	**120 hrs**	**18.5 days**	**Thu 1/29/04**	**Tue 2/24/04**		
17		**4.1 Develop Request for Proposal (RFP)**	**64 hrs**	**8 days**	**Thu 1/29/04**	**Mon 2/9/04**	4	
18		4.1.1 Create Request for Proposal	32 hrs	32 hrs	Thu 1/29/04	Tue 2/3/04		Business Analyst
19		4.1.2 Approve Request for Proposal	24 hrs	24 hrs	Wed 2/4/04	Fri 2/6/04	18	Business Analyst
20		4.1.3 Distribute Request for Proposal	8 hrs	8 hrs	Mon 2/9/04	Mon 2/9/04	19	Business Analyst
21		**4.2 Process RFP Responses**	**24 hrs**	**1.5 days**	**Mon 2/16/04**	**Wed 2/18/04**	**17FS+5 days**	
22		4.2.1 Vendor RFP Responses Due	0 hrs	0 days	Mon 2/16/04	Mon 2/16/04		
23		4.2.2 Review and Summarize Vendor Responses	16 hrs	8 hrs	Tue 2/17/04	Tue 2/17/04	22	Technology Advisor,Business Analyst
24		4.2.3 Research Vendor References	8 hrs	4 hrs	Wed 2/18/04	Wed 2/18/04	23	Technology Advisor,Business Analyst
25		4.3 Develop Preliminary Fit Analysis	16 hrs	16 hrs	Wed 2/18/04	Fri 2/20/04	21	Technology Advisor
26		4.4 Determine Vendor Demonstration List	8 hrs	8 hrs	Fri 2/20/04	Mon 2/23/04	25	Technology Advisor
27		4.5 Schedule Demonstrations	8 hrs	8 hrs	Mon 2/23/04	Tue 2/24/04	26	Project Leader
28		**5 Evaluate Finalists**	**400 hrs**	**25.5 days**	**Tue 2/10/04**	**Tue 3/16/04**		
29		5.1 Develop Demo Test Scripts	48 hrs	24 hrs	Tue 2/10/04	Thu 2/12/04	17	Technology Advisor,Business Analyst
30		**5.2 Assess Performance**	**224 hrs**	**8 days**	**Tue 2/24/04**	**Fri 3/5/04**	16	
31		**5.2.1 Assess Package Performance**	**128 hrs**	**6 days**	**Tue 2/24/04**	**Wed 3/3/04**		
32		5.2.1.1 Working Session - Vendor A	12 hrs	4 hrs	Tue 2/24/04	Tue 2/24/04	16	Technology Advisor,Business Analyst,Project Leader
33		5.2.1.2 Working Session - Vendor B	12 hrs	4 hrs	Wed 2/25/04	Wed 2/25/04	32	Technology Advisor,Business Analyst,Project Leader
34		5.2.1.3 Vendor "A" Demonstration	48 hrs	16 hrs	Wed 2/25/04	Fri 2/27/04	32,29,27,33	Technology Advisor,Business Analyst,Project Leader
35		5.2.1.4 Vendor "B" Demonstration	48 hrs	16 hrs	Fri 2/27/04	Tue 3/2/04	34	Technology Advisor,Business Analyst,Project Leader
36		5.2.1.5 Record Demo Scores	8 hrs	8 hrs	Tue 3/2/04	Wed 3/3/04	35	Business Analyst
37		**5.2.2 Assess Vendor Performance**	**96 hrs**	**8 days**	**Tue 2/24/04**	**Fri 3/5/04**		
38		5.2.2.1 Research vendor references	48 hrs	16 hrs	Tue 2/24/04	Thu 2/26/04	16	Technology Advisor,Business Analyst,Project Leader
39		5.2.2.2 Possible Site visits	48 hrs	16 hrs	Wed 3/3/04	Fri 3/5/04	31	Technology Advisor,Business Analyst,Project Leader
40		**5.3 Develop Final Fit Analysis**	**80 hrs**	**5 days**	**Fri 3/5/04**	**Fri 3/12/04**	30	
41		5.3.1 Perform Fit-Gap analysis for each option	16 hrs	8 hrs	Fri 3/5/04	Mon 3/8/04		Technology Advisor,Business Analyst
42		5.3.2 Assess risk for each option	16 hrs	8 hrs	Mon 3/8/04	Tue 3/9/04	41	Technology Advisor,Business Analyst
43		5.3.3 Develop high-level schedule and budget forecast	16 hrs	8 hrs	Tue 3/9/04	Wed 3/10/04	42	Technology Advisor,Business Analyst

SoftwareSelectionExample(2004-01-12)v2.mpp — Page 1 of 2

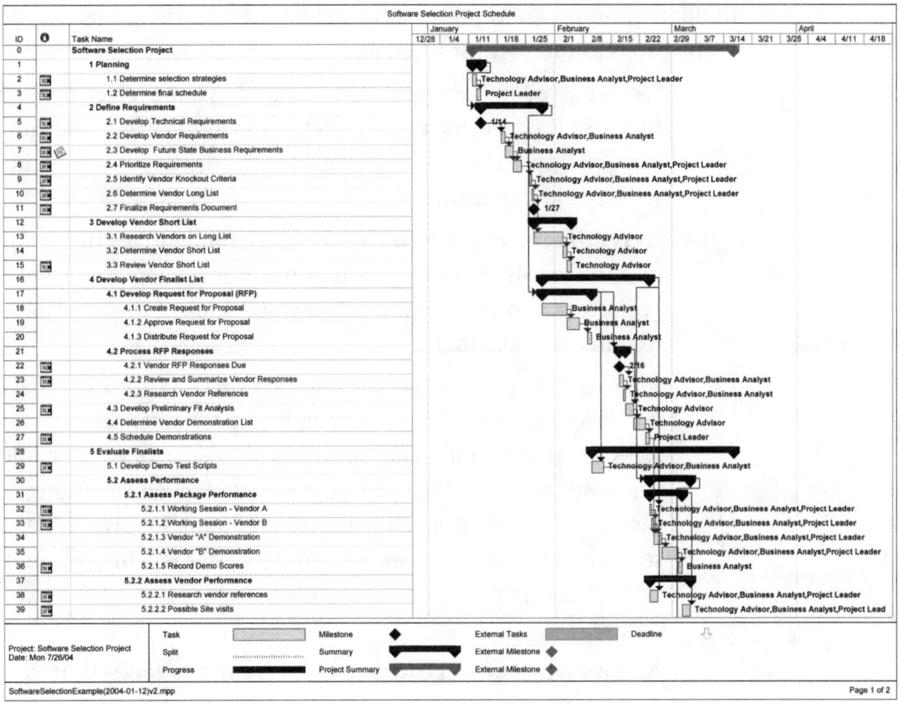

FIGURE 8.2

An example of a partial schedule displayed in Gantt chart form.

As mentioned earlier in the book, the project schedule is often referred to as the "project plan" in error. While not technically correct, it is easy to understand why this term is often used. The project schedule serves as the chief integration point for most, if not all, of your project planning efforts. The project schedule reflects (or should reflect when the schedule development process is complete) all the following:

- Work Breakdown Structure (WBS)
- Resource plan
- Work estimates
- Key milestones
- Responsibility assignments (RASIC)
- Quality management plan
- Risk management plan
- Communications management plan
- Procurement management plan
- Staff management (training) plan

In addition to providing this vital integration role, the project schedule is important to the project manager for these reasons as well:

- **Drives project budget**—Since most of your project costs are a factor of time (we'll cover this in more detail in Chapter 9, "Determining the Project Budget"), the project schedule is a main driver for your project budget. If the schedule is inaccurate, your budget is likely incorrect too.
- **Drives resource schedule**—Your schedule drives the timing of your resource needs. Especially in organizations where resources are shared across projects or centrally managed, the accuracy of the schedule is key to efficient resource management.
- **Essential for managing expectations**—With a well-developed schedule, you have the best tool for managing stakeholder expectations regarding the schedule-cost-quality equilibrium. A well-developed schedule illustrates the "earliest" date a project can be completed given the project's current requirements and constraints. This is an invaluable tool when negotiating the final schedule with senior management or customers and when assessing the impact of any change to equilibrium factors during the execution of the project.
- **Allows project performance to be measured**—With a well-developed and approved project schedule, you now have the capability to establish a baseline for how the project is actually performing. We discuss this in more detail in Chapter 10, "Controlling a Project."
- **Provides for "what-if" analysis capabilities**—Another important ability that a well-developed schedule provides is the ability to perform "what-if" analysis during the execution of the project. Over the course of a project, things happen that can negatively impact project performance. At these times, you will often be asked what corrective actions can be taken to possibly get the project back on schedule. Without a well-developed schedule, you will not be able to quickly determine the impact of implementing a given schedule compression technique, such as fast-tracking, crashing, or limited overtime.

The Goal of the Schedule Development Process

I've used terms like "realistic" and "well-developed" to describe the type of project schedule we want to develop. Before we continue, let's clarify what the goal of the schedule development process should be. The schedule development process should generate a project schedule that meets the following criteria:

- **Complete**—The schedule must represent all the work to be done. This is why the quality and completeness of the WBS is so important.

- **Realistic**—The schedule must be realistic with regard to time expectations.
- **Accepted**—The schedule must have "buy-in" from team members and stakeholders.
- **Formal**—The schedule must be documented and formalized.

After reviewing this list, you probably see why so many projects are troubled from the start. While there are many factors that can adversely impact project performance and cause us to re-plan, re-schedule, or take corrective actions, an improper schedule should not be one of them. Of course, by understanding the lessons discussed in this chapter and in this book, you will be well on your way to developing solid project schedules every time.

tip

To be final, a schedule must possess the following key attributes to be considered complete and ready to be used as a baseline for project performance:

- **Complete**—The schedule must represent all the work to be done.
- **Realistic**—The schedule must be realistic with regard to time expectations.
- **Accepted**—The schedule must have "buy-in" from team members and stakeholders.
- **Formal**—The schedule must be documented and formalized.

Key Inputs for Building a Schedule

The first step in building a schedule is to review the key inputs. Let's make sure we are clear on these and where we are in the overall schedule development and planning process. To build a project schedule, you need five key inputs:

- **WBS**—List of organized tasks, the work to be done (covered in Chapter 6, "Developing the Work Breakdown Structure").
- **Effort estimates**—Amount of effort and time each task will take (covered in Chapter 7, "Estimating the Work").
- **Task relationships**—The logical dependencies that exist between work tasks (depicted as the Sequence the Work step in Figure 8.1). We will review this step in this chapter.
- **Resources**—The actual personnel and equipment needed to perform the work between work tasks (referenced throughout these Planning chapters, and covered in more detail in this chapter).
- **Risk responses**—Measures taken to deal with the uncertainty surrounding effort and resource estimates. Usually, in the form of additional time (contingency buffer) added to the schedule.

Due to the amount of important information and the critical nature of two of these inputs (developing the WBS and estimating the work packages), we reviewed them in their own chapters. In this chapter, we will take these two key inputs together with the other three (sequencing the work, develop schedule, and finalize schedule) to develop a realistic schedule, as depicted in Figure 8.3.

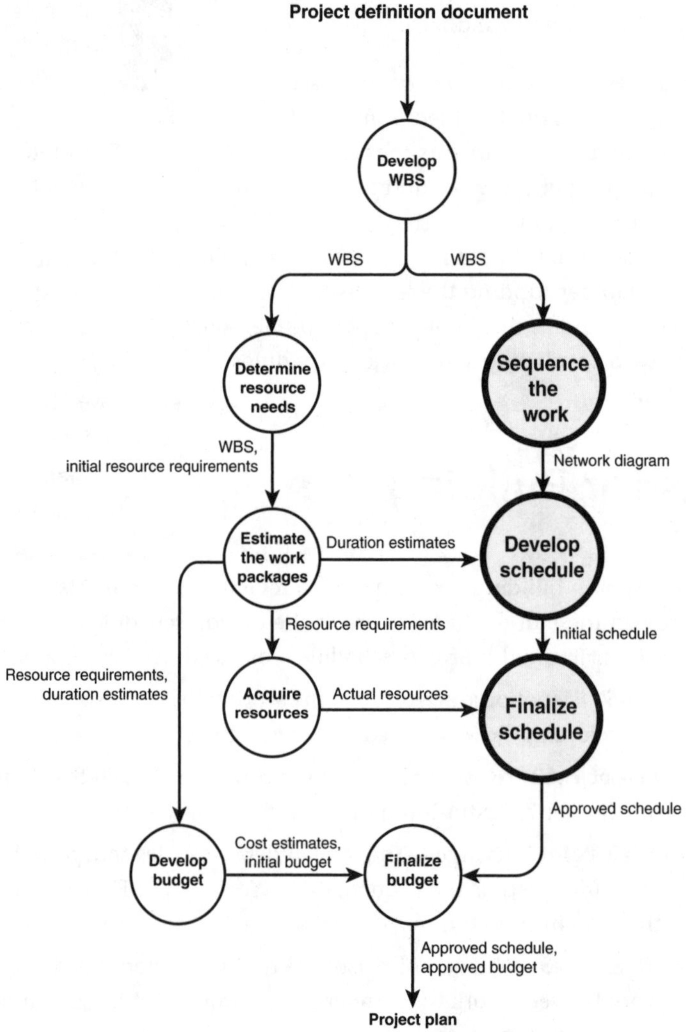

FIGURE 8.3
The schedule development points to be reviewed in this chapter.

Creating a Schedule

Since we are on this wavelength, let's go ahead and review the key steps involved in building a project schedule. The steps are also summarized in Figure 8.4. We will follow-up this section with a more in-depth look at a few of these:

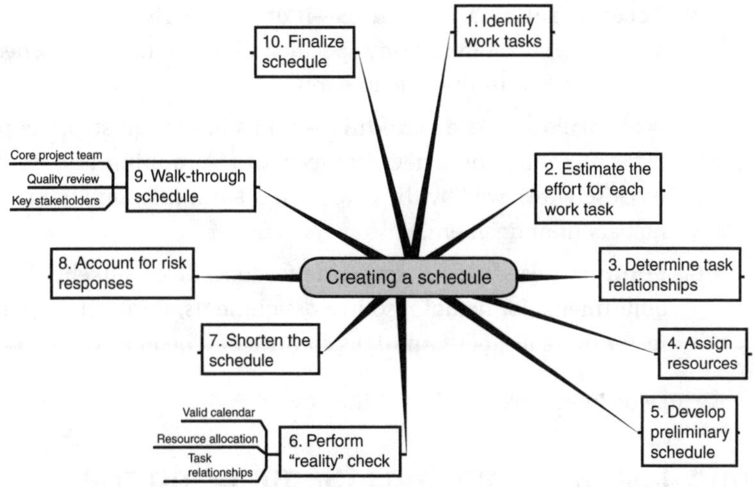

FIGURE 8.4

The ten steps involved in creating a schedule.

1. **Identify the work tasks (WBS)**—Identify the work tasks that need to be performed. Reviewed in Chapter 6, but may need to be revisited as you iterate through the process.
2. **Estimate the effort for each work task**—Based on specific resource types, estimate the amount of effort each task will require. Covered in Chapter 7, but may need to be revisited as well until resource assignments are finalized.
3. **Determine task relationships (network diagram)**—Identify which tasks have to be done before others can begin and which tasks can be done at the same time (in parallel).
4. **Assign resources**—Assign the roles, personnel, and equipment that will perform each task.
5. **Develop preliminary schedule**—If you have not already, capture all these inputs using your preferred scheduling software.
6. **Perform "reality" check**—A key, often overlooked, step in the process to make your schedule realistic. This step includes a review of resource allocation and calendar setup.
7. **Shorten the schedule**—In this step, you determine the critical path and look for ways to reduce the time required to complete the critical path tasks.

Due to the number of inputs, tradeoffs, and feedback points, the schedule development process is a natural, iterative process.

Expect to continuously loop back through this process and refine your inputs until a final, approved schedule is achieved.

8. **Account for risk responses**—If any of the risk responses includes adding a contingency buffer to any specific task or to the entire schedule, make sure to include this in the schedule too.
9. **Walk-through the schedule**—In this important step, the proposed schedule is presented for review and feedback. At a minimum, the schedule should be closely reviewed by the core project team first, and then by the key stakeholders (management, customers).
10. **Finalize schedule**—Incorporate feedback from stakeholders; make any adjustments for actual resource assignments, final risk responses, and success factor tradeoffs; get formal acceptance of schedule.

Let's take a closer look at a few of the key steps.

Determining Task Relationships (Sequencing the Work)

In this step, we think about what needs to be done first and what can be done at the same time. We want to capture the logical relationships that exist between the tasks in our WBS. The traditional technique used to capture these relationships is the network diagram. An example of a network diagram is pictured in Figure 8.5.

FIGURE 8.5
Example of a partial network diagram showing logical sequence of tasks.

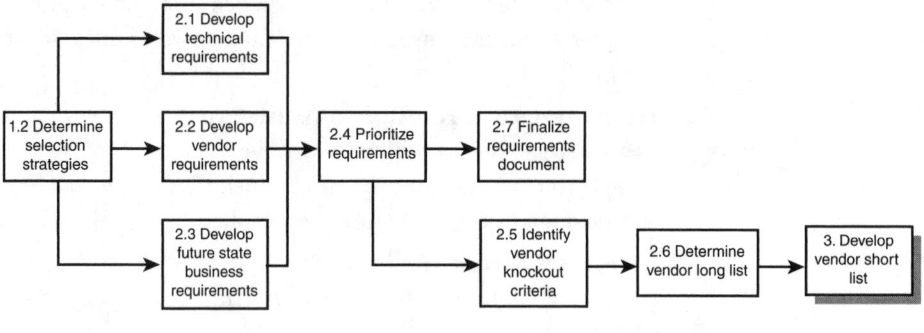

Unlike most introductory project management books, I'm not going to spend 5–10 pages (or more) on traditional network diagram topics such as types of network diagrams (Activity-on-Node, Activity-on-Arrow, GERT), dependency types (Finish-to-Start, Start-to-Finish, Start-to-Start, Finish-to-Finish), or mathematical analysis scheduling techniques (Critical Path Method, PERT, and Monte Carlo simulation). Why? Because unless you are in a specialized industry, these techniques are not used very often, and most project scheduling software will take care of this for you (if you know how to use it). Of course, if you plan to take the PMP, you will need to hone up on these concepts.

The whole idea here is look at your work visually and think about in what order (sequence) the work needs to occur. This is an exercise in logic. In many cases, this step is an excellent team activity. At this time, you don't want to concern yourself with resource constraints: just focus on logical sequence of the work. When you complete this task, you want to be clear on three things:

- For each task, what others tasks must be completed first?
- For the project, what tasks could be done at the same time (concurrently, in parallel)?
- For the project, where are your external dependencies? What tasks need an external event or task to complete, before it can start?

caution

A common reason for unrealistic schedules is that the schedule does not account for all the logical dependencies that exist. The schedule will generally reflect an earlier completion date than what is actually possible.

tip

Become knowledgeable and proficient at the scheduling software you use. Many unrealistic schedules originate with a project manager who does not understand how to best use the tool. For those who use Microsoft Project, make sure to check out Chapter 23.

Building the Preliminary Schedule

Now that we have our key inputs (WBS, task relationships, effort estimates, and resource assignments), we are ready to build our initial schedule. There are a few keys to remember here:

- Use scheduling software and get properly trained in how to use it.

VALUE OF SCHEDULING SOFTWARE

In case you are not an advocate of scheduling software, or you need to help convince someone else in your organization, please note the following benefits provided by scheduling software:

- Critical path analysis
- Project and resource calendars
- Schedule calculation
- Resource leveling
- Baseline management

- If you've completed the other steps well up to this point, this step is much, easier.
- For each task you want to schedule, you need to enter the following information:
    - Task name
    - Estimated effort
    - Predecessor task
    - Assigned resource
- Understand the relationship between work, duration, resources, and productivity.

  The duration of a task is dependent upon the number of resources (and their productivity rate) that are assigned to the total work effort.
- Using the scheduling software, locate the critical path. Often, the software will differentiate the tasks that comprise the critical path in some way, such as showing these tasks in red font.

  The critical path is the longest path through your network and represents the minimum amount of time it will take to complete the project.
- While the overall schedule development process should be a team-based activity, a single person generally performs the construction of the actual schedule, due to the nature of the software.

caution

Avoid entering start and end dates for tasks unless you have a hard, fixed milestone date that must be honored.

These dates establish constraints in the scheduling software and can give you unexpected results.

tip

A team-based schedule development approach should be pursued whenever possible for two primary reasons:

- Higher quality schedule
- Team ownership of the schedule

Team collaboration tools like Mindjet's MindManager can be very effective for these activities.

Perform "Reality" Check

In this step, we need to make sure the schedule is reasonable and is aligned with the organizational culture. The primary checkpoints are to check for proper allocation of resources and to check for proper use of calendars.

note

A schedule is considered "preliminary" until resource assignments are confirmed.

When checking for proper allocation resources, you want to do two things: remove unrealistic work allocations and optimize the use of your resources.

This activity is commonly referred to as *resource leveling*. Most scheduling software systems provide a function to do this for you, but proceed with caution—the software does not always get this right. As a result, you can have a less than optimal schedule.

I recommend, especially if you are just beginning, that you manually level the allocation of your resources. You will learn more about your scheduling software and become more intimate with your schedule.

Review the resource schedule and look for any allocation that is over the maximum hours per day or per week. In other words, if Joe Analyst is allocated for 16 hours on Monday, we have an unrealistic expectation. An adjustment needs to be made. The three common responses to resource over-allocation situations are

- Utilize other resources. Assign one or more of the affected tasks to an available resource.
- Establish a predecessor relationship. If Joe is the one who must perform each task, make the start of one task dependent on the finish of the other(s).
- Modify the priority level of one or more of the tasks and let the software perform its resource leveling function.

caution

Over-allocated resources and misaligned schedule calendars are two of the most common causes of unrealistic project schedules.

To check for proper use of calendars, verify the following:

- Are non-working days accounted for (holidays, weekends)?
- Are the number of work hours per day consistent with the organization's expectation? Are eight hours of productivity per day assumed or something different?
- For part-time resources or resources with special work schedules, are individual calendars assigned to them that reflect this reality?

Shorten the Schedule

On most projects, your preliminary schedule will not be the schedule presented to the stakeholders for approval. Due to either stakeholder expectations or an external deadline that must be met, an effort must be made to compress or "shorten" the schedule without reducing the scope of the project. The key to this effort is the critical path.

The critical path determines the earliest (the soonest) your project can be completed given the current task relationships and estimated durations. As a project manager, you want to be very clear about which tasks comprise the critical path for two reasons:

- If you can reduce this critical path (or change it), you may be able to complete the project sooner.
- Any slippage in the completion of a critical path task will push out the completion date for the entire project.

The only way to shorten a schedule is to compress the critical path time.

The common techniques to consider are detailed in Table 8.1.

Table 8.1 Techniques for Compressing the Project Schedule

Technique	Definition	Key Issue(s)
Crashing	Adding resources to critical path activities only.	Certain activities cannot be completed faster by adding resources. Additional resources often add overhead that can negate any time savings. Crashing can increase project costs.
Fast tracking	Performing critical path activities in parallel.	Fast tracking is a high-risk technique that increases the probability of rework.
Process improvements	Gaining productivity increases based on different work processes, technologies, and/or machinery.	New approaches can increase project risks. Process improvements are not always available.
Limited overtime	Increasing the number of hours per day or week available to work on project tasks.	Overtime is most effective when used for limited periods of time. Overuse can lead to team morale and quality of work issues.

Walk Through the Schedule

In our pursuit of both a more realistic schedule and a schedule that our stakeholders feel ownership for, we need to walk through the schedule with at least two groups—and if at all possible get a third quality-based review.

- **Review with project team**—First, present the proposed schedule to your project team. Seek their feedback on all aspects: complete task listing, correct resource assignments, logical task sequence, reality factors, and so on. Make any necessary adjustments.

tip

Techniques to shorten the project schedule can also be deployed during project execution as a corrective action to a schedule variance.

Clearly document and communicate all assumptions used in building the schedule.

- **Quality review**—This review is not always possible, but whenever possible, have an experienced and knowledgeable project scheduler review your proposed schedule before you submit it to your stakeholders. Especially if you are just gaining experience at this, this input and training can be invaluable.
- **Review with project stakeholders**—Present the proposed schedule to key stakeholders. Seek feedback and questions on all aspects: verify resource assignments, risk responses, key milestones, and so forth. There are two keys to this step. One, the form and manner in which the schedule information is presented (making it as reviewer friendly as possible); and two, investing the time to have a real-time, interactive review session.

Presenting the Schedule

One element of project planning and project management that is often overlooked is effectively communicating the project schedule to the various project stakeholders. Although presenting a detailed, tabular view of the schedule to the core team is acceptable, the use of visual summary representations of the schedule is highly recommended when presenting the schedule to other stakeholders. The common methods of presenting a project schedule summary are detailed in Table 8.2.

Table 8.2 Methods for Presenting a Project Schedule Summary

Method	Key Attributes	Benefits	Notes
Milestone chart	This is a bar chart that shows start and end dates, major deliverables, and key external dependencies.	Highlights key decision and completion points as well as any external dependencies.	Milestone tables are also used (same information, no bar chart).
Gantt chart	This is a bar chart that shows the various levels of the WBS.	Easy to read, incorporates the WBS, and can easily show actual progress against estimates.	Usually does not generally show interdependencies.

Table 8.2 (continued)

Method	Key Attributes	Benefits	Notes
Network diagram	A network diagram uses nodes and arrows. Date information is added to each activity node.	Highlights the critical path and shows project logic (flow).	For presentations, the summary task level of the WBS is generally used. Otherwise, a network diagram is best suited for wall display.
Modified WBS	Uses the project WBS organization with status information added to each node.	Shows progress against original work breakdown organization. Easy to read.	Similar to network diagram type representations.

THE ABSOLUTE MINIMUM

At this point, you should have a solid understanding of the following:

- Schedule development is an iterative, team-based activity.
- The project schedule is a critical component of the project plan and integrates all the key planning activities.
- The project schedule drives the project budget and the resource schedule.
- The project schedule is the project manager's most effective tool in managing expectations regarding the key success factors (time, cost, and quality).
- The five key inputs for the schedule are the WBS, the effort estimates, the task relationships, assigned resources, and the planned risk responses.
- Many reasons for an unrealistic schedule originate with an inadequate schedule development process and inadequate training with the scheduling software.
- Document and clearly communicate all scheduling assumptions.

The map in Figure 8.6 summarizes the main points we reviewed in this chapter.

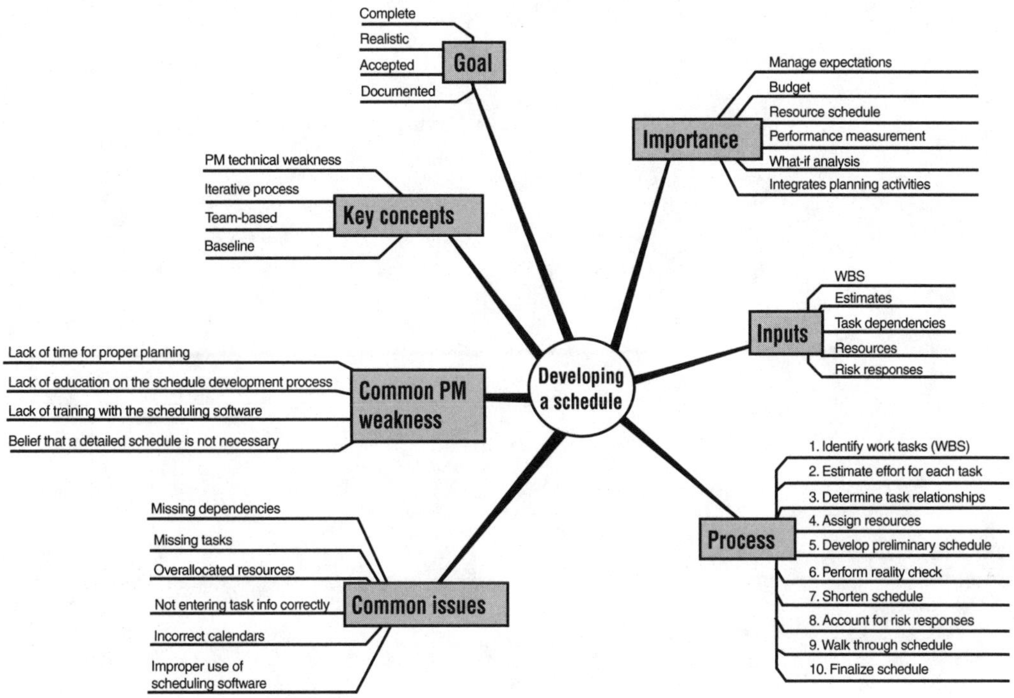

FIGURE 8.6

Overview of developing a schedule.

In This Chapter

- Understand why the project budget is important to project success
- Review the process for figuring a realistic budget
- Learn the key project budgeting principles
- Understand the common mistakes people make when building a project budget

9

Determining the Project Budget

It's one of the key success factors for projects—completing the project within budget. Yet, for many project managers, especially those managing internal projects, it's the success factor they have the least awareness about. There are several reasons why this occurs, and it does vary by industry, but most of the reasons have to do with organizational management structures and organizational budgeting and cost controlling policies.

For our purposes, in this age of increased accountability of project investment decisions, we will assume you need to establish a project budget and will need to track costs against it as the project is executed.

Because this is an introductory project management book, we will avoid any discussion of advanced financial topics and instead will put our focus on the "need to know" fundamentals for figuring your project budget. In this chapter, we emphasize the importance of the project budget, review the process and key principles for developing a realistic budget, and highlight the areas where people often go astray. This leads to a budget that has credibility with your stakeholders and provides you with the foundation to effectively track project costs and manage project execution.

The Impact of the Project Budget

Even if you find yourself in an environment where it is not expected that you develop a project budget (instead you are asked to primarily manage schedule and scope), I strongly encourage you to do two things:

- **Do it anyway**—Develop a project budget anyway. This exercise builds your project management skills, enables you to recognize project performance issues sooner, and better prepares you for senior management discussions about your project.
- **Follow the money**—You should have determined this as part of project definition, but just in case you haven't, make sure you are totally clear on who is financially sponsoring the project and who controls any financial-based decisions to be made about your project. This awareness is key in your efforts to manage expectations and to understand the political aspects of your project.

The project budget estimates all the costs the project will incur, when they will be incurred, and is a key component of the overall project plan. The project budget is important for the following reasons:

- **Planning validator**—Because the project schedule is a main driver for the project budget, the budget can serve as an excellent cross-reference for the validity of the schedule and vice versa. By looking at the schedule from a cost perspective, you may see resource or budget issues that were not obvious before. Inversely, the schedule input is key for validating the project budget, because the budget needs to account for all the time a resource is required on the project.
- **Performance measurement**—By measuring project progress against a cost baseline, you can better measure the true performance of your project along the way, and in most cases, identify issues and risks much sooner. This is the basis for an advanced project controlling technique called *earned value management*, which we will discuss in Chapter 10, "Controlling a Project."

- **Managing expectations**—The budget impacts stakeholder expectations in several ways. The initial budget sets the expectation on what the total project costs should be. If the budget is not developed properly then you are bound to have an expectation issue. If the project budget is predefined and serves as a cost ceiling for the project then it helps you to set stakeholder expectations regarding project schedule and project scope.
- **Cash flow management tool**—Your schedule drives the timing of your resource needs. Especially in organizations where resources are shared across projects or centrally managed, the accuracy of the schedule is key to efficient resource management.
- **Justifying project investment**—With more projects accountable to a project selection process and to financial return on investment expectations, it is increasingly important to establish the cost baseline for the project and monitor closely.

Principles of an Effective Budget

Before we get into the details of building a project budget, let's review the fundamental principles that will guide this process:

- **Iterative process**—Budget development is an iterative process just like all project planning. The various facets of project planning all interrelate and have natural feedback loops. With the project budget, there are strong dependencies on organizational policies and on the schedule development process. As a result, it usually takes several cycles to fully develop the budget and to get an agreement.
- **Total lifecycle**—The budget should address the total project lifecycle. This is a common oversight, especially for the operational phases of the project.
- **Time-phased**—Not only do we need to budget cost totals, but we need to know when these costs will be incurred for both cash flow management and project control reasons. The goal of the project budgeting process is to establish a cost baseline.
- **Comprehensive**—The budget should account for all project costs. There is a tendency to only account for obvious resources needed for the project (labor, new equipment). As part of our focus on making the budget (like the schedule) complete and realistic, we'll cover all the costs that need to be considered later in this chapter.

caution

Make sure your project budget accounts for all cost factors and for the entire lifecycle of the effort.

- **Include a buffer**—A buffer, normally referred to as management reserve, should be allocated to the project budget. The management reserve is primarily there to deal with known risks (a risk response), the estimating uncertainty factor, and the overall planning uncertainty factor (hidden work, re-work, hidden costs, change requests). In addition, if you have a long-term project or an international project, you may need a buffer for monetary factors such as inflation and exchange rates. Of course, these should be noted as risks in these situations.
- **Document assumptions**—Budget assumptions are documented like all other project assumptions. Any assumption made as part of the budgeting process should be documented and clearly communicated. As with all assumptions, you can document them within the targeted deliverable (in this case the budget document spreadsheet), or add them to the designated repository for project assumptions (commonly either a separate assumptions document, the project definition document, or project plan).

Creating a Project Budget

The actual process of developing a project budget is straightforward. The general challenges lie more with omissions and the foundation the budget is based upon. In this section, we will review the details of the development budget and finalize budget steps that we have depicted in our general project planning process flow (see Figure 9.1).

Sources of Project Costs

The first step in building a project budget is to identify your costs. This sounds easy enough, right? Let's review the cost sources that need to be considered. These cost sources are summarized in Figure 9.2.

- **Labor costs**—One of the key budget cost items. Budget should reflect a line item for each person or role—whichever makes the most sense for your project. Costs are based on resource rates and estimated work durations. When dealing with external labor, these costs are a key component of the business relationship and normally easy to obtain. However, it can be difficult getting rates for internal resources. In most organizations, either the human resources or finance department should have standard labor rates for internal resources based on role.
- **Equipment**—This category generally includes the tools that the project team requires to complete the work of the project. For budget purposes, the keys with the equipment category are twofold:

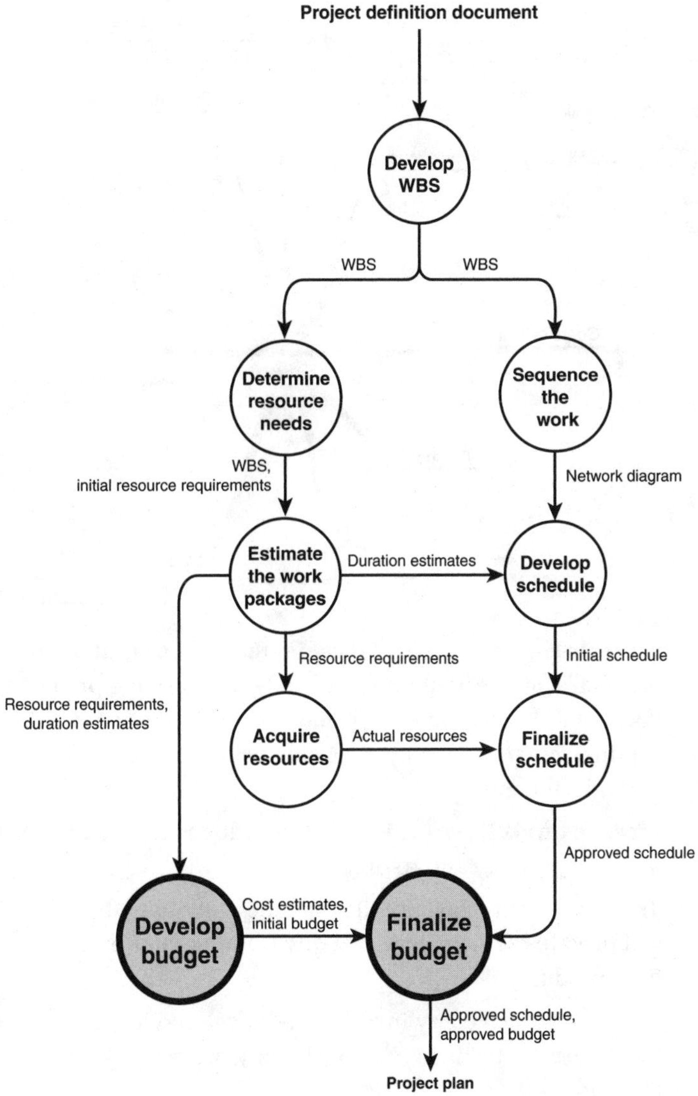

FIGURE 9.1
The budget-focused planning steps.

- **Completeness**—Using a bottom-up estimating approach should identify all equipment needs from a task perspective. For knowledge-based projects, you need to account for software-based tools too.
- **Expense versus capital**—You should work with accounting to determine whether your equipment costs need to be expensed at full cost against your project or whether your project just needs to reflect depreciation cost. Different factors can influence this decision, but the most common one is whether or not the equipment will be used by more than one project.

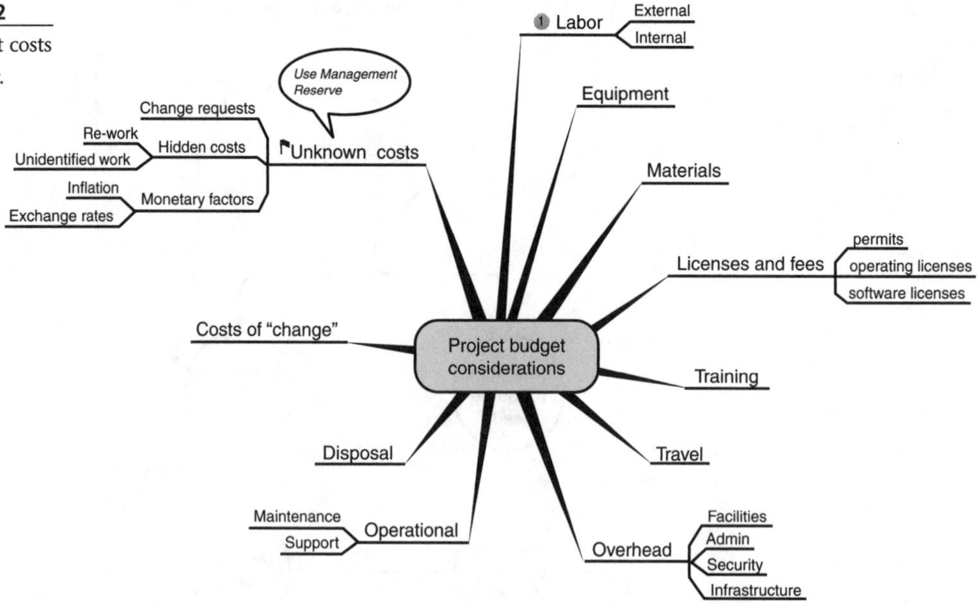

FIGURE 9.2
The budget costs to consider.

- **Materials**—This category includes those items that are needed to build the product. The information is generally found in the product specifications document. In dealing with vendor relationships, you would either acquire or confirm material costs by reviewing vendor responses to the formal procurement documents.
- **Licenses and Fees**—This category includes costs such as software licenses, building permits, and so on.
- **Training**—This category includes the cost of any training your project team will need to do their work and any training your users may need to use the final product.
- **Travel**—This category includes the travel and lodging costs to be charged to the project that will be incurred by any project team member while doing the work of the project.
- **Operational costs**—This category includes the costs associated with the maintenance and support of the final product. In addition, there may be costs to dispose of whatever the project is replacing.
- **Disposal costs**—This category includes the costs associated with the disposal or removal of whatever the project is replacing.
- **Overhead costs**—This category includes the common overhead costs incurred by any project. Items typically included are facilities, administrative assistance, security, and technology infrastructure. Depending on the organization, these costs may not be allocated to individual projects or there may be a pre-determined percentage or amount that is used by all projects.

- **Costs of "change"**—A focal point of project planning is to consider the "change" impact that the project will have. This category would include any costs (change management programs, initial productivity loss) that can directly attribute to the change factor. These costs should have been considered during the project selection phase as part of a cost-benefit analysis or return on investment analysis. In addition, these costs may be accounted for in the other budget categories. The important thing here is to think about these costs up-front during planning.

Develop Initial Budget

Once we have our resource requirements and work duration estimates, we can start to develop the budget. Like the estimates for work, it is best to estimate your costs at the work package level. By taking a bottom-up approach, you are in the best position to identify all your resource needs and develop a more realistic budget. In addition, many industries and organizations have cost estimate models that can be leveraged, too. These models are best used during initial planning activities and as a cross-reference and validation tool for your detailed planning efforts.

Unless your organization has invested in an enterprise project management application with an emphasis on project costing or you have advanced skills in project scheduling software, I recommend the use of spreadsheet software (such as Microsoft Excel) for your project budget. I favor the spreadsheet approach for three principal reasons:

- **Capture all costs**—The spreadsheet approach allows you to easily capture all your project costs (and not just labor costs, which is the primary cost element captured by your schedule).
- **Flexible**—The spreadsheet approach offers flexible options in how you set up and organize your budget. It can also be used to track your project costs during project execution.
- **Easy analysis**—The spreadsheet approach comes with built-in analysis and reporting capabilities that can be easily leveraged.

Most project scheduling software programs offer a resource schedule that shows the total hours (and total costs) that each resource incurs over the desired time period. This feature can be very helpful to your budgeting process.

The two keys for setting up your project budget are to set a line item for each cost source and to use columns for each time phase (period) that will be tracked.

Finalize Budget

Once the schedule nears completion and the actual resources have been identified, we can finalize the project budget. Besides firming up rates on resources and estimates on other cost factors, there are several objectives to accomplish in this step.

- **Validate procurement tasks scheduled**—Make sure that all the tasks dealing with procuring resources (labor, equipment, materials) are accounted for in the project schedule (and WBS). Common tasks include ordering, delivery, setup, and payment.
- **Reconcile task costs versus resource costs**—In most cases, there will be gaps between resource assignments on the schedule, or resources will not always be scheduled at maximum capacity. Much of this depends on how efficiently resources are leveled. Nevertheless, if your resource costs are based solely on assigned tasks, your budget may not reflect the actual resource costs you will incur. For example, Joe Analyst may only have 26 estimated work hours assigned one week, but is fully booked at 40 hours the following week. You can't afford to release Joe for the small gap that exists, so the project is generally accountable for all his time both weeks. This situation also depends on the level of responsibility the project has for maximizing resource usage, the level of resource planning done in the organization, and how time is reported.

  A good rule of thumb is to calculate personnel costs by taking their rates multiplied by a given calendar time period. For example, if I know Joe Analyst is on my project for 12 weeks, and I know he is generally a full-time resource, I will calculate a resource cost for Joe by taking Joe's hourly rate × 40 hours × 12 weeks. This is likely to give me a truer cost estimate—at least a more conservative one.
- **Finalize management reserve**—Based on all known risk factors, finalize the buffer amount to be added to the project budget. The specific amount will vary depending on risk level, industry practices, and management philosophy.

Common Budget Challenges

Let's take a quick review of the common challenges that a project manager faces when figuring a project budget. By increasing awareness of these factors, you can work proactively to avoid these in your own situation.

- **Based on weak foundation**—The budget is built on the planning foundation created by the WBS, resource estimates, effort estimates, and the project schedule. An inadequacy in any of these elements is directly reflected in the budget.

- **Missing cost categories**—The budget needs to reflect all the costs that will be incurred or at least all the costs that the project is accountable for by the sponsoring organization. See earlier section for the list of cost sources that should be considered.
- **No profit margin**—For projects that are sold to clients, do not forget to include the profit margin in your project budget and in your pricing decisions.
- **Budget is pre-allocated**—In many organizations, due to the nature of their budgeting cycles and level of project management maturity, the budgets for projects are established (from high level estimates) before the complete work of the project is defined. In these cases, the budget is often the dominant constraint on the project; as a result, it will limit the amount of work that can be completed and the resourcing options available.
- **Labor costs not tracked**—More of an issue for internal projects, but in many organizations it can be difficult for the project manager to define and track labor costs, especially for internal staff. The most common reasons for this include:
    - Organizational policy that project managers do not track internal labor costs
    - Organizational policy to treat internal labor as "sunk costs"
    - A mismatch between time reporting system/procedures and needs of the project

  This last reason is important to understand and may limit your cost tracking options, or at least the level of detail information you can obtain.

The Absolute Minimum

At this point, you should have a solid understanding of the following:

- If the other planning activities have been done well, establishing a project budget is a very straightforward process.
- The project budget is vital for managing expectations, accurately measuring project performance, and managing cash flow.
- An effective project budget is time-phased, addresses the complete project lifecycle, and accounts for all project costs.
- The project budget is a critical component of the project plan and integrates the project schedule, resource plan, procurement plan, and risk response plan.

- The WBS, work estimates, and project schedule provide the foundation for a solid project budget.
- Spreadsheet software is usually the best tool to use for project budgeting.

The map in Figure 9.3 summarizes the main points we reviewed in this chapter.

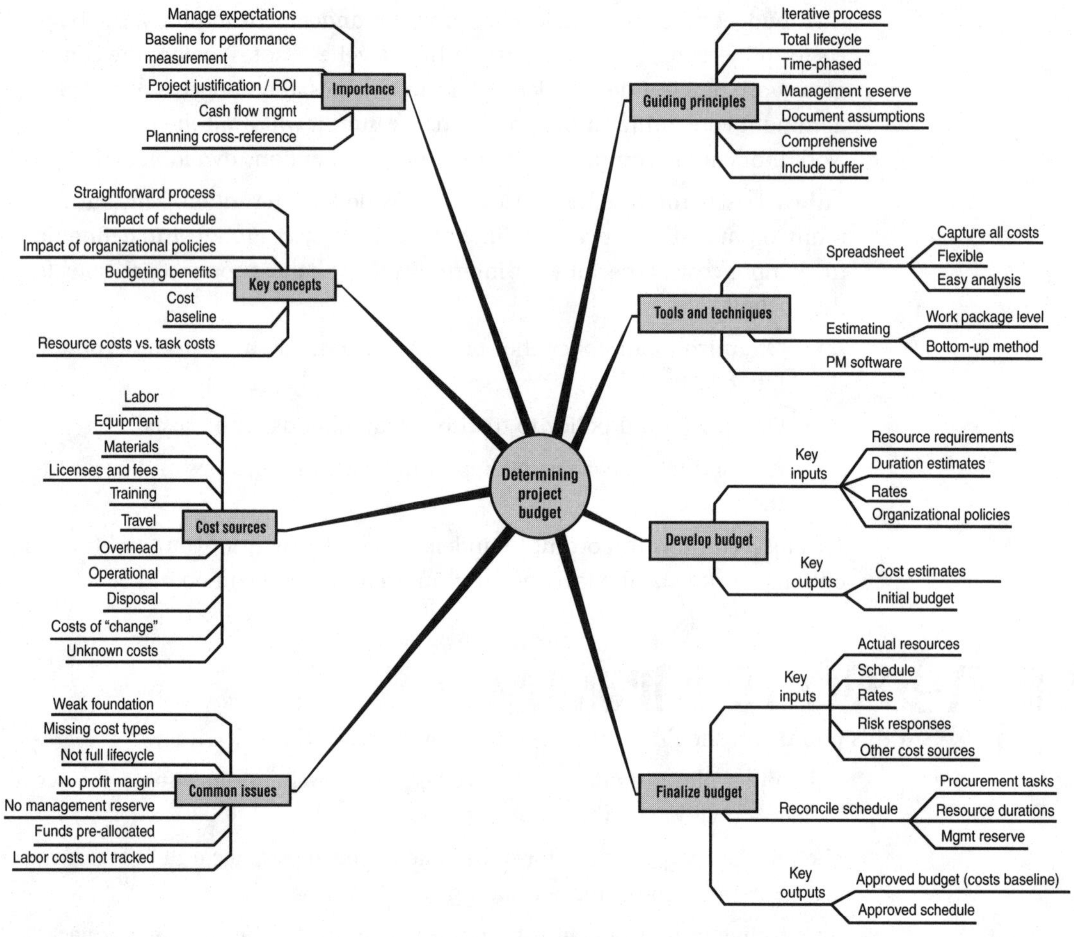

FIGURE 9.3

Overview of figuring a budget.

PART iii

PROJECT CONTROL

In This Chapter

- Clarify what we mean by "controlling" a project
- Understand why project planning is so important to controlling a project
- Learn the principles of an effective project control system
- Learn powerful techniques that simplify project control
- Understand why earned value management is the best technique for measuring project performance, yet the least used
- Review the essential principles of project status reporting

10

Controlling a Project

Now that we have our project plan, we are ready to implement it. From a project management perspective, implementing a project plan involves two general categories of activities: project execution and project control. These activities are performed in parallel to complete the work of the project, report project progress, and keep the project on track. For the purposes of this book, we will address the process-focused activities in Part III of the book, "Project Control," and the people-focused aspects in Part IV, "Project Execution."

While there are entire books and courses that address just single aspects of project control and project execution, we will focus on the "need to know" fundamentals that will greatly reduce your learning curve and accelerate your effectiveness as a project manager.

This chapter serves as an excellent bridge between the "Project Planning" part we just completed and the "Project Control" part we are just beginning. In this chapter, we will clarify what "controlling" a project" really means, emphasize the key principles of a project control system, highlight the impact that project planning has on this effort, review powerful techniques that should always be considered, and discuss how to avoid the common challenges faced by most project managers. Finally, to summarize the key fundamentals of controlling a project, we will study the lessons that can be learned from project recovery missions. This will lead to an understanding that will enable you to develop an appropriate project control system that best meets the needs of your next project.

What Is Project Control?

What do you think of when you hear "project control"? Micromanager? Confrontation? Inflexible? Military-style leadership? Theory X management? Fortunately, none of these terms accurately describe project control. Project control consists of the information systems and the management procedures that allow us to answer questions such as

- Are we on track?
- Are we on budget?
- Are we on schedule?
- Are we delivering what we said we would?
- Are we meeting quality and performance standards?
- Are we meeting stakeholder expectations?
- What have we accomplished?
- Will the project objectives be met?
- What deviations/variances exist?
- What corrective actions are we taking?
- What caused these variances?
- What risks are we monitoring?
- What issues do we need to resolve?
- What lessons have we learned?

Officially, PMI defines the controlling processes as those processes that ensure that project objectives are met by monitoring and measuring progress regularly to identify variances from plan so that corrective action can be taken, if necessary. While accurate, this definition does not clearly communicate all the aspects of project control that we need to understand, and does not emphasize the most important aspect—prevention.

PDA: The Principles of Project Control

An easy way to remember what project control is all about is to think *PDA*. PDA stands for Prevention, Detection, and Action. Let's take a closer look at these fundamental principles of project control:

- **Prevention**—As with your own health, the secret to wellness is strengthening your immune system and minimizing contact with harmful agents. In other words, don't get sick in the first place. The same principle applies to effective project control. The best way to keep your project on track is to prevent (or at least minimize) variances from occurring. How do you do this? This takes your entire array of project management skills, but a few key activities include investing in planning, communicating effectively, monitoring risk factors continuously, resolving issues aggressively, and delegating work clearly.
- **Detection**—For this aspect of project control, think "radar system" or "early warning system." Project control should provide early detection of variances. The sooner we can act on a variance, the more likely we are to get the success factor back on track. The key for early detection is to have the tracking systems and work processes in place that allow for the timely measurement of project results. Common examples of detection methods are performance reporting and review meetings. Two important concepts to note here are that to have a variance, you must be comparing actual results to a baseline of some type, and a variance can apply to any of the critical success factors, including stakeholder expectations and quality, not just schedule, cost, and scope.
- **Action**—While the prevention aspect has a strong action orientation too, this principle goes hand-in-hand with early detection. For project control to be effective, the detection of a variance must be able to trigger an appropriate and timely response. The three most common action types are corrective actions, change control procedures, and lessons learned.

tip

Controlling project performance is all about PDA—Prevention, Detection, and Action.

tip

"Lessons learned" are important resources for improving performance on the current project and on future projects.

Often, as part of the planning for project control, specific variance thresholds are established that dictate what variances and corrective actions can be managed by the project team and what ones need the immediate attention of senior level management.

Components of Project Control

To better clarify what is involved with project control, let's review some of the key project management processes that are involved. To reiterate, project control involves more than just these processes. Your leadership, communication, interpersonal, analytical, and team management skills are equally, if not more, important to this endeavor. However, without these fundamental management processes in place, as depicted in Figure 10.1, you will have a much more challenging time.

- **Performance Reporting**—The process for measuring and communicating project status to the targeted stakeholders. Information generally focused on the performance of critical success factors against baseline targets, key issues, corrective actions, and forecasted metrics.
- **Change Control Management**—The process for reviewing, approving, and coordinating any request to alter project scope schedule or budget. We will address this in greater detail in Chapter 11, "Managing Project Changes."
- **Configuration Management**—The process for controlling changes, updates, and versions of project deliverables. We will discuss this in greater detail in Chapter 11, and in Chapter 12, "Managing Project Deliverables."
- **Issue Management**—The process for identifying, tracking, and resolving issues that could impact the project critical success factors. We will address this in greater detail in Chapter 13, "Managing Project Issues."
- **Risk Management**—The process for identifying, monitoring, and responding to project risks. We will address this in greater detail in Chapter 14, "Managing Project Risks."
- **Quality Management**—The process for ensuring that work processes and project deliverables meet quality expectations. We will address this in greater detail in Chapter 15, "Managing Project Quality."
- **Procurement Management**—The controlling processes specifically used to manage any suppliers and vendors involved in the project.
- **Requirements Management**—The process to ensure all requirements are identified correctly, documented, and tracked throughout the project. This is an excellent scope and change control technique that we will mention again later in this chapter.

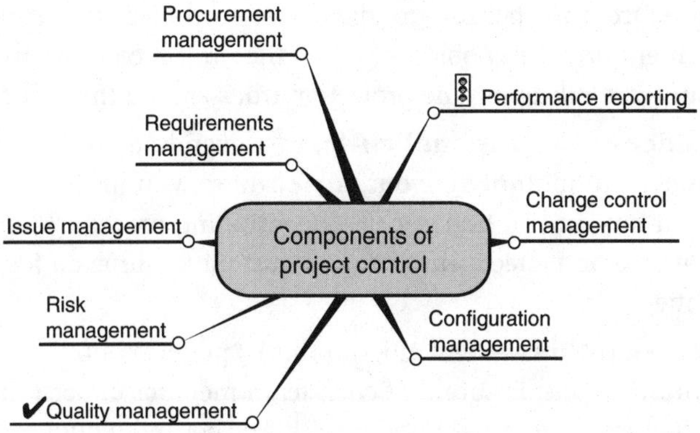

FIGURE 10.1
Summarizes the project management processes involved with project control.

Management Fundamentals for Project Control

caution

It is important to know that a project is the most at risk, and most likely to change, at the beginning of the project.

As a project manager, there are a few management fundamentals to consider when establishing your project control system.

- **Focus on priorities**—Understand what is important to the project and to the organization. Understand that whatever you do focus on, will become important. Make sure there is alignment between the two.
- **Scale to project**—The level of rigor and detail in your project control system should be consistent with the level of risk in the project. It should also be consistent with the project budget. In other words, projects with either low risk or small budgets should not be burdened with a project control system that is designed for larger, mission-critical projects.
- **Think "process"**—You do not want to spend all your time and energy putting out fires, trying to get basic status information, and feeling like you are not in control of your project. You want to establish a natural system of control for the project—you want to plan it in advance. This applies to the project as a whole and to each individual team member's contribution.
- **Expect changes**—Project control does not mean prevent changes at all costs. Conversely, project changes should be expected, planned, and well-managed.
- **Invest in thorough planning**—The more energy spent in planning, the easier it is to control a project. If the project is defined properly, work is

planned from the bottom-up, risks have been identified, stakeholders are in agreement on project objectives, and the project control system has been accounted for, keeping the project on track should take much less effort.

- **Consider organizational culture**—Depending on the level of project management maturity in your organization, you may need to consider a gradual implementation of project controlling procedures to achieve greater acceptance and effectiveness. Again, just make sure you focus on top priorities.
- **Set expectations**—Remember to think "project control" in your project communications. Ensure that each team member understands what is expected from the project and from his or her individual roles. In addition, make sure that the project team sees the discipline and priority that you place on all project control procedures.
- **Be consistent**—An important element to both effective project control and effective project communications is consistency. Project performance needs to be measured and reported on a consistent, regular basis. This approach is key for both early detection of variances and for establishing a culture of accountability to project assignments.
- **Pay attention early**—Just to follow-up on the last point—make sure to pay close attention to your project early on. Per a study of over 800 projects for the Department of Defense since 1977, the outcome of a project was no better than its performance taken at the 15% completion point. Thus, if a project was behind schedule and/or over-budget at the 15% completion point, it did not recover from this variance. The general consensus is that this happens for two key reasons: lax project controls in the early stages, and poor estimating. If the estimates were off for the immediate work efforts, they are unlikely to be more accurate farther down the timeline. We discuss how to handle a variance in the later "Variance Responses" section.

caution

15% Completion Rule—No project recovers from a variance at the 15% completion point. If you underestimated the near term, you are generally off on the long term too.

Powerful Techniques for Project Control

We emphasized the value and importance of planning your control system. In this section, we highlight some of powerful project control techniques that you want to consider during your planning efforts and then implement during the execution of your project.

- **Small work packages**—This was a point of emphasis during our discussion on building a WBS. If you recall, there were two primary reasons for advocating small work packages: more accurate estimates and better control. From a control perspective, if your work packages are scheduled to complete within one (or at the most, two) reporting periods, it is much easier to detect a delayed or troubled task. With earlier notice, you are more likely to resolve the variance and protect the project's critical success factors.
- **Baselines**—A fundamental control principle is to manage to baselines. First, establish a baseline. This is generally applied to the critical success factors of schedule and budget, but can be applied equally as well to product-oriented aspects of the project, especially requirements. Second, measure and report performance against the baseline. Third, maintain the baseline unless there is a formal agreement to reset the baseline. We will discuss this in greater detail in Chapter 11.
- **Status meetings**—The simplest, and most widely known, technique is the status meeting. Consistent and regular status meetings help to keep everyone honest, accountable, and on their toes—especially if work assignments are small and have clear completion criteria. In addition, status meetings are powerful tools for improving project communications and managing expectations.
- **Completion criteria**—This starts during project definition with defining the acceptance criteria for the project, and it continues for each deliverable and work assignment. Answer this question in advance for each deliverable and work assignment: "How will we know when it is done?" Understanding the completion criteria up front increases productivity and avoids many of the issues associated with status reporting on work tasks, especially the infamous "I'm 90% done" syndrome.

caution

Make sure your status meetings are scheduled and conducted in a purposeful, value-added manner. Be cognizant of the cost involved in pulling the targeted resources together. Focus on improving team synergy, project communications, managing expectations, and accountability to the team.

- **Reviews**—Reviews are a key technique for ensuring quality and managing expectations on project deliverables, and they can take many forms. The principle here is to plan for the review-feedback-correction cycle on most, if not all, of your key deliverables. Common examples of reviews are process reviews, design reviews, audits, walkthroughs, and testing. In addition, reviews can be combined with predefined milestones and checkpoints.

- **Milestones and checkpoints**—A key feature of most proven project methodologies is the use of predefined milestones and checkpoints. These markers are important points to stop, report progress, review key issues, confirm that everyone is still on-board, and verify that the project should proceed with its mission. Besides being a powerful expectations management tool, these predefined points allow project sponsors and senior management to evaluate their project investments along the way, and if warranted, redirect valuable resources from a troubled project to more promising pursuits.
- **Track requirements**—A simple, yet often neglected, technique to help control both scope and expectations is the use of a *requirements traceability matrix*. The traceability matrix provides a documented link between the original set of approved requirements, any interim deliverable, and the final work product. This technique helps maintain the visibility of each original requirement and provides a natural barrier for introducing any "new" feature along the way (or at least provides a natural trigger to your change control system). In addition, the trace matrix can link the specific test scenarios that are needed to verify that each requirement is met.
- **Formal signoffs**—Formal signoffs are a key aspect of change control management, especially for client-vendor oriented projects. The formal record of review and acceptance of a given deliverable helps to keep expectations aligned and minimize potential disputes. Most importantly, the use of a formal signoff acts as an extra incentive to make sure the appropriate stakeholders are actively engaged in the work of the project.
- **Independent QA Auditor**—The use of an independent quality assurance auditor is another specific example of the "review" technique mentioned earlier, and is often a component of project quality assurance plans. In addition, the quality audit can be focused on product deliverables, work processes, or project management activities. The power of this technique is in establishing the quality criteria in advance and in making the project accountable to an outside entity.
- **V method**—The "V method" is a term used for a common validation and verification approach that ensures that there is validation and verification step for every deliverable and interim deliverable created. The left side of "V" notes each targeted deliverable and the right side of the "V" lists the verification method to be used for each deliverable directly across. The diagram in Figure 10.2 helps illustrate this method.

FIGURE 10.2
V method approach for a software development project.

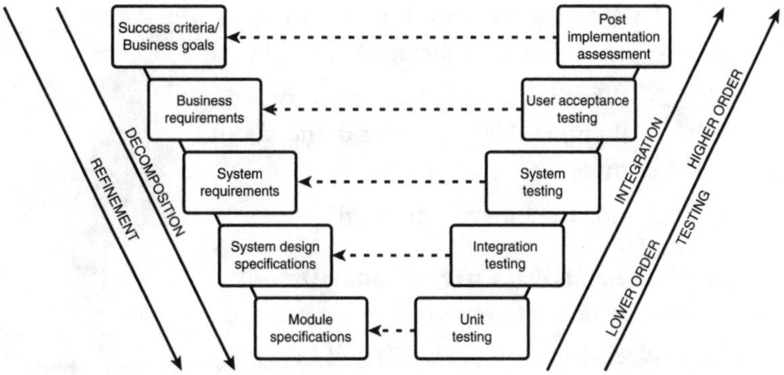

- **Escalation thresholds**—Escalation thresholds sound much more ominous than what they actually are. The purpose of escalation thresholds is to determine in advance what issues and variances the project team can handle and what issues or variances demand attention by senior management. Often, these thresholds are defined as percent variances around the critical success factors. For example, if the cost variance is greater than 10% or schedule variance is greater than 15%, engage senior management immediately for corrective action steps. The key value of this technique is that it helps define tolerance levels, set expectations, and clarifies when senior management should get involved in corrective action procedures.

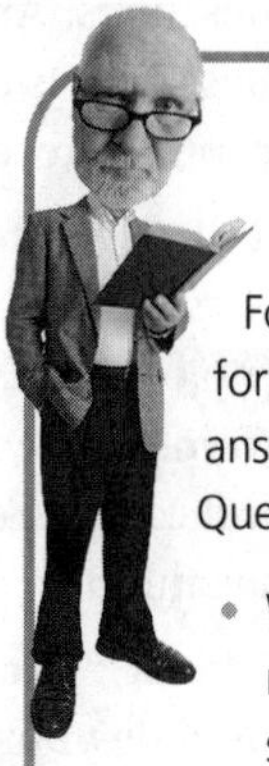

tip

Focus your project performance reports on answering the Big Three Questions:

- Where do we stand (in regard to the critical success factors)?
- What variances exist, what caused them, and what are we doing about them?
- Has the forecast changed?

Performance Reporting

As we have touched on several times already, another key aspect of project control is measuring and reporting project performance. We could easily spend an entire chapter (or two) reviewing the various options, factors, and challenges involved with this process. However, if you keep these following principles in mind, you can adapt your performance reporting process to best meet the needs of your project environment:

- **Answer the Big Three Questions**—As a rule, key stakeholders want to know the answers to these three questions when reviewing project performance:

1. Where do we stand (in regard to the critical success factors)?
2. What variances exist, what caused them, and what are we doing about them?
3. Has the forecast changed?

Performance reporting requirements should be captured as part of the project communications plan.

- **Measure from Current Baseline**—If you are going to report project performance with a variance focus, you must establish and maintain your performance baselines. Any change to the performance baselines is controlled via your change control procedures.
- **Think "visual"**—Another key concept in reporting is to think visually. Most people are visual and spatial learners and will grasp the important project performance metrics more quickly if they are presented in a visual format. The use of bar charts, graphical schedule summaries, and stoplight indicators (red, yellow, and green) for key metrics are good examples of this technique.
- **Think "summary page"**—Along this same theme, you generally want to provide your key status information in no more than 1–2 pages. If it is appropriate to have details that will take more than 1–2 pages, it is recommended that you provide a one summary page up front.
- **Highlight accomplishments**—A part of the status report's function is to serve as a public relations tool for the project, so make sure key accomplishments are highlighted prominently.
- **Show forecasts**—In addition to reporting how the project has performed to date, remember to show the forecasted schedule and cost metrics. Often, this information is shown as Estimated At Completion (EAC) and Estimated To Complete (ETC) figures. Specifically, highlight any changes to these figures from the last reporting period.
- **Highlight key issues, risks, and change requests**—A natural category when assessing project performance. Make sure any key issues, risks, and change requests are included on status reports. We will discuss these in greater detail in subsequent chapters.
- **Avoid surprises**—An important point about consistent, performance-based status reporting is that stakeholders are aware and knowledgeable regarding overall project status and are not caught off guard with project developments. To this extent, depending on the audience for any status report, you

may want to communicate with specific stakeholders in advance of any official report distribution. Always remember, don't surprise anyone—especially your sponsors and accountable senior management stakeholders.

- **Adapt to meet stakeholder needs**—This is an example of the customer service orientation and servant leadership qualities of effective project managers. Be prepared to offer examples of performance reports that have worked well for you in the past, but most importantly, go into any project looking to understand the information needs for this given environment. Show enthusiasm and willingness to adapt to the customer's standards or to develop custom formats to best meet the stakeholders' needs.
- **Appropriate frequency**—Consistent with a management fundamental mentioned earlier, the frequency of performance reporting needs to be appropriate for the project. The process of gathering information and reporting performance needs to be quick enough and occur often enough to be useful and relevant.

Variance Responses

As we have mentioned, the first goal of our project control system is to prevent any variance. However, we also realize variances and changes will occur—this is the nature of the project beast. Thus, the remaining goals of project control are centered on early detection and appropriate response. Let's review the general response options that are available to us (the project) when a variance occurs.

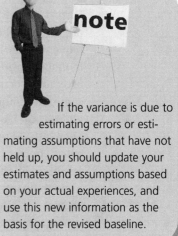

If the variance is due to estimating errors or estimating assumptions that have not held up, you should update your estimates and assumptions based on your actual experiences, and use this new information as the basis for the revised baseline.

- **Take corrective actions**—The preferred option, whenever possible, is to understand the root cause of the variance and then implement action steps to get the variance corrected. When performance measurement is frequent, it is more likely that action can be taken that will make a difference. Examples of corrective actions include adding resources, changing the process, coaching individual performance, compressing the schedule (fast-tracking, crashing), or reducing scope (this would be documented as a change request too).
- **Ignore it**—In cases where the variance is small (and falls within an acceptable threshold range), you may choose to take no action to resolve the deviation. Even in these cases, it would be advisable to log the variance as a risk factor.

- **Cancel project**—There may be times when the appropriate response is to cancel the project altogether. This response is more likely on projects where one or more key assumptions have not held or when one or more of the critical success factors has a very low tolerance for any deviations.
- **Reset baselines**—While taking corrective action is the preferred option for performance variances, there are times when the variance cannot be eliminated. This is common on knowledge-based projects and common on projects where the estimating assumptions have not held. In these cases, a decision to reset the performance baselines is made and approved. Then from this point on, performance is measured from this revised baseline. This is part of the change control procedures we will discuss more in Chapter 11.

caution

Approved change requests would cause a baseline revision too.

Leveraging Earned Value Management Concepts

Earned Value Management (EVM) (otherwise known as *variance analysis*) is the best project control technique for early detection of performance variances. The technique was developed nearly 40 years ago for the United States government to better manage contract payments to vendors. Ever since, it has grown in popularity and acceptance across many industries, and now is regarded as the preferred project control technique by PMI. However, it has not been accepted as standard practice in all industries, and it is usually a technique found in organizations or industries that are relatively mature in their management processes. Thus, we could spend an entire chapter on a technique that may not be part of your organizational culture yet. In addition, if you work in these process mature environments, you are less likely to be reading this book, and you will likely have many additional resources to address the details of earned value.

Still, there is tremendous value in a quick review of EVM. An awareness of the fundamental concepts will help you in your project controlling and performance reporting endeavors.

- **Assess cost performance and schedule performance together**—The main value of EVM is that it allows you to measure and track both schedule and cost performance together. Evaluating project performance on just one of these indicators does not always give you the true picture and does not allow you to detect variances as early.

- **Each work package has a planned value**—The planned value of any work package is the budgeted cost of the work scheduled to complete the work package. The important point here: Estimate the cost of each work package in your schedule. Also, this means that the project as a whole has a baseline schedule and budget.
- **At any point, the project has an "earned" value**—The earned value of a project is the budgeted cost of the work actually completed. In other words, how many work packages (or partial work packages) have been completed at this time? The value is expressed in budgeted cost terms, not actual costs. This allows you to perform cost analysis by comparing budgeted versus actual costs for the work completed. The important point to consider: Be aware of the costs you expected to incur for the work that has been completed.

tip

Earned Value Management (EVM) is the best project control technique for early detection of project performance variances.

Before we introduce an example EVM graph, let's review the other key terms and concepts that comprise EVM. Table 10.1 summarizes these key elements.

Table 10.1 Earned Value Management Elements

Element	Definition	Notes
Planned Value (PV)	Budgeted cost of work scheduled.	Performance baseline.
Earned Value (EV)	Budgeted cost of work performed.	For the work performed, what was the budgeted cost?
Actual Costs (AC)	Actual costs of work performed.	For the work performed, what were the actual costs?
Cost Variance (CV)	Earned Value – Actual Costs CV = EV – AC	A negative number means you are over budget.
Schedule Variance (SV)	Earned Value – Planned Value SV = EV – PV	A negative number means you are behind schedule.
Cost Performance Index (CPI)	CPI = Earned Value (EV) / Actual Costs (AC) Numerical representation of project cost performance.	CPI < 1 means your project is costing you more than you planned. CPI > 1 means you are taking less money to do the project.
Schedule Performance Index (SPI)	SPI = Earned Value (EV)/ Planned Value (PV) Numerical representation of project schedule performance.	SPI < 1 means your project is behind schedule. SPI > 1 means you are ahead of schedule.

Table 10.1 (continued)

Element	Definition	Notes
Budget at Completion (BAC)	Total baseline project budget.	
Estimate at Completion (EAC)	EAC = BAC / CPI	Based on current cost performance, what will your total cost be?
Estimate to Complete (ETC)	ETC = EAC – AC	Subtract Actual Costs from Estimate at Completion to get estimated remaining costs.

EVM takes the planned value (PV), or what you planned to do at an estimated cost, and compares it against the estimated cost of the work performed (EV) and against the actual cost of work performed (AC), or what actually got done. These metrics provide a wealth of information about whether the project tasks are taking longer than they should (schedule variance, or SV), or whether they are actually requiring more work effort to complete (cost variance, or CV). In addition, the estimate-at-completion metric (EAC) helps you forecast final project performance and determine if any corrective action needs to take place.

caution

A negative performance index value is not favorable. It means that you're behind schedule or over budget.

To illustrate how EVM could be used for performance reporting, please see Figure 10.3.

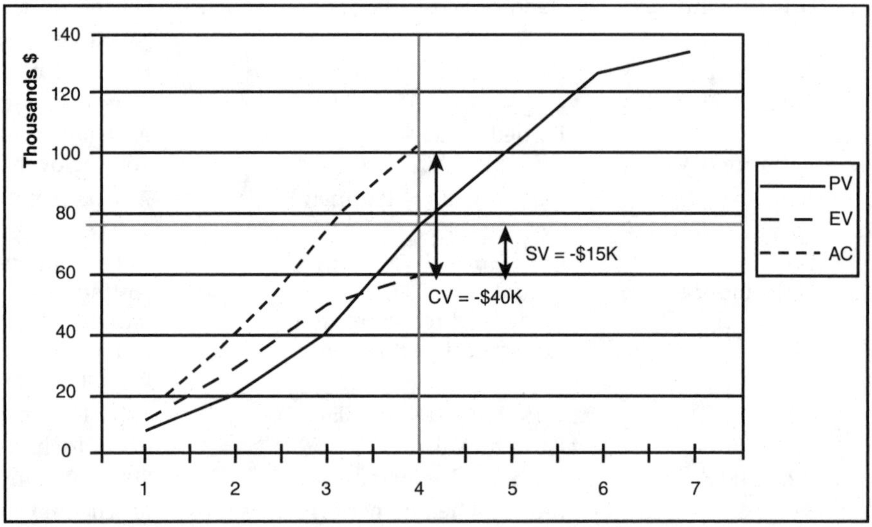

FIGURE 10.3
Depicts EVM metrics for the fourth time period on a sample project.

In this example, the report provides EVM data for the fourth reporting period. At this time, the Planned Value = $75K, the Actual Costs = $100K, and the Earned Value = $60K. On this project, we can tell the following by analyzing this report:

- There has been a cost variance from the start. It could be the actual resource costs have been higher.
- Also, for the first three weeks, the project was ahead of schedule. More work was completed than planned. This was a likely factor for the actual costs being higher too.
- During the past reporting period, something has occurred that delayed progress. The project is now behind schedule (and the cost variance has increased significantly).

Many of the project management software tools, such as Microsoft Project, include these EVM calculations. To be useful, the schedule must include all assigned resources, individual resource costs, and current progress measurements.

Common Project Control Challenges

While we've touched on several of the challenges facing project managers when attempting to control their projects, let's run down the top reasons for difficulty in the project control arena.

- **Time and cost accounting logistics**—The logistical and organizational culture issues relating to time reporting and project costs tracking can prove detrimental to timely and accurate performance reporting. During planning, you want to understand and clarify how project time and cost information is reported and how quickly you can get this data. You may need to establish project specific time reporting or approval procedures to ensure the integrity of your control system.
- **Project manager reluctance, multi-tasked**—The project manager may be reluctant to request WBS level time reporting by project team members, especially if this is not part of the organizational culture. In addition, the project manager may be over-allocated and may not be able to invest enough time to performing the project controlling duties. This is most common when the project manager has assigned other project roles to him/herself or when the project manager is assigned to multiple projects.
- **No change control**—The most popular reason is the lack of change control procedures. This is most problematic when the project scope has increased without the proper reconciliation with the project schedule and budget.

- **No completion criteria**—When clear completion criteria for work assignments is not established, you are more likely to have increased re-work cycles, more difficulty in accurately reporting progress/status, and more likely to experience the "90% done" phenomenon.
- **No baselines**—This should be obvious by now, but if a schedule and budget baseline are not established and controlled, then you will not be able to accurately measure for performance variances. Without this ability, you are less likely to detect problems early—when they are small and more manageable.
- **No requirements traceability**—Definitely an issue for controlling scope and stakeholder expectations. The lack of a formal tracking procedure between original requirements and final products increases the odds of missed work and scope creep.
- **Not consistent**—When control procedures are not consistently implemented, it is difficult to detect performance variances early, and it is more difficult to get project team members to follow the defined control procedures.
- **Measuring progress accurately**—Accurately measuring progress is a natural challenge on work assignments with intangible final products, especially on any project where status is "estimated." However, this challenge is further complicated when work definition is vague, completion criteria is not established, or when work efforts are not reported on a daily basis.
- **Impact of hidden work**—This hits at the heart of work definition and change control. Any effort spent on unidentified work, unplanned rework cycles or out-of-scope work adversely impacts the accuracy and effectiveness of project control procedures.
- **Virtual/distributed teams**—When project team members are not physically located together, it can be more difficult to get information, detect potential issues, measure work progress and ensure understanding of work expectations. We will talk more about this in Chapter 20, "Managing Differences."

The "90% done" phenomenon refers to the phenomenon where task progress is reported as on-schedule up to the 90% complete point. Then, the last 10% ends up taking most of the total task time to complete.

This can occur on projects when task status is reported subjectively by the resource assigned to the task and when there is no clear completion criteria for the task.

Lessons from Project Recoveries

To really understand what is important for controlling a project, let's review what occurs during a typical project recovery. For clarification, a project recovery is an attempt to turn around a troubled project. If there is ever a case where project control is absolutely critical, it is when you are trying to heal a sick project.

The first thing that senior management will do to recover a project is to make sure there is an effective project manager in charge. This may mean anything from validating the current project manager, bringing in someone new, pulling someone up from the project team, or providing a mentor to the current project leadership. After the project leadership is solidified, most recovery missions involve the following activities:

- **Review planning principles**—The planning principles are revisited. A focus is placed on establishing priorities and objectives, clarifying acceptance criteria, gaining consensus, and reviewing roles and responsibilities.
- **Reset baseline**—As a final step in the re-planning step, key milestones are set and new baselines are set for cost and schedule performance.
- **Frequent status checks**—To facilitate better communications, prevent additional obstacles, reinforce the visibility of the recovery mission, and emphasize individual accountability, team status meetings are conducted daily. In some situations, these checkpoints are even more frequent. It depends on the nature of the project.
- **Aggressive issue resolution**—One purpose of the frequent status checks is to gain visibility of any new or potential issue. The resolution of any new issue is aggressively pursued. These become top priorities for project leadership.
- **Ensure clarity**—Another technique normally employed in successful project recoveries is an extra effort to ensure clear understanding of all communications, expectations, and work assignments. When focus and efficiency is of paramount importance, the criticality of clear communications and mutual understanding is obvious.
- **Increase visibility and accountability**—This has been referenced indirectly already, but it is worth emphasizing again. A major reason that project recoveries often work is because people know they are more accountable for their efforts due to the increased visibility with senior management. For both the individual and the organization, the recovery mission helps to prioritize efforts and align resource allocations.

THE ABSOLUTE MINIMUM

At this point, you should have a solid understanding of the following:

- The principles of project control are prevention, detection, and action.
- Project control consists of the information systems and the management procedures that allow us to answer the key questions regarding project performance.
- Key components of project control include performance reporting, change control management, configuration management, issue management, risk management, quality management, procurement management, and requirements management.
- The key management fundamentals of project control include focus on priorities, scale to project needs and organizational culture, set up natural control processes, expect project changes, be consistent, and pay particular attention to early project performance.
- Powerful project control techniques include using small work packages, managing to project baselines, conducting regular and effective status meetings, establishing clear completion criteria for each deliverable (and the project), conducting proper reviews, tracking requirements, and getting formal signoffs.
- Performance reporting should communicate status in regard to critical success factors, any variances, and any changes to the performance forecast.
- The possible responses to an identified variance include taking corrective action, accepting it, resetting the performance baselines, and canceling the project.
- Earned Value Management (EVM) is the best project control technique for early detection of project performance variances.

The map in Figure 10.4 summarizes the main points we reviewed in this chapter.

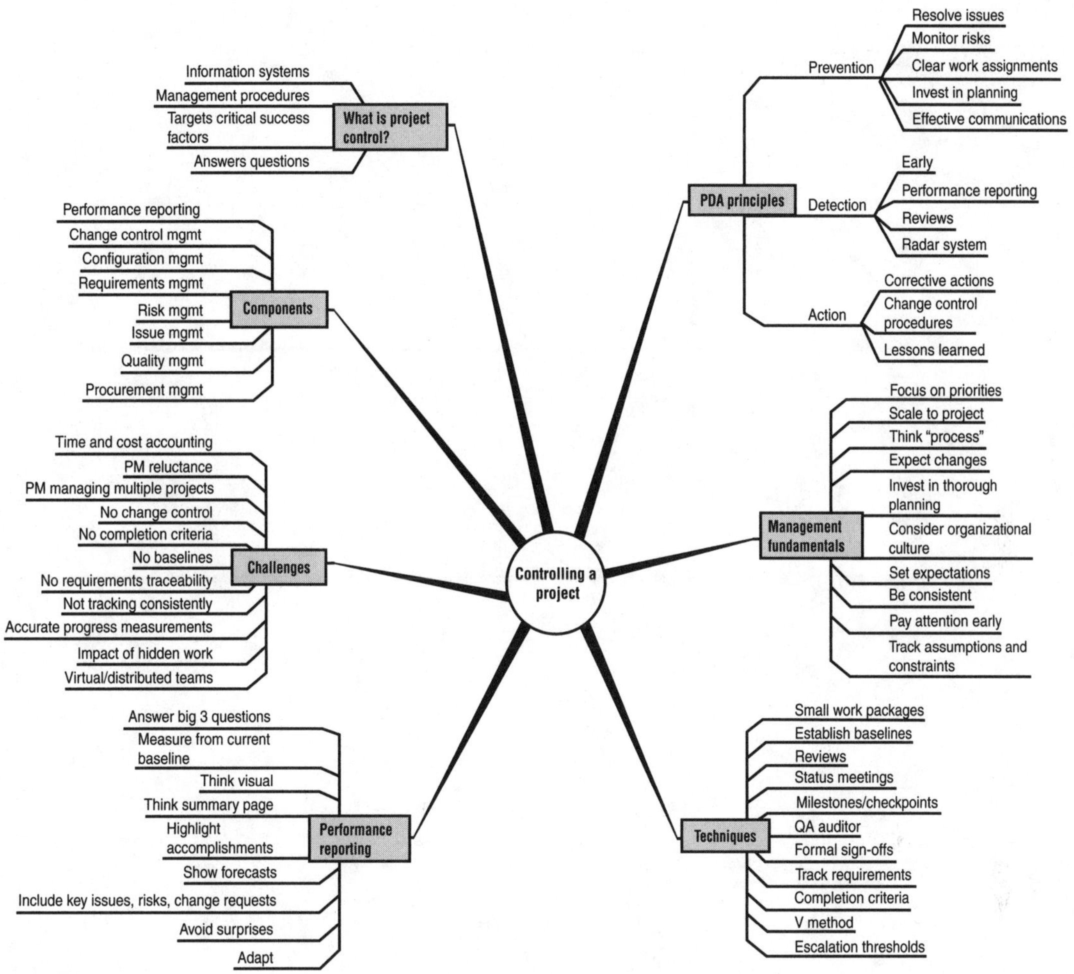

FIGURE 10.4

Overview of controlling a project.

IN THIS CHAPTER

- Understand what is meant by a project "change" and project change control
- Understand why scope changes occur
- Understand why good project managers take project change control seriously
- Learn the key management fundamentals for successfully handling project changes
- Review the essential components of an effective project change control system
- Learn how to reduce project changes
- Understand the common mistakes with managing project changes and how to avoid them

11

MANAGING PROJECT CHANGES

For many people, project control equals "managing project changes," and managing project changes equals preventing "scope creep." While this belief is not completely accurate, the perception cannot be ignored. The ability to manage and control the change elements on a project, particularly the project scope, is a key to project success and a key performance indicator for a project manager. To manage project changes effectively, a project manager must utilize all of his/her skills and demonstrate project leadership. In addition to being an insightful measure of individual project management maturity, it is not uncommon for organizations that are in the early stages of adopting project management business approaches to look at how well project changes are being managed to determine whether project management is making a difference.

While it sounds like there is a lot riding on this ability to manage project changes (and there is), the process is not difficult if you follow the key success principles and understand how to avoid the common errors.

In this chapter, we will continue our review of project control by taking a focused look at managing project changes. We will clarify what we mean by "managing project changes," understand what drives most project scope changes, review the success principles of managing project changes, emphasize the essential elements of a project change control system, review powerful techniques that should help reduce the number of changes we need to manage, and make sure we are aware of the common challenges faced by many project managers in this arena in the past.

tip

The ability to effectively manage and control project changes is a trademark of a mature project manager.

What Exactly Is a Project Change and What's the Big Deal Anyway?

A project change is a change in any of the critical success factors (scope, schedule, costs, quality, and project acceptance criteria). The "big deal" is not that there is a change. In fact, for many projects, changes—especially scope expansions—are expected and encouraged. The big deal is uncontrolled change. Why? Because a change in any of the critical success factors impacts the other factors, which will then impact project performance and the project's ability to achieve the success criteria, which will then impact stakeholder perceptions and satisfaction levels. For example, an expansion in project scope increases the work of the project. At a minimum, the increased work impacts project schedule and project costs. In many cases, the increased work also impacts resource plans and adds new risks. On projects with contractual arrangements, the increased scope will likely have contract implications and needs to be formally managed to protect all parties involved.

Scope Creep is a common term used to describe uncontrolled expansion of project scope. Scope Creep is legendary for causing project delays and cost overruns.

Thus, any time a change occurs, the project needs a way to recognize the change, evaluate the impact of the change, communicate the change, and make planning adjustments if the change is accepted. This mechanism is commonly referred to as a *project change control system*. We will review the key elements of this system later in this chapter.

A project change is a change in any of the critical success factors (scope, schedule, costs, quality, and project acceptance criteria).

Project Change Types—More Than Scope

As we mentioned before, a project change is a change to any of the critical success factors and not just scope. While scope changes are generally responsible for 80% or more of the project changes, and we will discuss these in greater detail in the next section, it is important to recognize that any of the following would also constitute a project change (and should be controlled using the project change control system):

- An expansion or reduction of project scope
- An expansion or reduction of product features
- An expansion or reduction in performance requirements
- An expansion or reduction in quality requirements
- A significant change in the target milestone dates
- A shift in the implementation or deployment strategy
- An increase in resource costs
- An expansion or reduction in the project budget
- A change in any of the project objectives
- A change in any of the final acceptance criteria, including return on investment forecasts
- A change in any of the project assumptions, constraints, or dependencies, especially regarding resources and work effort estimates
- A shift in project roles or responsibilities, especially on projects with contractual arrangements
- A decision to reset the performance baselines due to an unrecoverable performance variance

Relation to Configuration Management and Organizational Change Management

To further clarify what is meant by a project change, let's review two other change-related components of project management: configuration management and organizational change. This is a common area of confusion, because they are somewhat interrelated, they all deal with change, and they all are a part of project management. As illustrated in Figure 11.1, we are focused on change control management in this chapter. Table 11.1 summarizes the key differences between the three.

FIGURE 11.1
Highlights this chapter's focus on change control management.

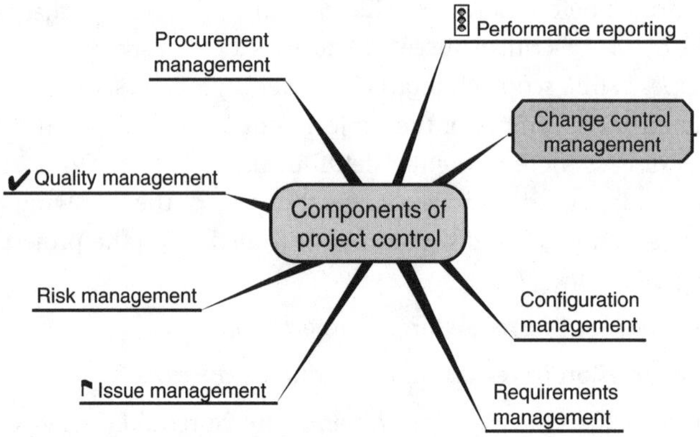

Table 11.1 Comparison of Change-Related Components of Project Management

	Change Control Management	Configuration Management	Organizational Change Management
Target	Project critical success factors.	Project deliverables, product.	Organizational impact of the project results.
Primary Concern	Project performance; stakeholder expectations.	Integrity of project deliverables; tracking changes in project deliverables.	Preparing individuals, organizational units, and customers for the changes.
Related Terms	Change control; scope management.	Document management, versions, builds.	Change management.
Discussed In	This chapter.	Chapter 12.	Chapter 18 and 20.
Notes	Focus on scope can overlap with configuration management.	Can be part of project's Overall Change Control Plan.	Not regarded as a project control activity.

Fundamentals for Managing Project Change

There are seven key management principles for effective project change control:

- **Plan for changes**—Change control does not mean preventing changes at all costs. Conversely, project changes should be expected, planned, and well managed. The two keys here are selecting the proper project approach (methodology) and setting up a project change control system (to be discussed next). For projects with an innovation focus or a volatile set of requirements, an iterative development-type approach that expects deliberate scope expansion or scope clarification should be utilized.
- **Set up a change control system**—If your organization does not already have a defined procedure for project change control, then you need to set up a change control system for your project. We will discuss the details later in this chapter. The key benefits for establishing a formal change control system include the following:
    - Helps protect the integrity of the project performance baselines
    - Ensures the right people are involved in the decision-making process
    - Helps manage stakeholder expectations
    - Enhances the credibility and professionalism of the project manager
    - Avoids issues and confrontations when changes do occur
- **Educate stakeholders**—Whether you adopt an existing change control system or develop your own, you need to step through the change control process with your stakeholders. Do not assume that because the procedure is documented that individuals understand it or their roles and responsibilities within it.
- **Use the system**—This may seem obvious, but it is a common pitfall. Make sure to utilize the change control system that you have defined. If the project manager does not consistently follow the process, no one else will either.
- **Minimize scope changes**—This is the great balance of managing project changes. On the one hand, you plan for changes and set up a system to manage those changes when they do occur; on the other hand, you work diligently on influencing those factors that are responsible for project changes, especially scope changes, to minimize their occurrence. The keys here include
    - Keep the team focused on the project objectives, the big picture.
    - Listen carefully. You need to understand immediately when a critical gap is identified.
    - Limit, if not totally avoid, any unnecessary changes by either the customer or the team.

- Educate stakeholders on the impact of their change request.
- Encourage any scope change request that is not an absolute, must-have feature to be scheduled for a follow-up project (cycle, iteration, or phase).

- **Over-communicate**—For effective stakeholder management, make sure that all project changes are clearly communicated and understood by all key project stakeholders.
- **Be a watchdog**—As a project manager, you must be continuously alert and mindful to anything that could impact your critical success factors. In particular, you need to understand what can cause unplanned scope changes to occur—and then work to prevent their occurrence.

What Causes Unplanned Scope Changes?

To better manage project changes and project risks, and to minimize the number of scope changes, it is important to understand the leading causes for unplanned scope changes on a project.

- **Shift in business drivers**—Due to the dynamic nature of the business world today, things can change quickly. These business changes can have an immediate impact on existing projects. Examples of business drivers that can alter a project's scope include
  - Available budget/funding for the project
  - New government regulations
  - Changing target market for the product
  - Time-to-market pressures
  - New business opportunities
  - Changing customer priorities
  - Unexpected market or world events
- **Shift in project acceptance criteria**—Addresses changes in either the targeted completion date, financial return on investments, client satisfaction ratings, quality levels, other expected benefits, or the stakeholders who need to approve.
- **Shift in technology**—With the move to shorter duration and phased projects, this is not as much of an issue as it has been in the past. However, there are still times when new technology becomes available during a project that will significantly meet the needs of the customer much better than what is currently planned.

- **Poor scope statement**—If the scope statement is incomplete, ambiguous, inconsistent with project assumptions, or does not address the complete business workflow process, you are much more likely to have project scope changes. Of course, this would only happen on projects that you inherited and would never happen on projects that you helped define. Right?
- **Poor requirements definition**—There are entire training courses on requirements definition and requirements management due to the importance they play on project success. Suffice to say, the more gaps that you have in your requirements, the more scope changes you are likely to have. For your awareness, here is a list of the leading reasons for poorly defined requirements:
    - Ineffective or wrong techniques used to gather requirements
    - Communication breakdowns between analysts and stakeholders
    - Requirements are not aligned with project scope
    - Requirements do not address complete process work flow
    - Documented requirements are not meaningful to targeted audience
    - Requirements not reviewed for inconsistencies
    - Requirements not verified for correctness and completeness
    - Missing stakeholders
    - Users signoff without a "real" understanding of what the documented requirements mean

Essential Elements of a Project Change Control System

At the heart of managing project changes well is a project change control system. The specifics of project change control systems can vary depending on industry, organization, and project importance, but there are essential principles, guidelines, and components that every change control system should possess.

Principles

Effective project change control systems follow these key principles:

- Any proposed scope change is documented, evaluated, and approved before it is implemented.
- The appropriate stakeholders are involved in the evaluation and approval process.

- Any change request is thoroughly assessed for impact to other project critical success factors, especially project schedule and budget.
- The appropriate management level approves any change request before it is implemented.
- All project changes are documented and communicated to all stakeholders.
- Any stakeholder is permitted to submit a project change request.
- The rules are firm, the roles and responsibilities are clearly defined, and the workflow process meets the needs of all stakeholders.

Guidelines

In addition to the principles we reviewed, these guidelines should be considered for an effective project change control system:

- **Re-baseline**—The project plan should be updated to reflect the acceptance of any change to the critical success factors. A new performance baseline should be established.
- **Multiple paths**—The change control system should consider multiple process paths based on estimated impact of the change request and the thresholds negotiated with senior management. This allows the appropriate stakeholders and management levels to be involved when needed and at the right time.
- **Focus on "buy-in"**—Especially on proposed scope changes, make sure the right stakeholders are involved, understand the need and impact of the proposed change, and agree to the action plans before proceeding.
- **Aligned with contract**—If your project involves contractual arrangements, make sure the project's change control process is aligned with the change control process used to manage the contract with the vendor(s).

Components

There are no requirements from a technology perspective when it comes to project change control systems. They can leverage manual processes or utilize enterprise software packages. The key is that the following components are present, understood, and utilized:

- **Change Request Form**—This form is used to capture the pertinent details of the proposed change and the key information resulting from the impact

tip

Capture completion criteria for any scope-related change request.

assessment. Recommended form sections and data fields are listed in Table 11.2.

Table 11.2 Recommended Change Request Form Sections and Fields

Section	Data Fields
Identification	Change Request Number (ID) Date Received Date Revised Project Number (ID) Project Name Organization/Client Reference
Requester Information	Requestor Name Organization/Department Contact Info (email, phone, etc.)
Change Information	Description of Change Request Reason for Change (Issue, Benefits, etc.) Priority
Impact Assessment	Stakeholders Impacted Deliverables Impacted Required Work Tasks Estimated Effort Impact (Hours) Estimated Cost Impact Estimated Schedule Impact Expected Benefits Completion Criteria
Status Information	Status (Submitted, Assigned, Evaluated, Pending Decision, Closed) Assigned To Assigned Date Decision (Approved, Deferred, Rejected) Decision Date Target Implementation Date/Milestone
Approvals	Approval Signatures

- **Unique Identification Number**—When a change request is submitted for evaluation, a unique identification number should be assigned to facilitate better communications and tracking.
- **Change Request Tracking Log**—The tracking log communicates summary information on all project change requests. Minimal information will include identification, impact summary, and current status. Spreadsheets and databases are common tools for tracking logs.

- **Change Control Board (CCB)**—The minimum set of project stakeholders who need to review and approve any change request impacting the project's critical success factors.

note

Ultimately, the determination of any change request is a consensus-based, cost-benefit decision made by the stakeholders accountable for the project.

Powerful Techniques for Minimizing Project Changes

While we want to be prepared for project changes when they occur, we want to spend most of our energy preventing the need for changes in the first place. The following techniques are powerful change prevention actions you can take:

- **Clear project definition**—The more effort spent up-front to get agreement on clear project objectives and success criteria from the appropriate stakeholders, the less likely we are to get change requests during the project.
- **Solid requirements definition**—Mentioned before when we looked at the common reasons for scope changes.
- **Trace requirements**—There is nothing like linking any work specification to its original source to control project scope. By tracing and showing the relationship from the original business objectives down to the detail design specification, you can identify (and possibly eliminate) any scope expansion when it is first proposed. If the proposed feature does not link directly to a higher level specification, it is a potential scope change.
- **Formal acceptance sign-offs**—Formal sign-offs are a key aspect of change control management, especially for client-vendor oriented projects. The formal record of review and acceptance of a given deliverable helps to keep expectations aligned and minimize potential disputes.
- **Engaged stakeholders**—While formal signoffs do act as strong "stick" incentive to get stakeholders involved, there is nothing like having

tip

Make sure your CCB is comprised of stakeholders who can represent each business process or functional group impacted by your project. This organization helps provide a holistic, objective evaluation of each change request, and it helps prevent the addition of changes with marginal business value.

professional, knowledgeable, engaged stakeholders who are committed to doing their best as the best weapon against unplanned scope expansion. A team of people who want to work together and get the job done can accomplish the work at hand with a "less formal" level of project management.

- **Use the right project approach**—This technique is more about risk management, but change control and risk management are very intertwined. As mentioned before, if you know there is likely to be a high degree of change, structure your project in a manner that allows for deliberate, planned scope expansion (prototyping, iterations, cycles, and so on). For all projects, the following approaches help reduce the number of project changes:
    - Emphasis on project definition and planning
    - Shorter timeframes (1 year or less is preferred)
    - Pilot tests
    - Phased implementations
    - Go-NoGo decisions at phase-ends
- **Use WBS to illustrate impact**—This technique may not prevent change requests from being submitted, but it can help you classify something as a change (and not part of the intended scope), and it can help you communicate the impact of the proposed change. By reviewing your detailed WBS, you can show that the work for the proposed feature was never accounted for, and you can show what other work items will be affected by adding the proposed change.
- **Defer to post-implementation**—Another technique that will not prevent change requests, and that may not be applicable to all project situations; however, if it does, it can reduce impact on the project success factors. If the change request is legitimate, but is not absolutely critical to the initial release (there is not a workaround, it does not adversely impact the customer experience), you can guide the CCB to defer the request to a future project or a post-implementation phase.
- **Track assumptions and constraints**—This is definitely part of your risk response plan too, but part of your "watch dog" mindset is to keep a close eye on the project assumptions and constraints. If these change, your project will definitely be impacted.

tip

Rather than capturing assumptions and constraints in various project documents, capture them together in a single document. This makes it easier to communicate, update, and track throughout the project.

Common Project Change Control Challenges

One more thing before we end this chapter on managing project changes. Let's look at the challenges faced by many project managers. Here's a list of things to either avoid or be on the lookout for:

- **The Obvious**—Be sure to set up a change control system as part of your approved project plan—and then use it.
- **Can't Say "No"**—Use your change control system and don't automatically agree to accept a scope change request without running it through the process. This is a common issue with project managers who have a fear of confrontation. Use your system as an objective third party to minimize direct confrontations.
- **Can't Say "Yes"**—Some project managers take the other extreme. They are so paranoid about "scope creep" that they do not listen to consider legitimate scope changes, often overlooking changes that are needed to meet the project objective. Again, keep the focus on the "big picture" (the project objectives) and exercise your change control system.
- **Over-reliance on formal signoffs**—Formal signoffs are important and valuable. However, they should represent genuine agreement and understanding. Verify that you have real understanding and buy-in before proceeding.
- **Not the "gold" you want**—Be on the lookout for "gold-plating." This is the term given to extras or features added to the work product by the project team but not requested by the customer. This is a common reason why schedule delays occur and why unnecessary risks occur on projects. Also, the same issue can manifest itself in a work process. A technician may want their work to be perfect rather than just meet the specifications for the project. This is another reason why a team approach to estimating and planning can be so valuable.
- **Is it really a change?**—Not that this ever happens, but sometimes stakeholders do not agree on what really is an official change. I know—it's hard to believe. Especially in contractual arrangements, the issue isn't always "is it a change?" but rather "do I have to pay for it?"—a slightly different matter. There are no silver bullets here. Most of the disagreements occur because of ambiguity or inconsistencies in the specifications. Just do the other things we mentioned, and you should have a solid foundation to deal with this, if it ever happens.
- **The "impact" of the impact**—In most cases, the individuals who need to assess the impact of a proposed change, especially scope changes, are members of the existing project team—who have current work assignments. Be aware of the impact that this "unplanned" effort could have on the project and guide the CCB accordingly.

- **Inadequate impact analysis**—You are exercising your change control system. The change request is being assessed. You are in good shape—right? Probably. Just make sure the analysis performed on the impact is complete. At the minimum, verify the following on any change request assessment:
  - Has the total work effort been accounted for? All supporting processes? All impacted deliverables?
  - Have the implications of the request been completely considered?
  - Have all impacted stakeholders been considered?
- **Beware of the little guys**—On most projects, there will always be one or more of those small, minor scope changes. Sometimes they are clear changes; other times, they fall into a gray area. In an effort to build relationships and please the customer, many project managers will not document these if they feel the change will require minimal effort to implement. Be very careful here. Before you know it, you can easily have a series of these little changes that "when added up" can impact your project. In addition, you must manage the expectations you are setting if you overuse this technique. As a rule, I would encourage you to at least document every change—no matter how small. For small ones, you may choose to group them into a single change request.

The Absolute Minimum

At this point, you should have a solid understanding of the following:

- The ability to manage and control the change elements on a project, particularly the project scope, is a key to project success and a key performance indicator for a project manager.
- A project change is a change in any of the critical success factors (scope, schedule, costs, quality, and project acceptance criteria).
- The seven key management principles for effective project change control are
  1. Expect and plan for changes
  2. Set up a change control system
  3. Educate stakeholders on process
  4. Use the system
  5. Work to minimize scope changes
  6. Ensure all changes are communicated and understood
  7. Be alert to anything that could impact the critical success factors

- The chief causes of unplanned scope changes include shifts in business drivers, project acceptance criteria, and technology; and inadequate scope statements and requirements definition.
- Completion criteria should be captured for any scope-related change request.
- Powerful techniques for minimizing project changes include a clear project definition, a solid requirements definition, effective traceability of requirements, getting formal acceptance signoffs, implementing the right project approach, and assembling a team of engaged stakeholders.

The map in Figure 11.2 summarizes the main points we reviewed in this chapter.

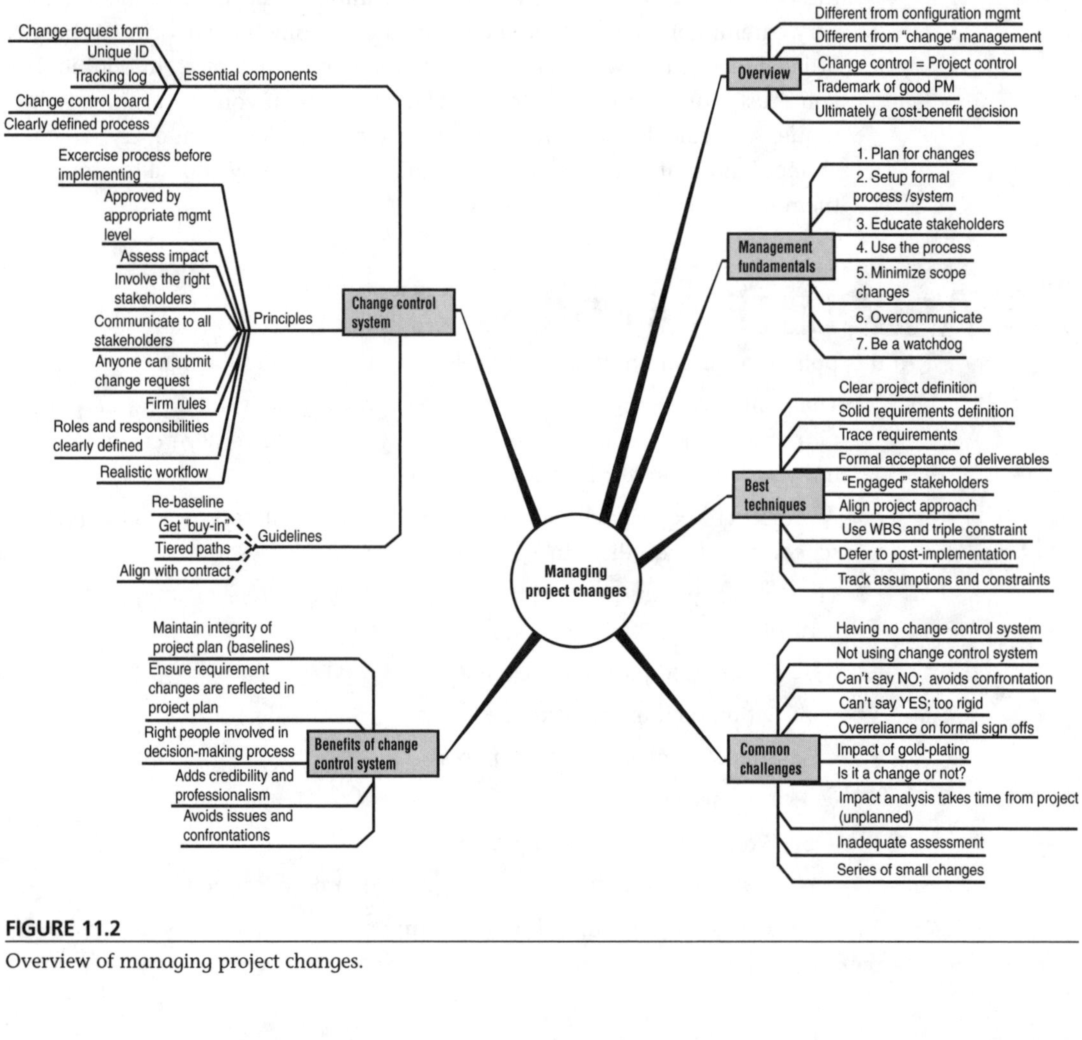

FIGURE 11.2

Overview of managing project changes.

In This Chapter

- Understand why managing project deliverables is integral to customer satisfaction
- Learn the key principles for managing project deliverables
- Understand the value of a configuration management plan
- Learn the best practices related to managing project deliverables
- Review the common challenges related to managing project deliverables

12

Managing Project Deliverables

An excellent indicator to the experience level, professionalism, and overall project management maturity of an individual is how much effort and thought they give to the management of the actual project work products (deliverables).

Why do I say this? This area of project management is one of the most neglected, yet it is a foundational element of managing risk, quality, and stakeholder expectations on any project. Without it, you will inevitably incur additional work efforts, lower quality, and more costs—which generally lead to missed project objectives and disappointed stakeholders.

In this chapter, we clarify what we mean by "managing project deliverables," emphasize the key principles of a project deliverable management system, review the best tips and techniques for keeping your deliverables under control, and discuss how to avoid the common challenges faced by most project managers in this area.

"Managing Project Deliverables" Means What Exactly?

By *managing project deliverables*, we mean the process by which the project work products are controlled. The work products can include anything resulting from project activities, including any deliverable, document, or project management item. And by *control*, we mean managing the changes to the actual work products themselves. The most common term for this process is *configuration management*. As discussed in Chapter 10, "Controlling a Project," this process is related to the project change control system, yet it is different. The change control system manages changes to a critical success factor (time, cost, scope, quality) for the project.

tip

Other terms related to configuration management include document management, software configuration management, and content management to name a few.

The exact nature and details of this process will vary by project and the types of deliverables involved. The project planning document that defines this process is generally called the *configuration management plan*.

Configuration management is often neglected because it is a non-glamorous, mundane aspect of project management that requires a certain discipline to carry out. In addition, this area of project management tends to fall victim to many ill-advised assumptions and to the notion that this is just common sense and it will just happen automatically. Real-world experience would say otherwise. Especially in the digital age, if you do not think about where your project files will be stored, who has access to them, how they will be protected, how changes will be made, and how changes will be tracked, your project is carrying a significant risk—and in most cases an unidentified risk.

In many organizations today, enterprise configuration management tools are being implemented to better protect and control all digital assets of the organization, especially documents. However, this movement is still in the early adoption period, so you will likely still need to develop your own project-specific procedures to address the needs of your project.

Why Do This? It's Too Much Work

You may work in an environment where configuration management is an integral part of the project management approach, so this is not even an issue for you. For others, it is often tempting, as we mentioned before, to not give this area proper attention. So let's answer the question, why should we do this? Why should we plan out the details for how specific work products are going to be managed? From the collective experience of project managers across the land (not that any of these have happened to me or anything), here a few reasons why:

- **Where is that file?**—The ability to quickly locate project information for a key stakeholder or to help resolve an important issue.
- **Lost productivity**—Avoid instances of lost productivity when the work of one team member is over-written by another team member, or when the product configuration you are testing does not have the latest versions of all components—thus making the test run invalid.
- **Baseline? What baseline?**—Avoid instances where you cannot "go back" or "restore" previous versions of work products.
- **Who made that change?**—Avoid instances where you cannot clearly tell (or explain) when changes were made and who made them.
- **Who approved that change?**—Avoid instances where changes are made to work products that are not properly reviewed and approved. To say the least, this can lead to quality and customer satisfaction issues.
- **That will never happen to us**—A major or minor disaster occurs that wipes out one or more work products. Where is your backup copy? Can you recover?
- **We said we would do what?**—On projects with numerous deliverables and work products, it is easy to lose sight of the minor or auxiliary work items. A basic deliverable tracking mechanism can go a long way to prevent this from occurring.

tip

If not using digital signatures or email confirmations for work product acceptance, make sure to scan the signed acceptance forms and store them within the project repository.

- **I've got your official sign-off right here...now where did that go?**—Assuming you have official client acceptance of your key deliverables, make sure you have a way to protect this evidence going forward.

- **You have no choice**—In many environments, there are legal, regulatory, or process compliance requirements that must be met. In each of these cases, having control over work product changes is an absolute must. Most of this activity is focused on protecting the integrity of the work product and providing associated audit trials (evidence).
- **The ultimate reason...negotiating power**—There is tremendous political power in having tight control over project work products. If targeted work products are officially approved, you have a clear audit trail on any changes to those work products, and those official signoffs are protected, you are well-positioned to deal with any scope or requirements dispute. In addition, a historical record of all project management work products, such as project schedules, issue logs, status reports, and meeting minutes can be very valuable in negotiating new issues.

The entire concept of document management started with the legal industry.

Identify, Protect, and Track: The Principles of Managing Work Products

Managing project work products is a strong example of the preventative aspects of project control. If you have a solid process in place, and you are using it, everything rolls along as expected. It's only when you have a "gap" in this arena that it attracts attention from stakeholders—generally unwanted attention. The principles of managing project work products are simple and can be boiled down to three management fundamentals:

- **Identify**—Define all the work products that need to be managed. Make sure all the work products are identified, not just the major ones and not just the product deliverables. For each deliverable type, you may need a different configuration management process. This is often true when dealing with both digital and tangible deliverables and when dealing with documents and software components. This can also be true when there

tip

The three fundamental principles of managing project work products are identify, protect, and track.

Managing project deliverables can also be summarized by another important principle, CYA—Cover Your Assets.

Assume you will have to legally prove your project's case in court someday.

are limitations with the configuration management tools that are available.

- **Protect**—Protect the integrity of the work product. This means that you need to control who has access to the work product, what changes can be made by each person, and that you can recover the work product in the event of an unexpected accident or disaster. The access control can have several layers, but the most common aspects are facilities access and network access. In addition, this means protecting any contractually significant approvals or sign-offs.
- **Track**—The ability to trace your steps and track the changes that are made to a work product. Common terms used associated with this principle are "version control" and "revision history." The other important aspect of this principle is the ability to provide status on the current state of all managed work products.

Depending on the type of work products you have, and the type of configuration management tools that you are utilizing, you may have more than one project repository, such as one for all digital documents, and another for software modules.

Best Practices

Whether you utilize manual or automated processes, here is a list of techniques that should be considered for your configuration management process:

- **Establish central repository**—First and foremost, define a central repository for the project where all project work documents will be stored. Make sure access to the repository can be controlled and that the appropriate stakeholders have access to it.
- **Define review/revision/approval process**—Define which work products need to be reviewed and approved when any change is made, who can make those changes, who needs to approve those changes, and the associated workflow that needs to be followed.
- **Define a "gatekeeper"**—Experience has shown tremendous value in establishing someone as the official librarian for the project repository. This person is responsible for controlling access to the repository, updating the repository, and ensuring that the configuration management procedures are being followed.
- **Implement access controls**—Ensure that the project repository is only accessible to authorized stakeholders and the granted access level is aligned with their role on the project.

- **Establish common directory structure**—To better organize work products and to make it easier to find them when you need them, it is recommended that a directory structure be defined that is aligned with the project phases and workflow process.
- **Establish file-naming conventions**—Also in the spirit of better organization of work products, it is recommended that a common convention be defined for naming project work products. The convention(s) provide consistency and help improve project communications and stakeholder expectations as well.
- **Establish version numbering scheme**—If these guidelines do not exist for your organization already, determine the rules that will govern the versioning scheme for each category of work product. Common elements to consider include version number format, differences between major and minor versions, and conventions to be followed.
- **Establish baselines**—A key best practice, especially before any milestone-type event on the project, such as phase-end, tollgate, start of a testing phase, or releasing work product to a client. To effectively deal with any quality issues and client expectations, you must be able to clearly define (and maintain) the configuration of a work product at a given point in time.
- **Use standard document sections**—To help encourage effective configuration management practices, it is recommended that work product templates be developed which contain standard document sections. Document sections that are recommended include the following:
    - Title page
    - Revision History page
    - Approval page
    - Standard Header and Footer formats/data
- **Use a Deliverable Tracker**—A powerful technique that can be utilized regardless of the sophistication of your process. Develop a mechanism to identify and track the status of your project work products. For lack of a better term, I will call this your deliverable tracker. This can be done with a simple spreadsheet program. Table 12.1 summarizes the key recommendations for your Deliverable Tracker.

Table 12.1 Deliverable Tracker Recommendations

Element	Definition	Notes
Work Product Name	Targeted work product.	Can be a column/field, or you can use separate tab/ sheet for each project phase.
Project Phase	Name of the project phase.	
Modification Type	For this phase, is the work product created or updated?	
Work Product File Name	Actual file name of the work product.	Tip: Hyperlink to its repository location.
Version	Current version number of work product.	
Status	Current status of the work product in this project phase.	In-process, Completed, Approved. Tip: Use color to visually represent the work product status.
CM Indicator	Flag indicating whether this work product is under CM control.	Most will be YES.
Owner	Person responsible for the change.	
Target Completion Date	Scheduled completion date.	
Completion Date	Actual completion date.	
Approver	Person/group who must approve the change.	
Target Approval Date	Scheduled approval date.	
Date Approved	Actual approval date.	

- **Back it up**—Make sure that your project repositories have proper backup procedures in place and that they are actually working. You will be glad you did.
- **Address needs of different work product types**—A single configuration management process may not be adequate for your project. You should develop specific configuration management procedures for each type of work product you are managing.

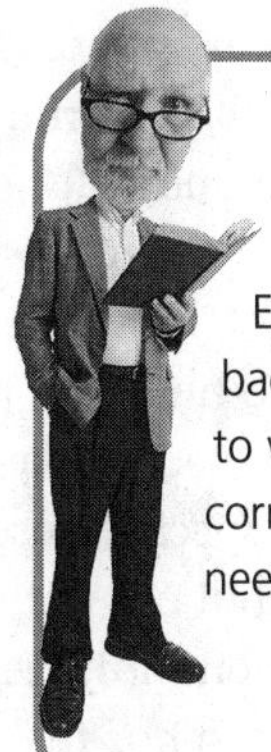

tip

Execute a test of your backup recovery procedures to verify they are working correctly—before you actually need them.

- **Leverage configuration management tools**—While effective configuration management procedures can be executed using clearly defined manual procedures—and a fair amount of discipline and a central control point—the process is much easier with configuration management tools. The tools allow you to control access to the repository, control the revision process (only one person can check out the work product for edit at a time), and provide an automatic audit trail.

note

Configuration management tools include document management tools, software configuration management tools, enterprise project management tools, enterprise (and web) content management tools, records management tools, and workflow/ collaboration tools.

- **Define product configuration build/release process**—On any project that deals with a product that is composed of multiple components, a process is needed that properly integrates the components into a final product. This is especially true for any product that represents a system. This process allows for a baseline configuration to be established.
- **Develop Configuration Management Plan**—This is where you document all of the configuration management best practices you are going to utilize for your project. The configuration management plan allows you to communicate the procedures and rules that the project will follow and to gain agreement on the plan. We will discuss some recommended sections for the configuration management plan in the next section.
- **Leverage archive folders**—A simple but powerful technique to help you manage (and not lose) project information is to always create an "archive" folder within a specific project directory to hold any previous versions, as illustrated in Figures 12.1 and 12.2. This is especially useful for digital work items that are not managed by a configuration management tool. This practice also has the added benefits of better organization and better visibility of the most current work items.

tip

Ensure appropriate team members are properly educated and trained on the configuration management tools and procedures.

Use archive folders to maintain access to previous versions and to improve organization.

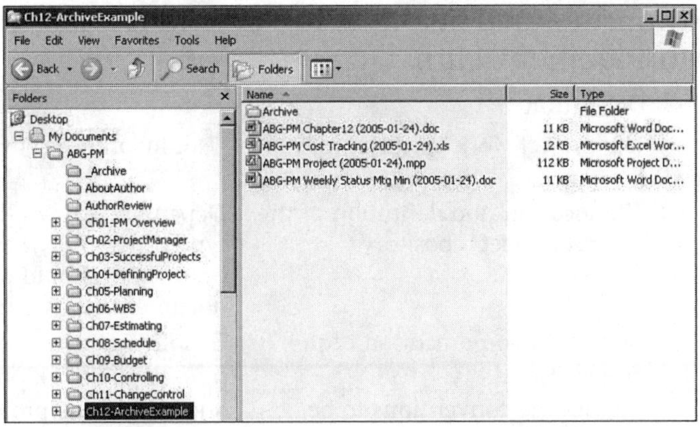

FIGURE 12.1
Sample use of archive subfolder.

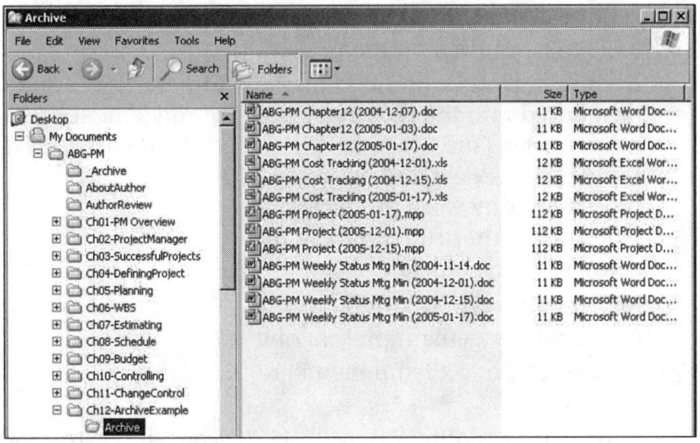

FIGURE 12.2
Sample contents of archive subfolder showing previous versions.

Configuration Management Plan

The configuration management plan (CM Plan) is first defined during the project planning process and is part of the overall project plan. Like all planning documents, the level of detail included in the CM Plan should be consistent with the risk levels, compliance requirements and composition of the project team. As a guide, Table 12.2 lists the minimum topics that should be covered in a CM Plan.

TABLE 12.2 Recommended Sections for Configuration Management Plan

Element	Definition	Notes
Targets	The project work products to be managed.	Usually all project work products.
Repository	The location and definition of the central project repository.	Depending on work product types, there may be more than one. There should only be one document repository.
Directory Structure	Defines the organization of the project repository.	Usually organized by project phases and work product type.
File Naming Conventions	Defines the conventions to be used for naming project files.	Should include project name and work product name at a minimum.
Tools	List the configuration management tools to be utilized on the project.	
Process and Procedures	Defines how work products are introduced into the repository and how revisions are made to them. Defines the review and approval process for any work product requiring authorization before a change can be official.	May reference sub-configuration management plans if multiple tools are used/needed.
Roles and Responsibilities	Defines the key roles in the configuration management process and what each project team member can do.	The key role is the Librarian.
Reporting	Defines how configuration management status will be reported and what metrics are needed for this project.	Deliverable Tracker.
Audits	Defines how the configuration management process will be audited for compliance and when those audits will occur.	Often a part of the QA Review process.
Relation to other CM Plans	Indicates whether configuration management plans are involved and how they integrate with the overall project plan.	Supplier CM Plans. Specific work product type CM Plans.

Common Challenges and Pitfalls

We've addressed the challenges you will have on your project if you do not have a CM Plan, but even with a CM Plan, there are still some remaining pitfalls that you need to be on the lookout for:

- **Not Following the Plan**—One of the first things to go when the realities of the project hit is execution of the CM Plan. There are two things you can do to help make sure the CM Plan is executed. One, use an independent auditor (such as a QA Lead) and include the CM activities as part of the quality review process. Two, make sure to include the CM activities in the WBS and project schedule.
- **Tool Difficulties**—As stated before, configuration management tools should be leveraged whenever possible, and in some cases, they are absolutely mandatory. That being said, the proper use of these tools is not automatic. If you are going to use a tool, you need to make sure the right team members are trained on how to properly use the tool(s), and you to verify that the tool works correctly (not that this is ever an issue or anything).

caution

A common planning oversight is not factoring the CM activities into the task assignments or not allocating specific CM roles. As a result, the individuals assigned to CM activities are often over-allocated. Thus, when time is tight, the CM activities are the first to go.

tip

For whatever CM tools you leverage, make sure there is a CM tool expert either on your team or available to the core project team.

The Absolute Minimum

At this point, you should have a solid understanding of the following:

- The benefits of properly managing project work products include increased productivity (by avoiding lost work), enhanced professional credibility, audit-proofing your project, and increased customer satisfaction.
- The principles of managing project work products are identification, protection, and tracking...and, of course, CYA.

- The configuration management plan documents the processes and procedures that will be utilized to ensure project work products are protected and that changes are controlled.
- Like other elements of the project, make sure stakeholders understand the value of the CM plan and are properly trained on how to use the process.
- Make sure your back-up recovery procedures work correctly before you actually need them.
- Consider web-enabled configuration management tools for virtual project team environments.
- For other helpful information on configuration management, check out CM Crossroads at http://www.cmcrossroads.com.

The map in Figure 12.3 summarizes the main points we reviewed in this chapter.

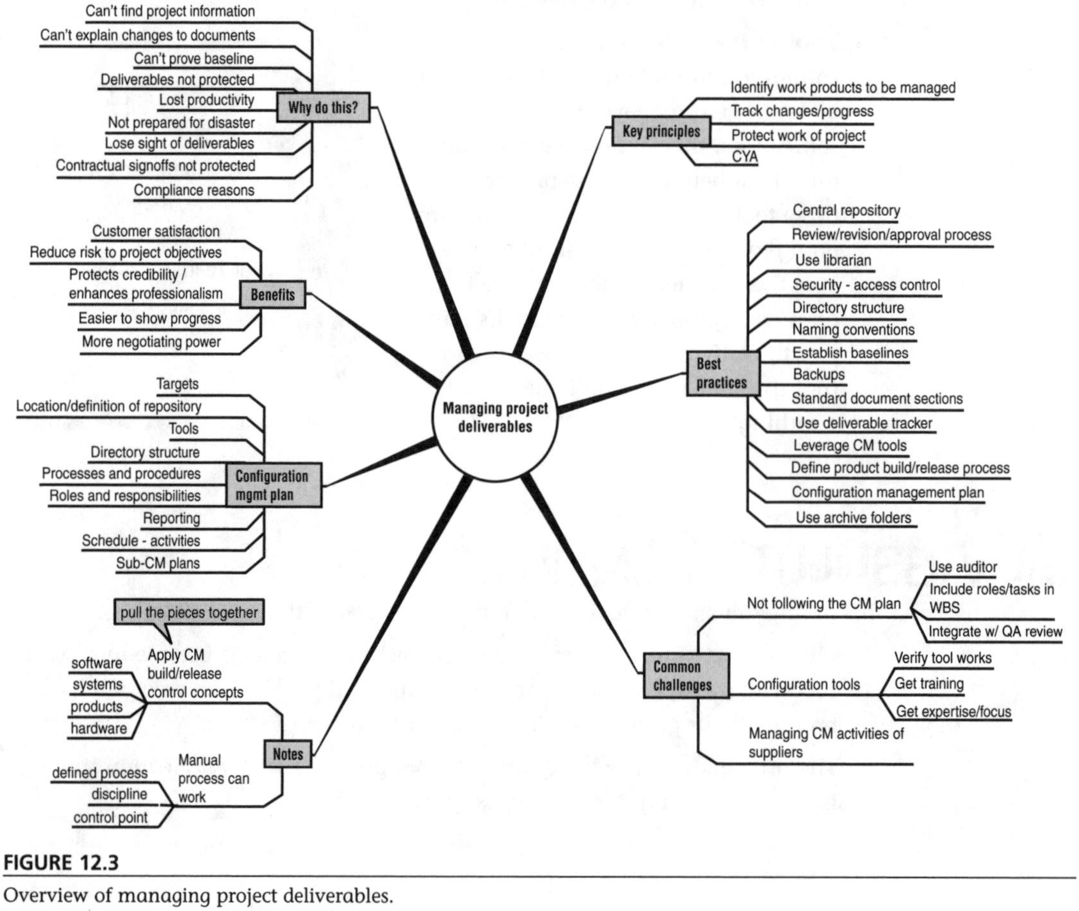

FIGURE 12.3

Overview of managing project deliverables.

In This Chapter

- Learn why an effective issue management process is vital to project success
- Understand why the project manager is the most important element in the issue management process
- Understand the subtle differences between managing risks, issues, and defects
- Learn the key principles and best practices for managing project issues
- Learn which data points are essential to your issue management system
- Understand the limitations of the common Issue Log approach

13

Managing Project Issues

Projects are dynamic, projects often deal with the "new" and the "leading edge," and projects involve people. As a result, circumstances are going to change, misunderstandings occur, assumptions don't hold, political agendas collide, problems arise, and risk events happen. These situations are categorized as *project issues*, and they all have the potential to adversely affect the project's ability to accomplish its objectives.

To minimize the potential impact of these obstacles on our project objectives, we need to have a proactive plan for effectively managing project issues. In this chapter, we will focus on the key elements of that plan. We will review the principles, best practices, and project manager skills that are essential to effectively managing project issues. In addition, we will touch on the important elements of your issue management system and make sure you are aware of the common challenges faced by project managers in this arena.

The Goals, Objectives, and Principles of Project Issue Management

Managing project issues is an example of proactive project management. Through solid planning, effective stakeholder management, and insightful risk management, you can reduce the number of issues your project will encounter, but you cannot eliminate them. The goal of project issue management is to detect issues as early as possible. The earlier an issue is identified, the greater the chance of resolving the issue before it can impact any of the project's critical success factors.

The objective of project issue management is to identify, record, track, resolve, and communicate all issues that may adversely impact the project. Translated—write them down (so you don't lose sight of them) and take care of them (get on it). To accomplish this objective, we need to review the associated principles. The principles of issue management fall into two main categories: an administrative process and a project manager mindset.

- **Administrative Process Principles**—To properly manage project issues, there are a few administrative fundamentals to adhere to:
    - **Document the issues**—You need somewhere to log the issues as they are identified. We'll discuss the log details later on.
    - **Track until closure**—Use the log to make sure issues remain visible until they are resolved.
    - **Align with project needs**—Ensure the overall process matches the communication and workflow needs of the project.
    - **Cost-effective approach**—Keep things in perspective. Don't buy a BMW when a Chevrolet is all you need.
- **Project Manager Mindset Principles**—More than anything, effective issue management is an attitude and an approach. The following terms describe the mindset principles that a project manager needs to have in this arena:

A common source of confusion in the project management arena is the terminology used for project issues. For our purposes, we are differentiating between issues, risks, and defects.

Issues are events that have occurred or situations that exist which will adversely impact the project outcome if not resolved.

Risks are potential issues (more on these in Chapter 14, "Managing Project Risks").

Defects are issues that result from the project's quality management procedures (testing, reviews, and so on).

The workflow processes for each are slightly different.

- **Ringmaster**—As the project manager, you operate as the focal point for tackling project issues. You are the gatekeeper. You are the one who must get the right people involved at the right time to make sure issues are resolved. In addition, some issues will require the input of several different parties to resolve. You will need to facilitate this process.
- **Smiling Bulldog**—Your goal is to resolve issues as quickly as possible and to stay with them until they are resolved. Be persistent. This is the "bulldog" mentality. However, you need to do this with a smile. Leverage your interpersonal strengths to do this, while still building relationships.
- **Swivel-Head**—Just like with risks, you need to constantly be looking for trouble. That is, trouble for your project. Sometimes issues come disguised as questions or non-verbal communications. When in doubt, ask questions and verify. The impact of most issues can be mitigated if they are detected early and resolved quickly with the right buy-in.
- **Goaltender**—Just as a good goaltender does not let anything get by him, a good project manager will let no issue go unnoticed or unresolved. In addition, the subtle intensity displayed by the project manager here helps to set expectations with the project team and signals to all stakeholders that they will be held accountable for getting issues resolved.
- **Disciplined**—To be effective, you will need a fair amount of discipline. You need the discipline to log the issues and follow the process. In the whirlwind of most project environments, it is easy to let this slip.

Key Features of Issue Management System

The actual details of the issue management system are not complicated, and in most situations will share many similarities with your change control system and risk tracking system. While issue management systems will vary in complexity and sophistication depending on your organization and the needs of your project, there are key features that they should all possess.

- **Clear Process**—Clearly define and communicate how issues are submitted, how they will be resolved, how and when

While the spreadsheet approach to an Issue Log has limitations, just the fact that you are documenting issues and actively managing them will put you light years ahead of many project environments.

outstanding issues will be reviewed, and what is needed to officially close an issue. Not complicated; generally very common sense stuff here.

- **Escalation Procedures**—Part of the overall issue resolution process, but not always thought about in advance. Define the types of issue that warrant escalation to higher levels of management. Generally, there is a single escalation process for a project that is leveraged for anything impacting the critical success factors (issues, changes, risks).
- **Issue Log**—The mechanism used to document and track project issues. Most common mechanism is a spreadsheet, but there are limitations to this method. Other options include database systems and collaboration tools. There are pros and cons to each choice. The important thing is to use a tool that matches the needs of your project. We'll discuss this in greater detail.
- **Issue Log Administrator**—Someone needs to serve as the central control point for the Issue Log. Usually, this will be you, the project manager.
- **Issue Data Points**—While the specific mechanism used for the Issue Log and the exact information needs will vary across projects, there are a core set of data points that should be considered for any issue logged. The recommended data points are listed in Table 13.1.

Table 13.1 Recommended Issue Log Data Points

Element	Definition	Notes
Issue ID	Unique ID that can be used to clearly track this issue.	Best practice.
Issue Type	Category of issue—domain values will vary depending on project.	Example set—Technical, People, Business, Supplier.
Issue Name	The short name for the issue.	Generally less than 40 characters.
Issue Status	The current state of the issue. This should be aligned with the process workflow established for issue resolution.	Example set—Open, Assigned, Resolved, Closed. In some settings, Open and Closed values may be sufficient.
Issue Priority	Summarizes the importance and severity of the issue.	Typical domain—Critical, High, Medium, Low.
Issue Details	The full details of the issue.	
Potential Impact	List the potential impact to the project critical success factors if issue is not resolved.	
Date Submitted	Date issue is identified and accepted.	
Submitted By	Person who originated the issue.	
Date Assigned	Date issue assigned to someone for follow up.	

Table 13.1 (continued)

Element	Definition	Notes
Assigned To	Person assigned to take action on the issue.	
Target Due Date	Target date for issue resolution.	
Date Updated	Date that Issue Log entry was last updated.	
Date Resolved	Date that issue is resolved.	This field may not be needed in many cases. Date Closed may suffice.
Date Closed	Date the issue is closed.	
Progress Notes	Contains updates and information regarding actions items, findings, and steps to resolution.	
Related Items	In many cases, one issue is associated with other issues or spawns other issues/action items. It is good to track this association.	May also be used to link to supporting documents.

Options for Issue Log

Let's take a look at the available tool options for our Issue Log. The most popular options are word processor, spreadsheet, database, and collaboration/workflow tools. There are advantages to each and each can be appropriate in the right scenario. Table 13.2 provides a comparison summary for our Issue Log options.

The details of the Issue Log will depend on the intended audience and general communication needs of project.

Table 13.2 Comparison of Issue Log Options

Options	Pros	Cons	Best Scenario
Word Processor	Low cost. Simple. Portable. "Quick and dirty."	Limited filtering. reporting capabilities. Limited access, visibility. Cumbersome as log grows. Manual processes needed.	Cost is key factor. Team is co-located. Only one person needs to update log. Collaboration needs are minimal. Low complexity level in issues tracked.

Table 13.2 Comparison of Issue Log Options

Options	Pros	Cons	Best Scenario
Spreadsheet Simple.	Low cost. Leverage sorting, filtering, and reporting capabilities of spreadsheet pgm. Portable.	Limited access, visibility. Cumbersome as log grows. Manual processes needed.	Cost is key factor. Team is co-located. Only one person needs to update log. Collaboration needs are minimal. Some need for sorting and filtering of data.
Database	Allows for multi-user updates. Better data relationships. Better reporting. Enforce process and business rules.	Increased setup and admin time. Increased costs. Not as portable. Training may be needed.	Many team members need to have access and update capabilities.
Collaboration Tools	Web-enabled. All advantages of database tool. Map process flow. Automatic notifications.	Increased setup and admin time. Increased costs. Training may be needed.	Workflow process is more involved. Team is distributed, virtual Communication needs are non-trivial.

Best Practices

The work of project issue management is straightforward. However, there are several techniques that are proven to be effective and will help you avoid the common mistakes in this aspect of project control.

caution

Complex issues tend to linger and can come back to bite you. Take charge of these right away.

- **Assign Unique ID**—Make sure to assign a unique number to each logged issue. This simplifies the ongoing communication and tracking process.
- **Assign one person responsible**—As with other work tasks, assign a specific person responsible for any follow-up action items and for complete resolution to the issue.
- **Facilitate resolution to complex issues**—There are times when issues do not have a clear owner or will need the collaboration of several parties to resolve. As the project manager, you must either assign someone to facilitate this process or take ownership of the facilitation process yourself.

- **Resolve issues at the lowest level**—Always attempt to deal with problems at their lowest level. You can resolve issues faster and at less cost. More importantly, you will earn the confidence of upper management by protecting their time and only engaging them when it is warranted. Again, make sure to establish the escalation triggers with your senior management stakeholders during planning, so you are clear about their expectations.
- **Go after "root cause"**—A common error in dealing with issues is not to deal with the actual source of the problem (root cause). Sometimes, political reasons may hamper your efforts to deal with the root cause, but whenever possible, do the proper analysis to get to the real problem, and address it. If you do not, the issue will likely return for another visit.
- **Get buy-in on due date and ownership**—Apply the same approach to assigning issues, as you do (or should) with assigning scheduled work tasks. For better issue management, make sure to spend the time with the person designated to take action on the issue and get their agreement on when they can have the action completed and that they are the right person to do it.
- **Adapt process and data points**—Even if your organization has a standard approach or methodology for issue management, don't be afraid to adapt the workflow process or the tracked data points to better fit the needs of the project.
- **Review issues frequently**—At a minimum, review any outstanding issues during each status review meeting (this should be included in your Communications Plan). As a good practice, follow up on outstanding issues every day and make sure the necessary steps/actions are occurring to get to a resolution.
- **Train project team on process and tools**—This is not as important for projects where the Issue Log is more a management tool just for the project manager (you). However, in any situation where collaboration tools are being utilized or multiple people are involved in the process, make sure the project team is properly prepared to leverage the system.

tip

As with all aspects of project management, always be looking for ways to improve your processes to better fit the needs of your current project and future projects.

Due to strong relationship and natural links between them, some organizations use a common log for all project issues, action items, risks, defects, and change requests. Just add a data point called Item Type.

This approach can make logging and tracking simpler, especially if one person is responsible for maintaining the log in each of these areas. However, you will need to know how to properly use your tool to best report information from this central log.

Some Special Situations

On this subject of managing project issues, there are a couple of special situations that often come up. Let's discuss them briefly.

- **Visibility of Issue Log**—Usually on projects where there are multiple organizations (especially vendors, suppliers), you will want to manage multiple issue logs (same for risk logs too). Why? Quite simply, there are things you are concerned about that may impact your project, which you need to bring to the attention of your organization's management, but that you are not ready to share with all project stakeholders. This is simply a matter of expectations management and not sharing your dirty laundry prematurely. A common example is with resource productivity on a fixed price engagement—a definite issue for your organization, but not a real concern of the customer.
- **Logging issues that cycle less than a reporting period**—Depending on how often the issue log is updated, there are often cases where an issue is identified, evaluated, and resolved before it can actually be logged. Of course, on many projects, this is a standard operating procedure. However, it is often difficult to exercise the discipline to log these issues after the fact. It is strongly recommended that you find the willpower (or assign someone) to get this accomplished. From a lessons learned and audit perspective, you will be glad you did. Plus, it boosts your "what did we accomplish" section of your status report.

The Absolute Minimum

At this point, you should have a solid understanding of the following:

- Managing project issues has two key components—an administrative process and a project management mindset—the mindset is far more important.
- The terms that best describe the desired project manager mindset are ringmaster, smiling bulldog, swivel-head, and goaltender.
- The difference between project issues, risks, and defects:
  - Issues are events that have occurred or situations that exist that will adversely impact the project outcome if not resolved.
  - Risks are potential issues.
  - Defects are issues resulting from the project's quality management procedures (testing, reviews, and so on).
- Project issues need to be identified, recorded, tracked, resolved, and communicated.

- Key issue management best practices include resolving issues at the lowest possible level, going after the root cause of any issue, assigning a specific person responsible for each issue, getting buy-in on ownership and due date from the person assigned the issue, and frequently reviewing the Issue Log with the project team.
- Whenever an issue needs the input of more than one person to resolve, the project manager should facilitate the resolution process.
- The issue management system needs to match the specific communication and workflow needs of the project team and the project stakeholders.

The map in Figure 13.1 summarizes the main points we reviewed in this chapter.

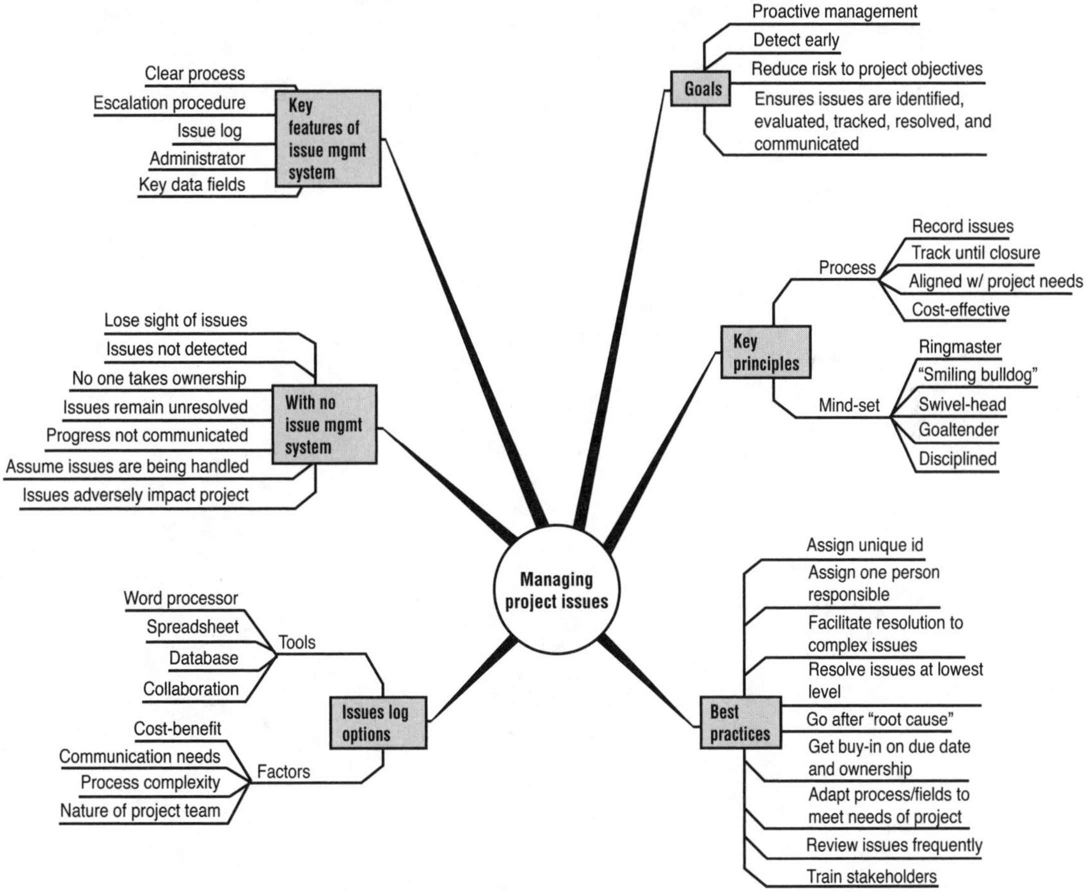

FIGURE 13.1

Overview of managing project issues.

IN THIS CHAPTER

- Understand why managing risks is what project management is all about
- Learn the key principles of controlling project risks
- Learn the value of managing project risks in a systematic manner
- Learn the essential steps and tools for effective risk management
- Realize that there is a common set of project characteristics that are responsible for most project risks
- Understand why many project risks are actually self-inflicted during the project planning process

14

MANAGING PROJECT RISKS

Managing project risks is the ultimate in proactive project management. It is the project manager's radar system. The goal of project management is to achieve the project's critical success factors, including meeting the targeted business objectives and client expectations. The goal of managing project risks is to identify and prepare for any potential threat to the project's critical success factors before it actually occurs. As a result, risk management is the essence of managing projects. Nothing impacts the decisions we make regarding general project approach, level of planning rigor, staffing, project control procedures, and overall contingencies more than the risks facing the project. Yet, there may be no aspect of project management that has a wider array of "real-world" implementations.

As a result, there is often a sense of confusion and uncertainty regarding the proper project risk management approach to take. In this chapter, we will clarify all of this. We will review the core principles, key process steps, and best practices that are essential to managing project risks. We will share insights on how to identify common project risks, review the proven strategies that work best in controlling project risks, and highlight the typical risk management problems, so you can avoid them.

tip

The essence of project management is "risk management."

Key Risk Management Principles

A proactive management philosophy underlies the key principles of project risk management. By effectively managing project risks using these principles, a project manager remains in control of the project at all times, enables better project decisions, and provides the project the best opportunity for success.

The key principles to managing project risks include the following:

- **It's all risk management**—All project management is risk management. The current approaches and rules of modern project management, especially the ones surrounding portfolio management, project definition, and project planning, are all risk management focused. From past experiences, we now know how to structure a project for total success and how to greatly increase the likelihood the project will achieve its objectives.
- **"Healthy paranoia"**—It's all attitude, even if it is a little psycho. Effective project managers take responsibility for managing risks on their project—believe me, no one else wants the job. As a result, you must strike the balance between having a paranoid outlook about your project (constantly thinking about what could go wrong) and doing everything you can to make sure the project is executed as planned.
- **Appropriate**—The level, type, and visibility of risk management should be consistent with the level of risk and the importance the project has to the organization. The cost of the risk response should not be greater than the impact loss the risk event might cause.
- **Systematic**—Any factor or risk that could impact the project should be identified, quantified, and assessed for possible impacts to the project. This includes all people, process, technology, organizational, and environmental influences.

- **Continuous**—The identification of risks is an iterative process. Risk identification is repeatedly performed throughout the project, not just at the beginning.
- **Relentless**—The project manager and the organization must be committed to risk management for the entire project lifecycle.
- **Focused**—Focus on the risks that you can control—starting with the high priority risks.

Per PMI, project risks can be reduced up to 90% if they are properly managed.

The Essential Process for Managing Project Risks

To be consistent with our principles, we need a systematic approach that allows us to focus time and resources on the highest priority risk elements. The power in the process is not in its complexity—it's relatively simple and straightforward—the power is in the management approach it inspires.

The best risk profiles are ones that are specific to your industry, organization, and project type.

Let's review the essential steps for managing project risks:

- **Identify**—This is the critical step of identifying the risks to the project. The best way to start this process is also the best way to leverage the lessons from the past—use a *risk profile*. A risk profile, also referred to as a risk checklist or risk assessment form, lists the common sources of project risk that you need to consider. While most risk profiles help you evaluate the majority of risk factors that are common to all projects, including the listing we have later in this chapter, the best risk profiles are ones that are specific to your industry, organization, and project type. In addition, the less experience that you have in project management or in the project domain, the more you will want to facilitate this process with the key stakeholders and subject matter experts on your project team.
- **Determine probability**—For each risk factor that has been identified, determine the likelihood that the risk event will occur. The goal is to quantify the uncertainty as much as possible, although in reality, this is still a judgment call. Common methods include numeric scales (1–5, 1–10), and subjective scales (High, Medium, Low).

- **Assess impact**—For each risk factor, determine the potential impact the risk event would have on the project critical success factors if it occurred. Like the probability element, the goal is to quantify the potential impact as much as possible. Generally, the same type of scale is used here too. It is a good idea to document the specific impact (which critical success factor) and the magnitude of the impact.
- **Prioritize**—Now that we have a probability and an impact level, tabulate a final ranking for each risk factor by combining the two values. If you have used numeric scales, this is straightforward; just multiply the two values together to get a final score. If you have used qualitative scales (L, M, H), you should be able to easily translate these to numeric values (1, 2, 3) to figure your final score. This step shows you the highest priority, most important risks, and the ones that we need to focus your initial efforts.
- **Develop responses**—Document a response plan for each risk using one of the five risk response options detailed later in this chapter. Since risk response strategies may entail the allocation of additional resources, tasks, time, and costs to the project plan, this is why the planning efforts are iterative in nature.
- **Get buy-in**—Review the risk response strategies with the key stakeholders to increase their awareness, get their feedback (if you have not already), and get their acceptance of the planned approaches.
- **Monitor**—Don't stop. Nothing stays the same. Continue to keep your eye on the risk factors—watch for triggers to activate other planned responses, be mindful of the appearance of new risk factors, and don't totally forget about the low-level risks. Either via circumstances changing or initial miscalculations, you may find some of these have a higher probability of occurring (or higher impact) than originally perceived.

caution

These steps are focused on qualitative analysis and are more than sufficient for most projects, especially if a team approach is taken for this process. However, if you are in a situation or industry that requires more precise risk analysis, you will need to leverage a second phase of analysis called numerical (or quantitative) analysis. Techniques such as decision tree analysis and Monte Carlo simulations are frequently used here. Please consult an advanced project risk management course or text for instruction in this area.

Risk Response Options

Most people tend to think "mitigation" when they think of risk management. However, there are also five risk response options. Table 14.1 reviews each response strategy and provides examples of each.

Table 14.1 Summary of Risk Response Options

Risk Response	Description	Examples/Notes
Avoidance	Avoiding the risk. Changing the project plan to eliminate the risk. Changing the project plan to protect a project objective from the impact.	Reducing the scope to remove high-risk tasks. Adding resources or time. Adopting a proven approach rather than new one. Removing a "problem" resource.
Acceptance	Accepting the consequences of the risk. The project plan is not changed to deal with the risk. A better response strategy cannot be identified.	Active acceptance. Passive acceptance. No action. Contingency allowance (reserves). Notifying management that there could be a major cost increase if this risk occurs.
Monitor and Prepare	Accepting the risk for now. Closely monitor the risk and proactively develop alternative action plans if the event occurs.	Contingency plan. Fallback plan. Establish criteria that will trigger the implementation of the response plans.
Mitigation	Taking action to reduce the likelihood the risk will occur. Taking action to reduce the impact of the risk. Reducing the probability is always more effective than minimizing the consequences.	Adopting less complex approaches. Planning on more testing. Adding resources or time to the schedule. Assigning a team member to visit the seller's facilities frequently to learn about potential delivery problems as early as possible. Providing a less-experienced team member with additional training. Deciding to prototype a high-risk solution element.

Table 14.1 (continued)

Risk Response	Description	Examples/Notes
Transference	Transferring ownership of the risk factor. Shifting the consequence of a risk and the ownership of the response to a third party.	Outsourcing difficult work to a more experienced company. Fixed price contract. Contracts, insurance, warranties, guarantees, and so on. Used most often for financial risk exposure. Does not eliminate the risk.

Key Risk Management Tools

One aspect of the risk management process described in the PMBOK® Guide (PMI 's *A Guide to the Project Management Body of Knowledge)* that many people find difficult to grasp is the reference to *unfamiliar tools and techniques*. Table 14.2 summarizes many of these tools and techniques to assist your learning and review process.

The risk assessment questionnaire contains questions that pertain to project size, structure, and technology. The risk assessment questionnaire is broken down by risk categories, subcategories, and criteria that rate risk level according to low, medium, or high.

Table 14.2 Summary of Risk Management Tools

Risk Tool	Description	Notes/Examples
Risk profile	A questionnaire or checklist to guide the identification of project risk factors.	Should be industry, organizational and project type specific.
Risk assessment	Generally synonymous with risk profile. Frequently will contain criteria to establish Low, Medium, High risk levels.	Often used interchangeably for risk profile or risk checklist.
Risk log	Used to document the identified risks, probability score, impact score, priority, and planned response strategies.	May be combined with other project logs.
Risk management plan	Describes how the risk management process will be structured and performed.	Describes the process to be used.

Risk Tool	Description	Notes/Examples
Risk response plan	Describes the response strategies for identified risks.	Risk Log. Details action steps to be taken if risk event occurs.
Probability/impact matrix	Used to establish general High, Medium, and Low classifications for a risk factor. Cross-references the probability score with the impact score.	Generally developed at the organizational level to improve the consistency of risk rankings.

The Common Sources of Project Risk

caution

As the project size and complexity increases (see size and complexity factors in Table 14.3), the level of risk can increase exponentially.

The first key to managing risk on your project is to know where to look for it. The good news is that 80% or more of all risks originate from the same sources on every project. Once you know the project characteristics that contribute to higher risk levels and the common sources of most project risks, you can quickly and effectively identify risk factors for any project. These factors should be first evaluated during project definition and will be the main reason why several iterations of planning are often necessary. In Table 14.3, most of the key project risk factors are listed to better guide your risk identification activities. You will note that many of these are emphasis points for project definition and detail project planning.

Table 14.3 Common Sources of Risk

Risk Source Category	Examples/Factors
Project Size and Complexity	Effort hours. Calendar time. Estimated budget. Team size (number of resources). Number of sites. Number of business units. Number of system interfaces. Number of dependencies on other projects. Number of dependencies on other systems. Degree of business change.

Table 14.3 (continued)

Risk Source Category	Examples/Factors
Requirements	Volatile requirements. Unrealistic or aggressive performance standards. Complex requirements.
Change Impact	Replacement or new system. Impact on business policies. Impact on business processes. Impact on organizational structure. Impact on system operations.
Organization	Changes to project objective. Lack of priorities. Lack of project management "buy-in" and support. Inadequate project funding. Misallocation and mismanagement of resources.
Sponsorship	Lack of strong executive commitment. Lack of clear ownership. Loss of political support.
Stakeholder Involvement	All key stakeholders not identified. Missing "buy-in" from a key stakeholder. Stakeholder needs not completely identified. Key stakeholders not fully engaged.
Schedule	Estimate assumptions are not holding true. Schedule contingency is not adequate.
Funding	Reduction in available capital. Cash flow issues. Inflation or exchange rate factors.
Facilities	Adequate for team productivity requirements. Adequate for project security requirements.
Team	Full-time or part-time roles. Location of team members. Can't find desired resources. Lack of experience. Lack of business knowledge. Lack of skills. Lack of commitment. Personal issues. Lack of prior experience working together.
Technology	Missing technical data. Use of unproven technology. Use of non-standard technology. Development approach. Level of complexity.

Absolute beginner's guide to
31318019039220
p10376495

...actors
...es.
... elements.
...t process.
...with vendor/supplier.
...veather conditions.
... legal and regulatory environment.
...from governmental agencies.
...anges.
...rket.
...d acquisitions.
...events.
...nditions.
...e schedule, costs, resource, or quality risks.
...perience.
...rship.
...nunications.
...ntingency plans.
...te risk management.

...inherent attributes of ...le the project man- ...g table summarized), ...ce of project risks ... These are the project ...ing adequate project ...nning.

Thu Dec 15
6161 R N P L

...planation of those ...I of this book. For a ...y factors are listed in ...ome risk source cate- gories ... table. This is intentional. In some areas, there are universal, inherent factors that contribute to project risk, and there are other risk factors that are introduced due to inadequate project planning. One example is the project schedule. Estimate assumptions not holding true and inadequate contingency buffer are inherent risks on any project. However, a poorly developed schedule is self-inflicted and a result of project planning deficiencies. Yet, it can be as devastating to your project critical success factors as anything.

Unidentified or unacknowledged project planning defects are the most popular source of unknown risks.

Table 14.4 Common Project Planning Sources of Risk

Risk Source Category	Examples/Factors
Project Management	Improperly defined project deliverables. Incomplete planning. Improper procedures. Not defining clear roles and responsibilities. Lack of contingency plans. Inadequate risk management. Inadequate attention to the right details. Inadequate resource staffing.
Project Definition	Unrealistic objectives. Inconsistent objectives. Incomplete scope definition. Inconsistent scope definition. Improperly defined project deliverables.
WBS (and Project Schedule)	Not reviewed and approved by stakeholders. Missing tasks. Lack of team understanding. Missing project management activities. External dependencies not identified and understood.
Project Schedule	Missing task dependencies. Tasks not clearly assigned. Resources over-allocated. Calendar realities not factored. Inadequate contingency or reserve.
Project Budget	Poorly developed cost estimates. Missing cost sources. Inadequate contingency or reserve.
Requirements	Incomplete requirements; Poorly defined requirements.
Assumptions and Constraints	Not completely defined.

Typical Problems

Technically, these factors are actually planning defects. They only become project risks if they are not corrected before planning is complete.

As with any project management process, there are always challenges and things for which you should be on the lookout. Let's first review the four general problems that are typical with managing project risk:

- **Undetected risks**—These are the risks that will get you, because you didn't even see them coming. The most common reasons for this are project managers not having the proper risk management mindset, project team members not raising awareness to specific risk factors, and planning defects that are not detected.

- **Unacknowledged risks**—This occurs in dysfunctional organizations or in immature project management organizations. For whatever reason, often political in nature, an obvious risk factor is not formally acknowledged, and as a result properly managed. This is the proverbial "elephant sitting in the middle of the living room." A common example of this is an impossible schedule deadline.
- **Not enough process**—It is not uncommon to see this area of project management totally ignored, at least from a systematic standpoint.
- **Too much process**—On the other end of the spectrum, I have often seen gung-ho, analytical project managers over do the risk management process. They can spend so much time here that planning is never completed, or they get so focused on risks that they become so cautious and won't take on any chances. Remember—project risk management is not about avoiding all risks.

caution

In some cases, organizations knowingly accept the risk of abbreviating the project definition and planning steps to meet other objectives.

In addition to the major problems typically found, there are a number of other smaller issues that are common to the risk management process we discussed earlier. Table 14.5 summarizes those common gaps.

Table 14.5 Summary of Common Risk Management Gaps

Risk Management Process	Common Gaps
Risk Management Planning	No risk management plan. Risk management plan equals risk response plan.
Risk Identification	Performed only once and not proactively managed. Process is incomplete. Missing entire types/categories of risk. Confusing issues with risks.
Risk Qualitative Analysis	The organization has not established standard practices/tools. The probability of occurrence is not calculated for each risk. The impact of each risk is not determined. Risks are not prioritized. Risk Quantitative Analysis is not limited to high-priority risks.

Table 14.5 (continued)

Risk Management Process	Common Gaps
Risk Response Planning	Response strategies are not documented. No risk response plan. Response strategies are not appropriate for risk severity. The project plan is not updated to implement and monitor responses.
Risk Monitoring and Control	The risk response plan is not maintained. Risk identification is not continued. The project plan is not updated to implement and monitor responses. Responses are not reevaluated. Progress is not tracked, or task owners are not held accountable.

Powerful Risk Control Strategies

Let's break out of the strict risk management process and consider some powerful strategies you should consider to either deal with the high priority risks you now have or to reduce the number of new risks from occurring as your project goes.

- **Tackle high risks first**—Develop a work plan that attacks your high risk factors right out of the gates. Why? If you are going to have a problem, it is best to know sooner than later. If something is not feasible or acceptable, determine this as soon as possible, so senior management can decide whether the project is worthy of organizational investment and resources.
- **Use iterative, phased approaches**—By breaking the work of the project into multiple iterations and phases, you provide a systematic method of providing tangible output to the stakeholders sooner and more often. The multiple points of review and feedback with the stakeholders allow you to better control your greatest risk—stakeholder expectations and satisfaction.
- **QA the planning process**—Mentioned before, but worth mentioning again—make sure to do a quality review on the planning process. This step helps identify planning defects that if undetected will become unknown risks with a high impact potential.

caution

For those planning on taking the PMP exam, note that risk management planning and risk response planning are two distinct activities.

- **Leverage independent QA audits**—Leveraging an independent, experienced, objective viewpoint can be a powerful way to identify risk factors and to determine the best response strategies. This can be especially useful in project situations where the key stakeholders are inexperienced, the climate is very political, or when multiple vendors are involved.

Are You Sure It's a Risk?

Before we end our review of managing project risks, it is worth mentioning that one common problem associated with project risk management is terminology and the proper labeling of risks. This is more of an academic issue, and generally the subtle differences are not key factors on projects. To make sure you avoid problems here, let's quickly review the definition of terms closely related to project risk and clarify those distinctions in Table 14.6

Table 14.6 Summary of Risk-Related Terms

Term	Definition	Notes
Risk	An uncertain event that could negatively impact the project critical success factors, if it occurs.	A threat. Probability of occurrence must be between 0% and 100%.
Issue	An active problem that could impact the project critical success factors.	A risk event that has actually occurred.
Constraint	A limit that must be planned around.	Factual. Constraints can introduce other risks.
Assumption	Factor considered to be true, real, or certain.	Assumptions can include accepted risks. Assumptions can introduce other risks.
Dependency	An external event that must occur for the project to accomplish its objectives.	Identified during planning along with risks, constraints, and assumptions.
Defect	A discrepancy between what is (actual) and what should be (expected). Mentioned here because planning and overall project management defects can become project risks if not identified and corrected.	Detailed planning efforts are important here. The key source for many unknown risks.

THE ABSOLUTE MINIMUM

At this point, you should have a solid understanding of the following:

- The essence of project management is "risk management."
- The level of risk management should be consistent with the size, importance, and risk level of the project.
- Managing risks is an integral part of project planning.
- Risk management is a continuous, iterative process throughout the project lifecycle.
- Project risks need to be identified, recorded, tracked, resolved, and communicated.
- Risk events that actually occur become project issues.
- The five risk response strategies include acceptance, avoidance, mitigation, transfer, and monitor.
- The best risk profiles are ones that are specific to your industry, organization, and project type.
- Unidentified or unacknowledged project planning defects are the most popular source of unknown risks.
- The best ways to control risk are through solid project management, effective project planning, and a relentless desire to protect the project.

Figure 14.1 summarizes the main points we reviewed in this chapter.

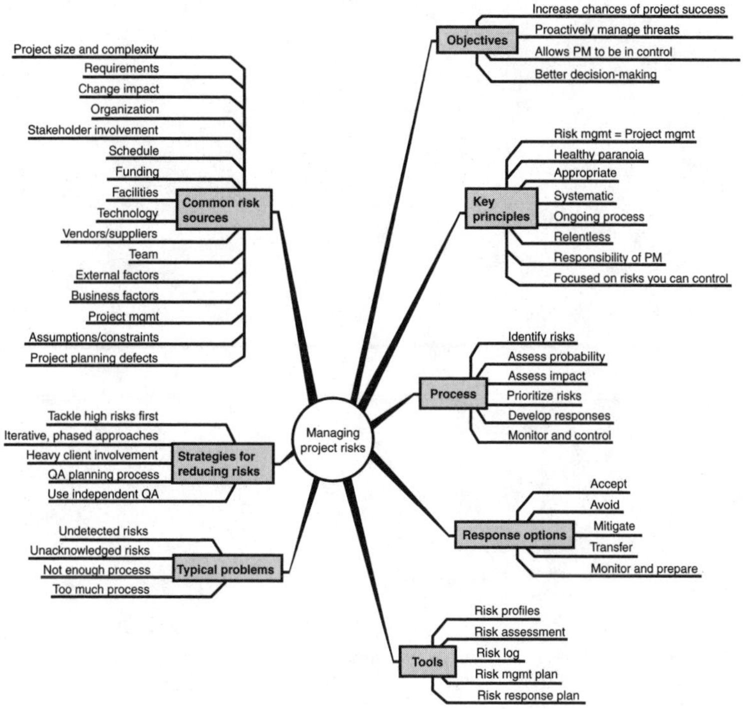

FIGURE 14.1

Overview of managing project risks.

In This Chapter

- Learn what comprises a "successful" project
- Understand why project quality starts and ends with the customer
- Understand how project quality management is integrated into all aspects of project management
- Learn the key principles of managing project quality
- Learn the essential tools and techniques for implementing project quality
- Project quality
- Review seven common challenges associated with project quality

15

Managing Project Quality

Quality is one of the critical success factors for any project and one of the key tenets of modern project management. Yet, project quality is often misunderstood and poorly managed. Why is this?

Suppose a project delivers a technically sound, zero-defect product, but the project is over-budget and the customer is not satisfied. Do you have project quality in this case or not?

Your organization must already comply with an industry quality standard (ISO 9000/10000, QS-9000, GxP, SEI/CMMi) or already employ one of the popular quality methodologies (Total Quality Management, Six Sigma, Continuous Improvement). Do you need to worry about project quality or not?

In this chapter, we explore these questions and address many more fundamental project quality topics. We clarify what *project quality* means and how it relates to managing project risks, project requirements, and client expectations. We review the core principles, key tools, and best practices of project quality management, including the critical quality techniques that are often overlooked by many project management texts. In addition, we share insights on the typical challenges surrounding managing project quality, so you can avoid these on your first (or next) project.

As mentioned in the book's introduction, this chapter does not address advanced quality management concepts that are more the domain of operational quality management programs. The review of quality control tools such as Pareto analysis, statistical sampling, control charts, fishbone diagrams, or trend analysis, and the review of quality management pioneers such as Dr. W. Edwards Deming, Dr. Joseph Duran, and Philip Crosby will be left to other textbooks and courses that have a primary quality management focus.

What Is "Project Quality"?

What do you think of when you hear the word, "quality"? Testing? Zero defects? Audits? Overhead? If you answered yes to any of these, you may be surprised to know how PMI defines quality. To PMI, *quality* equals, "conformance to requirements and fitness of use." Well, of course it does. Simply translated, this means that the project produces what it said it would and that what it produces satisfies real customer needs. In other words, did the project deliver on the targeted requirements and were the requirements on target? Did your understanding of client needs translate into client satisfaction?

You may be thinking, "Greg, isn't this what a project is supposed to do?" or "You know, Greg, this sounds an awful like managing requirements." Exactly. While there are aspects of managing quality that are unique, mainly verifying that the work is complete and correct, most elements of managing project quality are fused tightly with other aspects of project management, especially requirements (scope) management, expectations management, risk management, team management, and procurement management.

In the same way that we said project management is risk management in the previous chapter, we could also say project management is quality management too. After all, most of the best practices now recommended for project management (and discussed in this book) have quality concerns as their foundation. From clearly defining the project, to the approach we take to accomplishing the work, to the project team we assemble, to the focus on customer "buy-in," it's all there to give the project the best opportunity to deliver the solution requirements and to meet the expectations of the client—in other words, deliver project quality.

Unique Aspects of Managing Project Quality

While project quality management is tightly integrated with all aspects of managing a project, there are a few aspects that are unique to this endeavor (after all, there must be some reason we have a separate chapter on it). The unique elements of managing project quality include

- **Focus on quality-based requirements**—Ensure that all the quality and compliance standards that the project is accountable for are identified, both from the customer and other governing stakeholders.
- **Focus on value-added requirements**—Work to understand the requirements, often unspoken if not probed, that go beyond the base functional requirements and that will have the greatest impact on the customer satisfaction level of the final solution.
- **Focus on product and process**—Quality management addresses both *product* (goods and services) quality and *process* quality, especially the *project management* process.
- **Focus on verification**—Determine the game plan for ensuring that all the requirements will be met to the satisfaction of the relevant stakeholders. How will you validate if the work of the project is on target? How will you prove the work is complete and correct?

Principles of Managing Project Quality

The seven key principles of project quality management originate from a proactive, customer-focused management philosophy and are consistent with other project management practices we have reviewed. By utilizing these principles, a project manager keeps the quality requirements aligned with both the project and the key stakeholders and gives the project the best opportunity to deliver on quality success factor.

The seven key principles to managing project quality include the following:

- **Identify targets**—This is the critical first step in the process. Make sure you identify both the customer's quality expectations as part of the requirements gathering process and the quality/compliance expectations demanded from other key stakeholders, whether these are internal quality departments or external compliance agencies. This is the most common reason for not meeting quality expectations—they are never completely identified.

- **Plan it**—Quality is planned in, not inspected in. Once you determine the quality level requirements, you must then decide how to meet these requirements. With the quality targets clearly identified, you can structure the overall approach of the project, allocate resources, and assign necessary tasks to give yourself the best opportunity to meet the quality expectations. In some form or another, you should document and communicate your plan for quality management on the project. Often, this is accomplished using a Quality Management Plan document, which is part of your overall Project Plan.

tip

Quality is planned in, not inspected in.

Effective project management is quality-focused.

- **Right-size it**—Like other project management processes, use the appropriate level of rigor and formality to meet the needs of the project. In other words, match the investment in quality procedures with the risk level and other critical success factors. For example, does the project need to produce a zero-defect product that must pass FDA validation audits or is the project more exploratory in nature—a "quick and dirty" initiative.
- **Set expectations**—This principle focuses on two key aspects. One, make sure the customer's quality expectations are aligned with the project's needs and the quality management approach to be taken. And two, if the effort (time, costs) to satisfy all quality requirements conflicts with either the schedule or budget constraints on the project, then you must facilitate a compromise via risk analysis and planning scenarios that results in a prioritization of quality management efforts or an adjustment in critical success factor balance.
- **Stay customer-focused**—Underlying the entire project quality management philosophy is a focus on the customer experience. This means doing things such as defining requirements from the customer's perspective, asking the right questions to uncover the other requirements that will impact the customer's perception of the final solution, validating from the customer's perspective, and clearly communicating (and getting buy-in) on why "other" quality requirements must be satisfied too.
- **Trust, but verify**—This is tangible example of an overall project management principle—"assume nothing." Whether it is work assigned to a project team member, a supplier, or some other external party, always perform some level of verification to ensure the resulting work package meets the targeted completion criteria.

- **It's up to you!**—The project manager has ultimate responsibility for the project quality. While many aspects of quality management are organizational in nature, and you need the support of senior management to make it stick, you are still responsible for the quality success criteria, as you are for the entire project. To this extent, this is why this chapter is focused on elements the project manager can control or influence.

Powerful Tools and Techniques for Project Quality

We emphasized the value and importance of planning your quality management system. In this section, we highlight ten of the most powerful quality-focused tools and techniques that you want to consider during your planning efforts, document in your Quality Management Plan, and then implement during the execution of your project.

- **Requirements traceability matrix**—A simple, yet often neglected technique to help control scope, expectations, and quality is the use of a requirements traceability matrix. The traceability matrix provides a documented link between the original set of approved requirements, any interim deliverable, all testing (verification) methods employed, and the final work product. This technique helps to ensure that the final work product(s) satisfy the targeted requirements and all those requirements were properly validated.
- **Checklists**—Checklists are simple, yet powerful. They clearly capture and communicate the quality standards that must be met by the targeted work package, and they improve project team productivity. They are flexible—separate checklists can be developed for each work product or project management process. They provide a mechanism to capture the lessons learned from past projects. They provide a mechanism to document the verification performed on the work package.
- **Templates**—The development and use of templates provides a way to both communicate and control the use of certain standards and to help communize the resulting work packages and procedures across projects. In addition, templates can capture lessons learned information (mostly updates and improvements based on prior experiences), provide guidance, and greatly improve the productivity level of a project team.
- **Reviews**—Reviews are a key technique for ensuring quality and managing expectations, and they can take many forms. The principle here is to plan for the review-feedback-correction cycle on most, if not all, of your key deliverables. Common examples of reviews are peer reviews, inspections, client walkthroughs, audits, testing cycles, and milestone reviews.

- **Completion criteria**—This starts during project definition with defining the acceptance criteria for the project, and it continues for each deliverable and work assignment. Answer this question in advance for each deliverable and work assignment: "How will we know when it is done?" Understanding the completion criteria up front increases productivity and avoids much of the re-work that can occur when quality requirements are not understood up front.
- **Small work packages**—You've seen this one before too. In addition to reasons previously mentioned—more accurate estimates and better control—small work packages provide a finer level of quality control too. By establishing completeness and correctness completion criteria for each work package and verifying each work package along the way, we provide many more opportunities to detect quality discrepancies as early in the project as possible. By doing this, we can take corrective actions when the costs are lower, and when time is still available.
- **Independent audits**—The use of an independent auditor is another specific example of the "review" technique mentioned earlier. The power of this technique is in establishing the quality criteria in advance and in making the project accountable to an outside entity.
- **Standards**—In many situations, specific quality standards either do not exist or have not been formally developed. In these cases, it is my recommendation, that you establish project standards up front that will be captured in both work assignments and quality checklists. And if at all possible, facilitate this standards development with the project team—you'll be glad you did.
- **V method**—The *V method* is a term used for a common validation and verification approach that ensures that there is a validation and verification step for every deliverable and interim deliverable created. An overview of this method is illustrated in Figure 15.1. The left side of the "V" notes each targeted deliverable and the right side of the "V" lists the verification method used for each deliverable directly across. This method allows us to check quality along the way rather than waiting to the end to discover there are quality defects.

caution

Make sure the work and responsibilities associated with the project quality system are reflected in the WBS and project schedule.

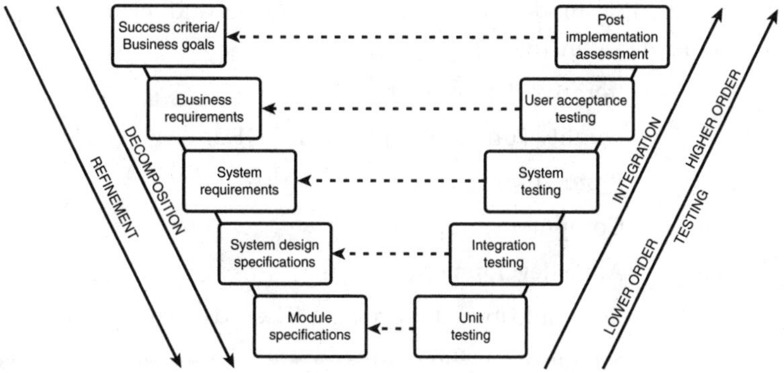

FIGURE 15.1 Illustration of V-method approach for software development project.

- **Quality Management Plan**—This is the document that describes and communicates the project's quality management system to the project stakeholders. Specifically, the Quality Management Plan should address most of these questions:
  - What is the scope of the quality management system?
  - How will either internal or external quality-based groups be involved?
  - What are the quality standards that must be met?
  - What approaches, tools, and techniques will be employed?
  - How will the standards be enforced?
  - How will quality defects/discrepancies be tracked and reported?
  - How will each deliverable be validated?
  - What are the expected costs?

Powerful Quality Strategies

In addition to the powerful quality tools and techniques we reviewed earlier, there are five other key strategies related to managing project quality that we need to discuss:

- **Use customer-focused project approaches**—This may be self-evident by now, but utilizing project approaches that accomplish the following:
  - Fully engages the customer throughout the project lifecycle.
  - Partners the project team with the targeted customers.
  - Allows the customer to provide feedback on "solution-like" deliverables as soon as possible.
  - Emphasizes prevention and early detection of quality defects.

Popular, modern-day project approaches and techniques that fall into this category include

- Iterative development
- Quality Function Deployment (QFD)
- Prototyping
- Computer simulation
- Agile development
- Rational Unified Processing (Use Case development)
- Scenario development
- Storyboarding

- **Take customer's perspective**—From the development of requirements to the testing approach, make sure to take the customer's perspective. In particular, the testing environment needs to simulate the real-world customer environment to the greatest extent possible. Without this approach, your verification procedures are incomplete at best and misleading at their worst.
- **Pre-verify deliverables**—To better manage client expectations, including confidence in the project team, make sure to conduct an internal quality check on any deliverable that will be reviewed by the client. Make sure to schedule these internal verification steps too.
- **Focus on the people**—There is no better quality management technique than to have people who are good at what they do, who take pride in their work, and who are focused on the customer experience. The project management processes of staffing, managing, and leading a team are key project quality factors.
- **Leverage expertise**—A great way to deal with unanticipated project quality issues is to structure the team with one or more mentors (or coaches). Because many organizations do not have an effective way to formally pass along the lessons from the past, this strategy is an effective way to leverage the wisdom that lies within the social fabric of the organization. The two positions that are most needed are a mentor for the project manager and a technical mentor for the technical aspects of the project. In many cases, the technical mentor may actually provide the QA function for the technical deliverables.

Typical Quality-Related Challenges

To both relate some additional experiences that you have endured or observed, and to re-emphasize some of the key points we have covered so far, let's take a quick look at some common project quality-related challenges:

- **Forgot to pop the question**—This problem can be found on projects that are guilty of no organized quality approach and on projects with formal methodology coming out their ears. Always ask the client what "quality" means to him/her. Again, do not assume anything, especially here.
- **"Good intentions, but..."**—Many projects start off great. The Quality Management Plan is fully developed and approved, but then...nothing. Stuff happens and the quality management procedures are never carried out.
- **"We can't afford it"**—There is a common misconception in many organizations that quality-focused efforts are overhead and cost too much. This perception originates from two main sources. One, projects in these organizations are likely managed very informally, so to add quality management seems like a major investment. Two, the quality standards seem non-value added. In some cases, this may be true. In either case, better understanding, communication, and salesmanship are needed. The real question to be asked is, "Can you afford not to focus on quality?" Historical data shows that in most cases the cost of poor quality (non-conformance) is much greater than the cost of prevention.
- **Not factored in the schedule**—Especially on projects where the quality procedures are an afterthought, the actual quality tasks (reviews, audits, and so on) are never factored into the project schedule.
- **Quality resources over-allocated**—In many project situations, the individuals who are designated for quality assurance roles are also fulfilling other roles. If the quality assurance role was not properly allocated and assigned to project tasks, you may have an over-allocated resource. In this case, or when other pressure events occur, the quality assurance hat is often the first to go for these multi-role team members.
- **Testing takes more than one cycle?**—An age-old dilemma on projects that require one or more testing phases on the targeted product is how much time to allocate for each phase. The common mistake is to officially schedule a testing phase as if it will be completed in the initial test cycle. I have yet to see this happen.

- **Avoid gold-plating**—Traditionally, gold-plating is a term associated with project scope management, and it refers to the practice of doing more (adding additional features) than what the requirements (specifications) call for without undergoing proper change control procedures. This is also an issue for project quality management for two reasons. One, the gold-plated features may introduce new quality risks into the equation. And two, the gold-plated features may do nothing to improve the actual deliverable quality, yet they can require additional time and costs.
- **No risk analysis**—While on the one hand, many projects are guilty of not identifying or being aware of the quality standards they are accountable for, there are other projects that blindly accept all the quality standards without properly assessing the impact to the project objectives and other critical success factors. Always assess the impact of meeting each quality standard, especially the schedule and cost impact. Decisions on priorities and risk response strategies may be needed to deal with the impact.

In summary, most aspects of managing project quality are interwoven into the fabric of solid project management practices. If you manage with a focus on

- The customer
- Requirements/scope
- Clear communication
- Clear completion/acceptance criteria
- Small work packages
- Prevention
- Skilled resources and high-performing teams

then your projects will be well-positioned to meet their quality objectives.

THE ABSOLUTE MINIMUM

At this point, you should have a solid understanding of the following:

- The level of quality management should be consistent with client expectations, project needs, and project risk level.
- Managing project quality is tightly connected with managing requirements, managing project scope, managing project risks, managing suppliers, and managing client expectations.
- The process of managing project quality allows you to go from identifying customer needs to achieving customer satisfaction.
- Specifically, project quality procedures answer the question: How do I verify that the work is complete and correct?
- Quality is doing what you said you would do.
- Quality management addresses both *product* (goods and services) quality and *project management* quality.
- The project manager has ultimate responsibility for the project quality.
- Effective quality management is consistent with effective project management.
- Two key aspects of project quality that are often overlooked are managing the project team and managing requirements.
- Historically, the costs of prevention are significantly less than the costs of quality defects.
- Essential tools for project quality management are the Quality Management Plan, checklists, reviews, Requirements Traceability Matrix, audits, verification procedures, and clear completion criteria.
- Checklists and templates allow quality expectations to be clearly communicated and enforced. They also provide a way to pass along lessons learned from past projects.
- To ensure overall project quality, ensure each deliverable along the way meets quality expectations.
- For additional information on quality function deployment visit the Quality Function Deployment Institute at www.qfdi.org.

The map in Figure 15.2 summarizes the main points we reviewed in this chapter.

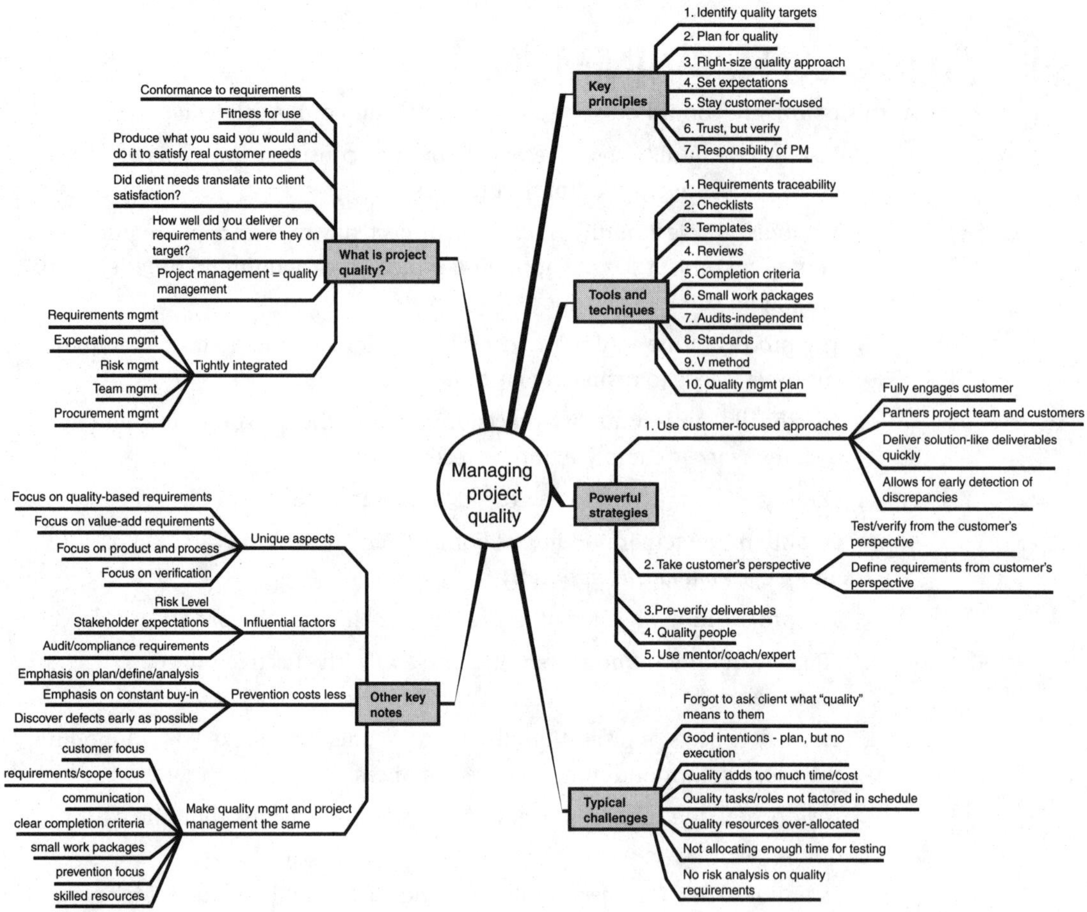

FIGURE 15.2

Overview of managing project quality.

PART IV

PROJECT EXECUTION

IN THIS CHAPTER

- Understand why project leadership is important
- Understand the difference between managing and leading a project
- Understand why "old school" management approaches don't usually work on projects
- Review the common behaviors of effective project leaders
- Understand where leadership is needed on a project
- Learn the 12 secrets to better project leadership
- Understand why a "servant leadership" approach gives you the best chance of doing the right work, the right way, for the right people

16

LEADING A PROJECT

Why do we include a chapter on "leading" a project when most introductory project management books won't go near it? Quite simply, a person "manages" processes, but "leads" people...and people accomplish projects.

While the skill set for effective project management consists of the project management fundamentals we have discussed so far in this book (along with general business management, communication, and technical skills mentioned in Chapter 2, "The Project Manager"), they are all interlaced with leadership skills as depicted in Figure 16.1.

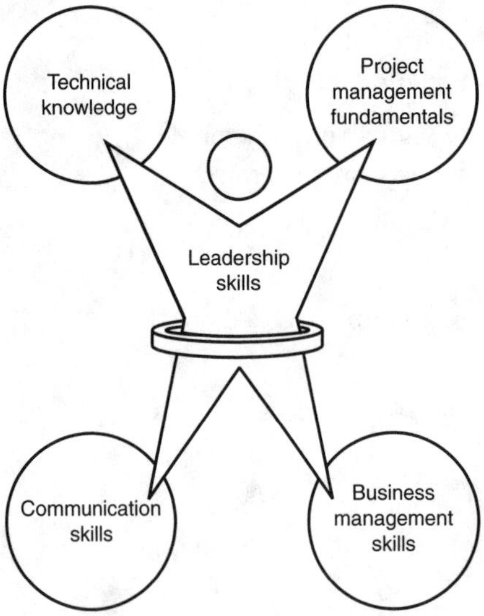

FIGURE 16.1
Integration of leadership skills.

In today's world, there is an overwhelming need for individuals who can serve both as project manager and project leader, yet it is a challenge to find individuals who can perform both roles effectively. Why is this? In general, it's the difference between the art and the science of project management. The difference between the soft skills and the hard skills and knowing how much of which one to apply. And on many unfortunate projects, the lack of leadership or the use of an ineffective leadership approach actually creates problems that did not otherwise exist.

In this chapter, we review the aspects of a project that need leadership and how leading a project is different from managing a project. In addition, we explore the key components of project leadership, the power of the servant leadership approach, and the common traits of effective project leaders. With this awareness and understanding, you will be much more prepared to serve as both project manager and project leader, even on your first assignment.

More Than Managing

The process of leading a project is more than managing the project. The process of leading a project entails the approach utilized to guide the people involved (team, stakeholders, organization) toward the accomplishment of the project's objectives. This process involves your mindset and leverages key skills like dedication, interpersonal, adaptability, and customer-orientation. If we look back at Chapter 2, many of the roles a project manager performs involve leadership, including

- **Planner**—Ensures the project is defined properly and completely for success, all stakeholders are engaged, work effort approach is determined, and processes are in place to properly execute and control the project.

- **Point Man**—Serves as the central point of contact for all oral and written project communications to key stakeholders.
- **Facilitator**—Ensures that stakeholders and team members from different perspectives understand each other and work together to accomplish the project goals.
- **Aligner**—Gains agreement from the stakeholders on project definition, success criteria, and approach; manages stakeholder expectations throughout the project while managing the competing demands of time, cost, and quality; gains agreement on resource decisions and issue resolution action steps.
- **Problem-Solver**—Utilizes root-cause analysis process experience, prior project experiences, and technical knowledge to resolve unforeseen technical issues and to take any necessary corrective actions.
- **The Umbrella**—Works to shield the project team from the politics and "noise" surrounding the project, so they can stay focused and productive.
- **Coach**—Determines and communicates the role each team member plays and the importance of that role to the project success, finds ways to motivate each team member, looks for ways to improve the skills of each team member, and provides constructive and timely feedback on individual performances.
- **Salesman**—This role is focused on "selling" the benefits of the project to the organization, serving as a "change agent," and inspiring team members to meet project goals and overcome project challenges.

In addition, many of the qualities of successful project managers we described in Chapter 2 have strong leadership elements too, including

- **Takes ownership**—Takes responsibility and accountability for the project; leads by example; brings energy and drive to the project; without this attitude, all the skills and techniques in the world will only get you so far.
- **Savvy**—Understands people and the dynamics of the organization, navigates tricky politics; ability to quickly read emotionally charged situations, thinks fast on the feet, builds relationships, leverages personal power for benefit of the project.
- **Intensity with a smile**—Balances an assertive, resilient, tenacious, results-oriented focus with a style that makes people want to help; consistently follows up on everything and their resolutions without "annoying" everyone.
- **Eye of the storm**—Demonstrates ability to be the calm eye of the project hurricane; high tolerance for ambiguity; takes the heat from key stakeholders (CxOs, business managers, and project team); exhibits a calm, confident aura when others are showing signs of issue or project stress.

- **Strong customer-service orientation**—Demonstrates ability to see each stakeholder's perspective, ability to provide voice of all key stakeholders (especially the sponsor) to the project team, strong facilitation and collaboration skills, excellent active listening skills.
- **People-focused**—Understands that methodology, process, and tools are important, but without quality people it's very difficult to complete a project successfully. Acts ethically; protects his team; takes teaching approach.
- **Always keeps eye on the ball**—Stays focused on the project goals and objectives. There are many ways to accomplish a given objective. Especially important to remember when things don't go as planned.
- **Controlled passion**—Balances passion for completing the project objectives with a healthy detached perspective. This allows him/her to make better decisions, to continue to see all points of view, and to better anticipate risks.
- **Context understanding**—Understands the context of the project—the priority that your project has among the organization's portfolio of projects and how it aligns with the overall goals of the organization.
- **Looking for trouble**—Constantly looking and listening for potential risks, issues, or obstacles; confronts doubt head-on; deals with disgruntled users right away; understands that most of these situations are opportunities and can be resolved up-front before they become full-scale crisis points.

Where Is Leadership Needed on a Project?

There are three key points to know about leading a project. One, there are many aspects of project leadership. Two, the project manager is not the sole provider of project leadership. And three, specific leadership providers will vary depending on project environment. To clarify this idea, let's take a look at project areas where leadership is needed and who could provide it in Table 16.1.

Table 16.1 Project Leadership Areas

Project Area	Leadership Provided By
Direction and Plan	Project sponsor Senior management Project manager Technical leader(s)
Organizational Influence	Project sponsor Senior management Project manager Technical leader(s)

Project Area	Leadership Provided By
Commitment	Project sponsor Senior management Project manager Project team
Stakeholder Expectations	Project manager Project sponsor Senior management
Facilitation	Project manager
Communications Point	Project manager Team leader(s)
Project Team	Project manager Team leader(s) Technical leader(s)
Conflict Resolution	Project manager Team leader(s)
Managing Business Change	Project sponsor Senior management Project manager
Technical Issues	Project manager Technical leader(s)
Business Issues	Project sponsor Senior management Project manager Team leader(s)
Managing Risks	Project sponsor Senior management Project manager Team leader(s) Technical leader(s)

We will explore more about managing stakeholder expectations, managing project communications, and building an effective project team in greater detail in Chapters 17, 18, and 19, respectively.

Twelve Keys to Better Project Leadership

In the modern day world of projects, project leaders cannot rely on position power or traditional, autocratic leadership approaches to get the job done. To guide a group of unfamiliar project stakeholders and project team members to accomplish something that has not been done before, you must rely on a different set of skills and leadership principles. As we review the 12 keys to more effective project leadership, please remember this is not an "all-or-nothing" deal—it is a continuum. The more of these that you demonstrate, the better leader you will likely be.

1. **It's about the people**—There are those who maintain that project management is about managing a process (or a workplan), and not about managing people. Are they serious? Who does the work? People. An effective project leader takes a holistic view that puts people first. This approach results in a focus on establishing and building relationships, and on a focus on gaining an authentic understanding and buy-in from each stakeholder.
2. **Visualize the goal...and the way there**—This is the traditional leadership ability of providing direction to the team. Not only does a project leader need to clearly see the end and be able to create this picture for everyone else, but they must also understand how the team is going to get there. The ability to see this big picture is vital to keeping the project focused on its primary objectives.
3. **See with "their" eyes**—A skill that is not natural for many, but an invaluable one if you can do it. Look at your project from the perspective of the other stakeholders. What do they see? What are they thinking? What do they need? This ability to "take another's perspective" is foundational to building better relationships, developing requirements, managing communications, managing expectations, and building a productive project team.
4. **Earn their trust**—Effective leaders are trusted by senior management to do the right thing and to get the job done. They are trusted by other stakeholders because they manage with integrity and consistently seek win-win scenarios to any project challenge.
5. **Earn their respect**—How do you earn the respect of project stakeholders, when you do not have position power? There are four key behaviors that affect the level of respect granted you by project stakeholders:
   - **Show respect**—First of all, show respect to each person you are dealing with. Listen to them—I mean, really listen to them, respect their time, and respect their knowledge, experience, and perspectives.
   - **Be real**—Deal with reality, not what it should be or could be. Your willingness to acknowledge and confront the realities of the project will be key to your overall effectiveness.

tip

The ability to effectively communicate (in all forms) is a fundamental skill for project leadership.

- **Be fair**—People may not always like final decisions, but they will respect the decision and you if they feel you handled the situation in a fair manner. An approach to team management, decision-making, and conflict resolution that emphasizes fairness is key to earning the respect of others.
- **Be consistent**—Lead by example, stick with your decisions, maintain your principles, do what you say you are going to do, and be emotionally steady.

6. **Facilitate progress**—As a project leader, you are focused on accomplishing the project objectives, and you realize that one of the most important jobs you have is to make it as easy as possible for your team to complete their work. How do you do this? Think of yourself as a conduit for progress, an enabler, a productivity-enhancer. Some key actions include

tip

Be the first to take responsibility and the last to take credit.

- Anticipate issues, work to prevent them, and confront and resolve the ones that do occur—quickly
- Create an open and honest team environment where members are encouraged and comfortable to exchange their thoughts and ideas
- Facilitate the decision-making process
- Get needed information quickly
- Ensure team has the structure, process, and tools to be as productive as possible
- Work to reduce the doubt and uncertainty factor for others

7. **Take ownership**—Let there be no doubt in anyone's mind who is responsible for this project. An "ownership" mindset manifests itself in a persistent, results-focused, no-excuses attitude that is undeniable and contagious to the other team members.
8. **Be resilient**—Like the proverbial willow tree that shows its true strength when confronted with a ferocious wind, a project leader is able to quickly adapt his approach and style to best meet the needs of the project. Through a creative and flexible mindset, a project leader understands that there are many ways to achieve the targeted goals and works to make it happen.

9. **Be a teacher**—A great model for the modern day project manager is that of a teacher. In many situations, you are literally educating all stakeholders regarding their roles and responsibilities in a project approach. But in all project situations, taking a teaching mentality—a mindset that sincerely wants others to learn, grow, and improve—rather than a judgmental view will be paramount to your leadership effectiveness.
10. **Strive for excellence**—An important trait of effective project leaders is their ability to create confidence that the project will be well-managed and that it will accomplish its goals. How do you do this? Be very good at what you do, know what you are doing—exclude competence and professionalism (note—I did not say arrogance). The three simple keys here: be prepared, be organized, and never stop learning and improving.
11. **Compensate for weaknesses**—A leader is humble enough, has enough self-awareness and is team-focused enough to recognize his weaknesses. From this recognition, he then builds a team and delegates responsibilities to properly compensate. Again, it is difficult to be proficient at everything, and it is much easier to leverage the strengths of yourself and of your team to get the job done.
12. **Showcase self-control**—As a rule, most effective project leaders are models of self-control. They are consistent and positive in their behaviors and are generally immune from egocentric approaches and significant shifts/swings in their emotional stability (especially negative ones). In addition, they are able to remain calm under pressure and serve as model for others during stressful times.

Depending on your experiences, organizational culture, and education, these project leadership keys may seem perfectly natural to you or they may seem like the ramblings of academia management theory. In either case, I can attest that each is important to your ongoing project leadership effectiveness.

Power of Servant Leadership Approach

While we discussed numerous project leadership keys in the previous section, it really boils down to a simple, practical mindset that drives the thoughts, words, and actions of an effective project leader. It is a mindset of "service-first" and not "me-first." Personally, I had served as a project manager for many years before I ever learned that there was a name for the natural approach that I took to managing projects. The approach is called servant leadership, and it was popularized by Robert Greenleaf in 1970 in his book *The Servant as Leader*. Since then, the philosophy of servant leadership has been steadily growing in popularity and now serves as the foundation for most modern-day leadership training programs.

One of the main reasons I took this type of approach naturally is because it just made sense. In a project environment, where you are stakeholder-focused, where you must rely on yourself, where you must effectively relate to others to get work done, and where you must completely understand the needs and requirements of your customers to deliver the proper solution, it just seems to be a very practical path to take.

The servant leadership approach to project management gives you the best chance of doing the right work, the right way, for the right people.

To me, it is a synergistic approach for any organization (or project) that values strong customer-service and team-focused approaches in their leaders.

To better illustrate what is meant by a servant leadership approach, and why I think this approach gives you the best chance of doing the right work, the right way for the right people on your project, let's look at the prominent characteristics of this philosophy:

tip

When dealing with people, nothing beats a face-to-face meeting and a humble spirit.

- Asserts a strong service-orientation; lead by expanding service to others
- Emphasizes listening, patience, respect, and responsiveness
- Takes the perspective of others; maintains the best interest of others
- Accepts responsibility; takes initiative
- Encourages collaboration and trust; empowers individuals
- Seeks growth and improvement in all team members, organization, and community
- Solicits input and feedback from all stakeholders; especially in decision-making process
- Insists on the use of skills to influence and persuade, not manipulate
- Spotlights a strong integrity principle—the ethical use of power

Again, like all project management and leadership skills, a servant-leadership mindset is not an "all-or-nothing" approach. It is spectrum between a total egocentric, leader-first mindset on one end and a complete servant-first thought pattern on the other end. The goal is to do your best, continue to learn and work to improve over time, just like the other skill set areas.

THE ABSOLUTE MINIMUM

At this point, you should have a solid understanding of the following:

- You lead people, but manage processes.
- All project management skill sets are interlaced with leadership skills.
- Project leadership is not the sole domain of the project manager.
- The 12 keys to better project leadership include
  - Focus on the people
  - Provide a clear picture of the project goals and how to get there
  - Look at the project from the perspective of the other stakeholders
  - Earn their trust
  - Earn their respect
  - Facilitate progress
  - Take ownership and responsibility
  - Be resilient, adaptable, and flexible
  - Be a teacher
  - Strive for excellence
  - Compensate for any weaknesses
  - Demonstrate self-control
- A servant-leadership approach to project management is practical, common-sense mindset that gives you the best opportunity for project success.
- For more information on Servant Leadership, check out the Greenleaf Center for Servant-Leadership at www.greenleaf.org/.

Figure 16.2 summarizes the main points we reviewed in this chapter.

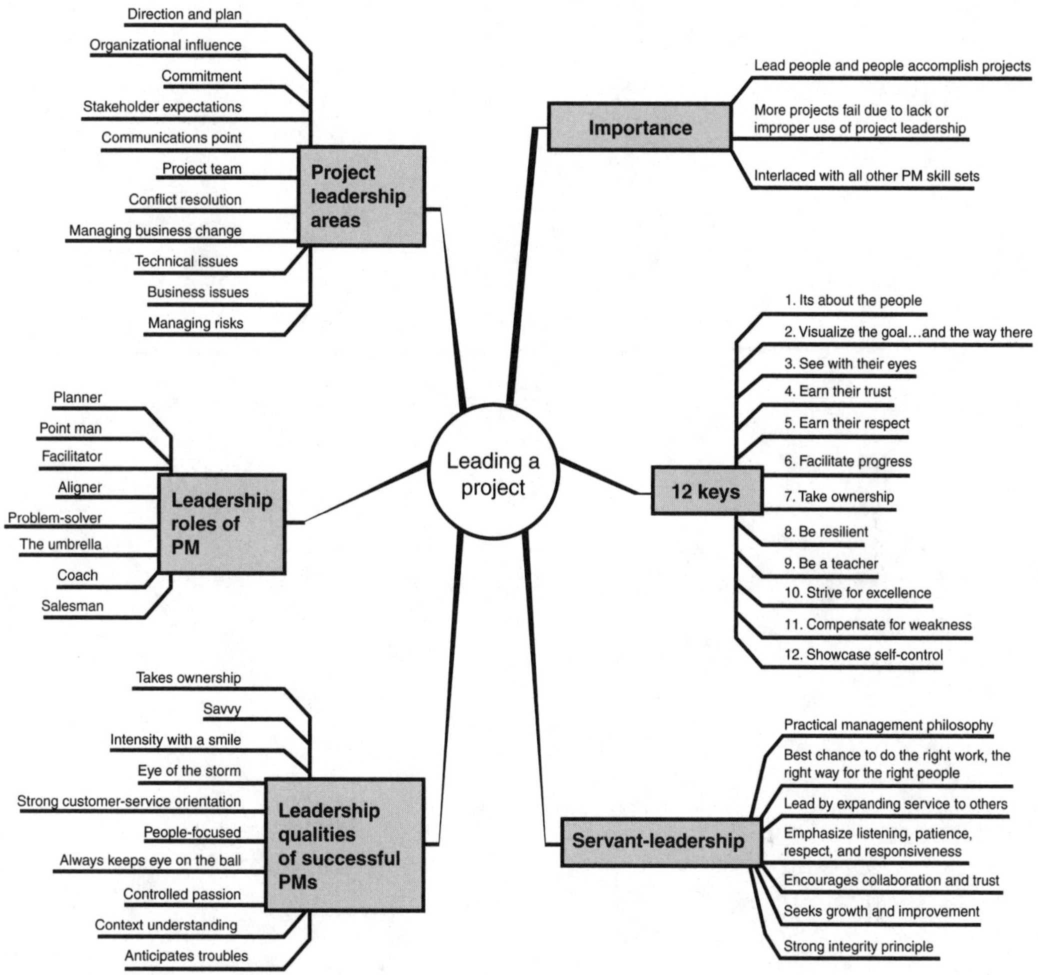

FIGURE 16.2

Overview of leading a project.

17

MANAGING PROJECT COMMUNICATIONS

IN THIS CHAPTER

- Understand why effective communications are so important
- Discover what makes effective project communications difficult
- Learn the key principles of managing project communications
- Understand what factors impact project communications the most
- Review the key interpersonal skills utilized by effective communicators
- Learn the best techniques for communications plan, meetings, and status reporting

Communication is the fuel that drives project success, and the mishandling of it is a top five reason why projects struggle. You've likely heard this mantra before, but what does this really mean, why is it true, and more importantly, how do we handle our project communications effectively?

In this chapter, we will answer these questions, review what we mean by project communications, think about why effective communication cannot be taken for granted, and study the key principles and best practices leveraged by effective communicators. With this knowledge, you will greatly increase your own personal effectiveness and position your project for the best outcome possible.

What Are Project Communications?

The communications of a project include all means and manners that the project interacts with all its stakeholders. This not only includes the standard, formal communication items such as

- Status reports
- Progress review meetings
- Kickoff meetings
- Executive reports
- Presentations
- Financial reports
- Government (or external agency) reports
- Issue logs
- Risk logs
- Change request logs
- Role-responsibility matrix
- Project organization chart
- Any project deliverable
- Project collaboration portals

Per PMI (Project Management Institute), project managers should spend 90% of their time communicating.

but can also include organizational change management communications such as

- Project name/identity
- Project website (portal)
- Organizational change management plan
- Frequently Asked Questions (FAQs) references
- Awareness campaigns
- Newsletters
- Public relation notices
- Roadshows
- One-on-one meetings with key stakeholders

While the nature of your individual project (number and type of stakeholders, location of stakeholders, and overall project risk level) dictates how many of these elements are part of your project, the next set of project communications are included on every project, and are likely the most important part of project communications: the day-to-day, interpersonal communications that occur between the project team and the project stakeholders. These include interactions in the following forms, plus others:

- Face-to-face
- Telephone
- Email
- Instant messaging
- Voice mail
- Conferencing (audio, web, video)
- Meetings

Later in this chapter, we will review simple but powerful tips to improve your interpersonal communication skills, and we will review important reminders to help you choose the best medium/tool for your desired message.

The Importance of Project Communications

Project communications are not only important for the obvious reason—keeping individual stakeholders properly and consistently informed on the status, progress, and impact of the project—they are a key determinant factor to the overall success of the project. Why is this? Here are a few key reasons:

- **Managing expectations**—We'll discuss managing expectations in greater detail in the next chapter, but for now, we'll just say that the quality and effectiveness of your communications will have a tremendous impact on stakeholder perceptions regarding the project and your role as a leader.
- **Managing the project team**—Your ability to communicate is the prominent factor affecting how well you manage and lead the core project team.
- **Reducing conflicts**—There are enough challenges executing your average project with the customary time, fiscal, and resource constraints without adding unnecessary conflicts that result from misperceptions, lack of information, or nonexistent issues. All of which result from ineffective communications.

Every solid project manager knows there are two skills that will carry him/her in almost any project situation: organization and communication.

- **The saving grace**—Every solid project manager knows there are two skills that will carry him/her in almost any project situation: organization and communication. Being excellent in these areas, especially project communications, will compensate for shortcomings in almost every other area.

Why Communicating Can Be Tough

Before we review key principles and best practices, let's make sure we understand why we cannot take communications for granted. On one hand, we know instinctively that there are many factors that impact the communications process—primarily, because we live it every waking minute. On the other hand, many of us don't seem to incorporate this reality into how we communicate.

The goal of any communication is to have the receiver end up with an understanding (resulting perception) that equals the meaning intended by the sender (intended message). It sounds so simple, doesn't it? Yet, as Figure 17.1 depicts, there are many challenges facing the accomplishment of this simple goal.

FIGURE 17.1
Challenges facing effective communications.

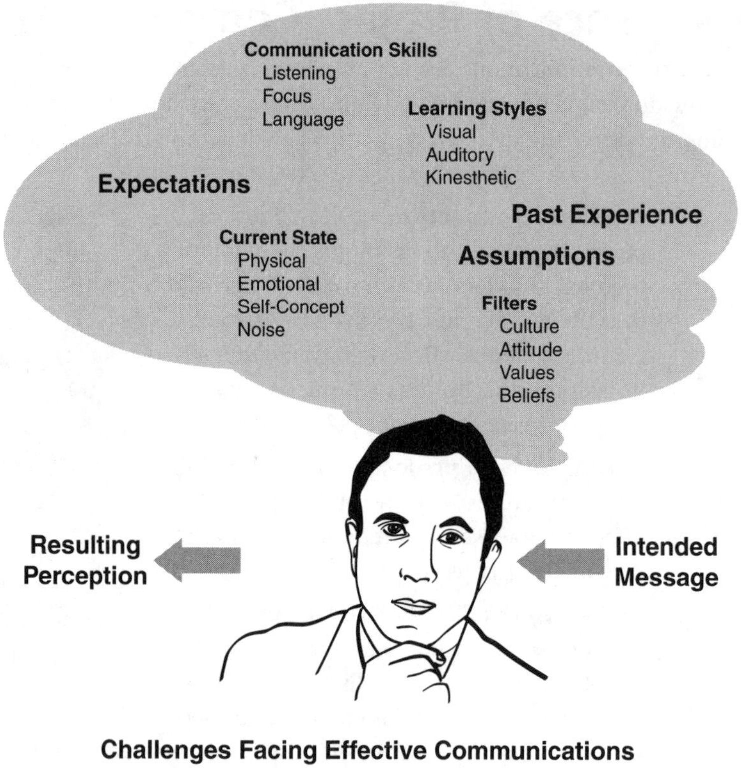

For any message to accomplish its goal, it must clear two key hurdles. First, it must register with the receiver—it must hit their radar screen. Depending on the current state of the receiver (physical state, emotional state), other things happening in the environment (noise), and ability of receiver to focus and listen to the message, this may or may not occur. Second, if it does land on the receiver's radar screen, the message must then pass through a series of filters in the receiver's mind, including past experiences, assumptions, expectations, culture influences, values, and beliefs. And then, even when the message clears these two primary hurdles without significant distortion, the receiver's general ability to decode the message will vary depending on their natural learning style (such as auditory, visual, or kinesthetic). Heck, when you think about it, it's a wonder we ever clearly communicate anything.

So why bring all this up? Three reasons:

1. As a sender, recognize that successfully getting your message across is not trivial and cannot be assumed.
2. As a receiver, recognize the factors that can impact your ability to accurately "understand" (or hear) what the sender is trying to communicate.
3. Most importantly, it gives your ego an out. Too many people let their ego get in the way of improving their communications. Don't take it personal if you are not understood the first time. As we have mentioned, there are many challenges. The more you can take your ego out of the equation and focus on understanding, the better your communication abilities will become.

Seven Powerful Principles

Let's take a look at the seven key principles employed by most effective project communicators:

1. **Plan your communications**—Like every other aspect of managing projects, you want and need to plan your project communications. The goal of communications planning is to ensure that all the stakeholders involved in the project have the information they need, when they need it, to fulfill their responsibilities. The key factors that affect communications planning and the communication requirements for a project include the following:
   - Sponsoring organizational structure
   - Results of stakeholder analysis
   - Reporting relationships
   - Functional areas involved in the project
   - The number of people involved in the project
   - Physical location of the project stakeholder

- Information needs of each stakeholder
- Experience level of project team members
- Availability of technology
- Immediacy and frequency of information needs
- Desired form of project communications
- Expected length of the project
- Organizational risk level of project
- Expected change impact on end users
- Organizational culture
- Level of external communications needed
- Procurement contracts
- Any constraints advised by legal counsel

caution

In organizations with standard project reports, don't assume these meet the information needs of your individual stakeholders. Be willing to adjust to better meet their needs.

After the specific communication requirements are determined for your project, make sure to do these two things:

- Document this information in a project communications management plan.
- Ensure that all formal project communications (and the work to produce them) is included in the WBS and project schedule.

2. **Remember the basics**—The three most powerful communication techniques are also the simplest. Why are these techniques powerful? They work and most people don't do them, so the contrast is very noticeable.
   - Make it a high priority—Don't shortcut project communications; show respect for stakeholders.
   - Use your manners—Be polite; show appreciation and gratitude.
   - Follow-through—If you say you are going to do something, do it.
3. **Five Cs of communication**—Keep the five Cs in mind when composing or delivering any project communication:
   - Clear—State the subject; stay on subject; hold the receiver's hand through the message; use appropriate terms.
   - Concise—Get to the point; limit scope of the message.

- Courteous—Be polite; watch your tone.
- Consistent—Use appropriate tone, medium for intended message; all message elements should support intended meaning.
- Compelling—Give them a reason to pay attention.

4. **Take responsibility for understanding**—This hits at the mindset you need for effective communications. Key points include
   - Invest the effort, patience, and determination to make sure you are clearly understood.
   - Employ effective listening skills to ensure you have clearly understood what the other person has intended.
   - Use the communication medium that is the best fit for the intended audience. Be flexible.
   - Tailor your communications content to best fit the information needs of each target audience (project team, customers, senior management, and/or personnel management).
   - Pay attention. Notice the feedback. If what you are doing is not working, be willing to adjust.
   - Don't assume understanding—always clarify, ask questions, verify. Focus on taking the other person's perspective in all communications.
5. **Build relationships**—Effective communicators know that the bridge between people is built upon trust, rapport, and personal connection. Be eager and willing to invest the time to build one-on-one relationships with your key stakeholders, especially early on the project. In addition, a relationship focus will help create an open and honest environment, which is better suited for dealing with natural project challenges.
6. **Be proactive**—Another key mindset and approach principle. Your enemies in project communications are surprise, doubt, and uncertainty. Per the communications plan, keep your targeted audiences informed on a consistent basis. Anticipate any additional information needs. Never leave stakeholders wondering or needing to call you first.
7. **People and politics go together**—Another name for this is "don't be naïve." Effective communicators demonstrate an understanding and savviness for the political nature of the project environment. They understand the political implications of any potential communication and make sure to look at it from other perspectives before delivering the intended message.

Best Practices of Effective Project Communicators

To better understand these communication principles and to improve your communication abilities, let's review the common, best practices used by effective project communicators. We'll look at general communications management, status reports, conducting meetings, interpersonal skills, and the best use for the common communication media.

tip

Responsibility for project communications is an excellent project management apprentice opportunity.

General Communications Management

First, let's review the best practices of general project communications management.

- **Assign a point man**—To ensure quality and consistency in project communications, make sure to assign specific project team members accountable for official project communications. On most projects, you (the project manager) will serve as the communications point. However, on larger projects, you may need to delegate responsibility for certain communication items or for communication to targeted stakeholders. This may include working closely with the company's human resources, marketing, and/or corporate communications departments.
- **Leverage natural strengths**—While you will always need to leverage many communication forms and media, take advantage of any natural communications strength you may possess and use the other methods to support those strengths.
- **Perform stakeholder analysis**—As part of your communications planning, perform a stakeholder analysis. This analysis should provide insights into the needs and motivations of each stakeholder. In addition, use this assessment to validate what type of project communications are needed to properly support each stakeholder audience and manage their expectations.
- **Use push and pull**—Effective project communicators use both push (send it to them) and pull (make it available to them) communication methods. With the advent of central project repositories, the pull method has experienced

tip

Send emails to stakeholders that contain direct URL links to the targeted project communication.

growing popularity. While the use of this method is excellent for anytime, on-demand information needs by stakeholders, do not rely on it for important or urgent project communications. Make sure to send (push) any important, urgent project communications directly to the targeted stakeholders. In addition, if you are using team collaboration technologies (such as Sharepoint), you can leverage both push and pull methods simultaneously by having stakeholders subscribe for alerts that notify them automatically (push) if there is an update to a given artifact. The alert contains a link that the stakeholder can use to access the targeted artifact (pull).

- **Make it easy**—If you want to score big points with your stakeholders, make it easy on them to understand what you are sending them (provide summaries) or asking them to do (provide context and purpose). Don't make them search for things (include referenced items with your communication). Your stakeholders are busy with many tasks and priorities, and they don't enjoy feeling confused and unsure. Any efforts you make that enable them to quickly understand what you're delivering or what you're asking them to do will always be appreciated, and these efforts will increase your value to the overall project.
- **Keep the information flowing**—A simple but powerful service provided by many effective project communicators is to make sure the right people have the right information to perform their roles. In many organizations, information tends to not flow easily from one group to another. An effective project manager looks for these bottleneck points and simply acts as a conduit for better information flow.
- **Take communication decisions seriously**—Consider your relationship, the message content, and available media options when making any communication decision. In general, certain communication options are better for different types of situations, and effective communicators choose wisely.

note

Researchers believe 50%–90% of a message is conveyed via nonverbal means (cues, signals, and symbols). Thus, the more nonverbal language present, the richer the communication.

tip

Set up distribution lists (voice mail, email, collaboration portals) to streamline communicating with project team members and project stakeholders.

- **Confirm technology and user training**—Always ensure that the technologies to be used for your particular communication are working properly and that the affected stakeholders understand how to leverage them correctly.

Communications Options

Now, more than ever, there are many communication media available to your project. To best manage project communications, you need to understand the strengths and limits of each option, so that you use the medium that is most appropriate for the type of relationship you have with the targeted audience and for the content of the message. The right choices can improve project productivity, facilitate open communications, and build stronger stakeholder relationships. The wrong choices create misperceptions, confusion, and weaker stakeholder relationships.

To assist your communications decision-making, let's review the best uses and important notes for the common communication options. This summary is captured in Table 17.1.

Table 17.1 Summary of Project Communication Options

Communication Option	Best Use(s)	Important Notes
Face-to-Face	Best method to start business relationships and to earn trust. Best for sensitive, interpersonal, or difficult messages.	Richest, most efficient method. Only way to do business in many cultures. "Showing up" demonstrates commitment.
Video-Conferencing	Best substitute for face-to-face meetings.	Not always available. Make sure technology works in advance.
Direct Audio (Telephone)	When interactive conversation is needed. When visual communication is not needed. When urgency is important. When privacy is important.	If placed on speaker phone, assume there are others in the room.
Voice Mail	Short messages. When common message needs to be sent to multiple people. When targeted stakeholder is auditory-oriented or is inundated with email.	If lengthy message, summarize message content up-front. Avoid for controversial or sensitive communications. Make sure stakeholder checks voice mail regularly.

Communication Option	Best Use(s)	Important Notes
Electronic Mail	When common message needs to be sent to multiple people. When supporting documents are needed. When targeted stakeholder is visually oriented or prefers email communications. When communication record is needed.	If lengthy message, summarize message content up-front. Avoid for controversial or sensitive communications. Make sure stakeholder checks email regularly. Use subject line wisely. Be cognizant of the size of attachments sent.
Instant Messaging	For daily interactions of project team. For virtual project teams. Can use IM conferencing to provide a record of meeting collaboration.	Helps to build community and project team intimacy. Not appropriate for formal work relationships. Keeps the office quieter. Monitor privacy and confidentiality concerns.
Audio Conferencing	When group collaboration is needed and face-to-face meeting is not possible.	More social presence than email or IM. Allows participants to multi-task and do other things, which makes full-attention an issue. Not as effective at building trust among participants. Most systems allow conference to be recorded.
Web Conferencing with Audio	When group collaboration is needed and face-to-face meeting is not possible. When data or presentation needs to be shared. Virtual training sessions.	Same challenges as audio conferencing. Invest more prep time on technology readiness and training. Able to record questions. Record and make available for later access.

tip

Send project documents as PDF files to reduce potential conflicts with software tools, minimize the size of email attachments, and to protect communication content.

Status Reporting

The best status reporting practices of effective project communicators include

- **Be consistent**—Provide progress status reports on a consistent, regular basis as defined in the project communications plan.
- **Target reports**—Provide the appropriate level of detail for the targeted audience.
- **Use bullets**—Use bullet points to summarize key facts; keep it short; enable the reader to quickly gauge the state of the project.
- **Employ visuals**—Because most people are visual learners and most senior management types need to get a thorough understanding of project status and/or the project issue quickly, look for opportunities to provide information in a visual format.
- **Use color-coding**—If not defined for the organization, establish three general threshold levels for key project metrics and critical success factors. For each level, associate the appropriate stoplight color: green, yellow, or red. Then use these colors to communicate the health of each key project metric on status report. This allows senior management to get a quick reading on the project's health.
- **Leverage exception-based approach**—Use the main (first part) of the status report to highlight any exceptions or variances to the project plan. Then provide details in the appendix section. This format should allow you to provide one status report that will meet the needs of most, if not all, of your key stakeholders.

There is a growing trend to leverage social networking tools (wikis, blogs, group chats, and so on) for managing project communications.

caution

Avoid using any recorded media (email, voice mail) for negative, sensitive, or controversial communications.

Meetings

The best meeting practices of effective project communicators include the following:

- **Know your game plan**—Determine the overall goal and objectives for the meeting; invite the right people; structure the meeting appropriately; determine what preparation is needed by the meeting participants to make the meeting useful.

- **Post an agenda**—Whenever possible, post an agenda in advance of the meeting. In either case, make sure to review the agenda at the start of the meeting and check whether any modifications are needed.
- **Facilitate**—Be the meeting director. Review and set meeting context; review meeting ground rules up-front; keep everyone engaged; keep the meeting flowing; solicit feedback; summarize key points; seek consensus.

tip

Establishing and building stakeholder relationships is a higher priority than enforcing a strict meeting protocol.

- **Stay on track**—Keep the meeting on topic; set time limits (timebox) agenda items; watch out for trying to solve problems in meetings—schedule follow-up meeting instead.
- **Take notes**—Delegate someone to take notes of meeting decisions and action items.
- **Attain closure**—Before adjourning meeting, review all actions items (including responsible owners and targeted completion times), summarize meeting results, schedule any necessary follow-up meetings, and thank attendees for their active participation and time.
- **Post minutes**—Distribute (post) meeting minutes within 24 hours of meeting whenever possible to meeting participants and affected parties. If action is required from non-attendees, seek their commitment before distributing minutes, or note items on which they have not been consulted.

Interpersonal Skills

The next set of best practices are likely the most important because they impact the quality of all your project communications—the formal and the more frequent day-to-day interpersonal communications that occur between the project team and the project stakeholders. The following list notes the key interpersonal skills demonstrated by effective communicators.

- Listen with a purpose
- Be humble
- Think before responding
- Take their perspective

Effective interpersonal skills are a trademark of servant leaders.

- Don't be judgmental
- Be interested in others
- Seek to understand what they do, why they do it, and what pains they are experiencing
- Validate perceptions before responding
- Show appreciation for their time and contributions
- Ask questions to confirm and improve your understanding
- Summarize what the speaker said
- Make people feel heard
- Focus on building relationships
- Stay in control of your emotions
- Don't assume that a negative response by others is personal—most of the time it's not
- Avoid interrupting, if at all possible
- Validate that you are being understood
- Avoid terms and tones that imply judgement, guilt, wrong doing on other parties

THE ABSOLUTE MINIMUM

At this point, you should have a solid understanding of the following:

- Effective communications are important to managing perceptions, managing expectations, managing the project team, reducing conflicts and overcoming any project management gap in other areas.
- The five Cs of effective communications are clear, concise, courteous, consistent, and compelling.
- The most important communication skill is listening.
- The three most powerful communication techniques are also the simplest: Give it your full attention, use your manners, and follow through.
- The most important mindset trait for effective communications is taking responsibility for understanding.
- Check out meeting collaboration tools, such as MindManager at www.mindjet.com to streamline your meeting management processes.

The map in Figure 17.2 summarizes the main points we reviewed in this chapter.

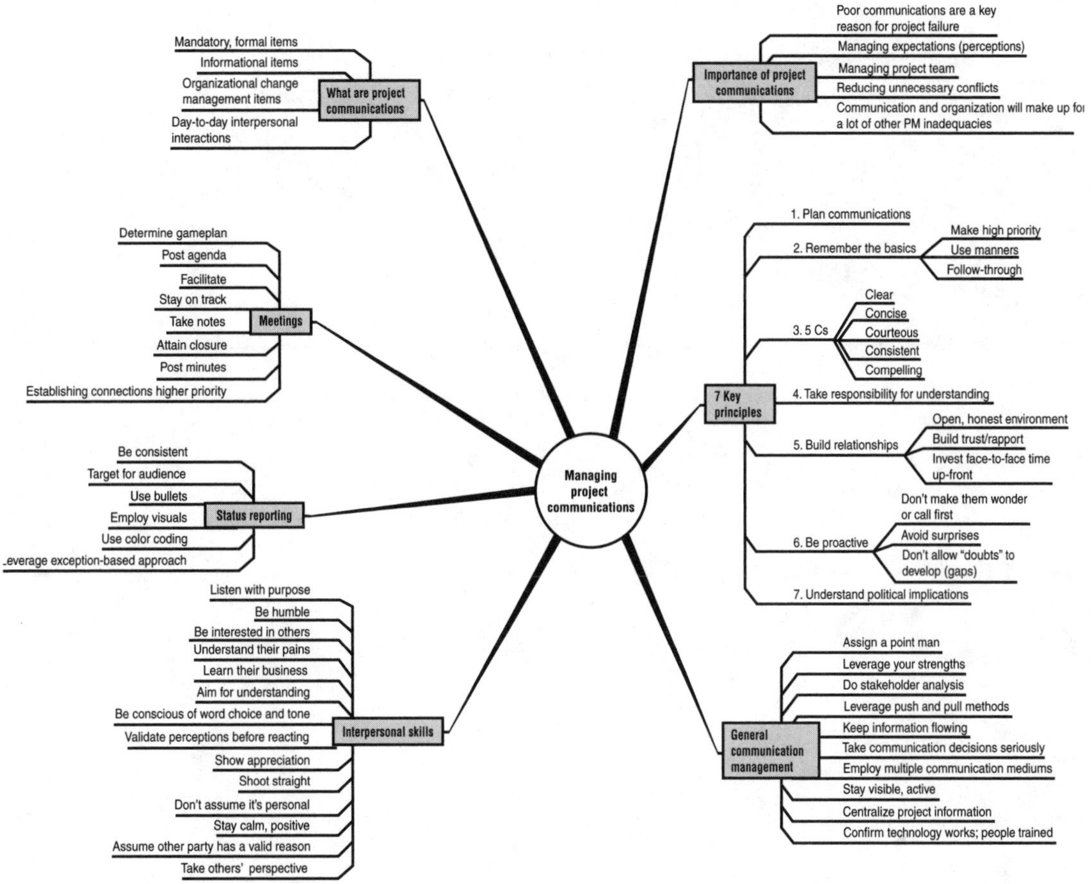

FIGURE 17.2

Overview of managing project communications.

In This Chapter

- Learn the essential components for successfully managing stakeholder expectations
- Understand why managing expectations is not the same as managing scope
- Learn the four critical aspects of stakeholder expectations
- Understand why completing a project on-time, on-budget, and within scope does not guarantee success
- Learn why many expectation issues originate during requirements definition
- Review proven guidelines to better requirements definition and management

18

Managing Expectations

Do you believe that managing stakeholders' expectations is nothing more than properly managing project scope? Do you believe that managing stakeholders' expectations is nothing more than effective project communications? Do you believe that every project is successful that completes on-time and on-budget? If you answered yes to any of these questions, then this chapter is for you.

Value of Reviewing Stakeholder Expectation Management

While managing stakeholder expectations speaks to the essence of project management and is a key objective of all project definition, planning, and control activities, it is often ignored in introductory project management books. Why? Well, I think there are many reasons, but there are two main ones. One, many consider it to be an advanced project management topic. Two, many people do not know how to manage expectations and thus just lump it with other project management activities.

While I agree that is very difficult to isolate strict expectation management activities or to talk about managing expectations without discussing other aspects of project management, there is tremendous value in taking a concentrated look at this:

- **Expectations are a critical success factor**—While scope, budget, and schedule are core elements of managing expectations, there is more—and if you ignore it, the odds for real project success are greatly diminished. We'll get into this more later in this chapter.
- **You can make a difference**—Because expectations deal with perceptions and often get into the "art" of project management, they can be less tangible, which makes it more challenging to offer guidance. This won't stop us. We will review several powerful, tangible techniques you can employ to better guide stakeholder expectations.
- **Sign of project management maturity**—Nothing says "experience" and "I'm not a rookie" more than a project manager who understands the importance of guiding stakeholder expectations and who constantly focuses on this aspect of his/her project.

While we have referenced many tools and techniques in earlier chapters that help manage expectations, this chapter provides the opportunity to highlight those important items one more time and the opportunity to take a focused look at this vital area of project management. We explore the critical aspects of expectations, the key components of successfully managing stakeholder expectations, the common mistakes to avoid, and the essential principles and techniques that will guide us in any project environment.

Critical Aspects of Expectations

If you are going to attempt to influence something, you first need to know what makes up that "something." For expectations, there is one key concept and four critical components that need to be understood for effective management.

Balancing Reality and Perception

The key concept is that expectations are shaped by both reality and perception. In an ideal project, both the reality and perception of project objectives, performance, targeted results, and expected impact are aligned up-front among all stakeholders during project definition and planning, and then remain this way throughout the project. However, this ideal situation generally eludes us. Even when expectations are aligned during planning, there are many influences and factors that can alter expectations during the course of the project. This relationship is depicted in Figure 18.1.

FIGURE 18.1

The expectation balance.

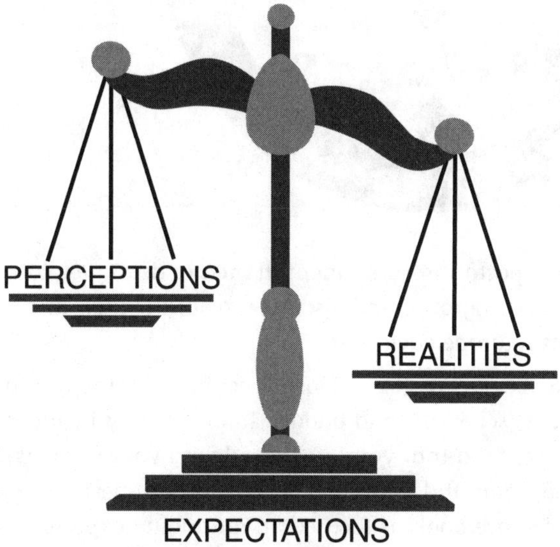

As a project manager, your challenge is to guide the actual "real" performance of the project, while simultaneously aligning and balancing the perception of each stakeholder. This work is a dynamic, on-going venture that is only complete when the project is closed.

Not Just Scope Management

There is more to managing expectations than just managing scope. Now, don't get me wrong; managing scope is a very important part of managing expectations, but it's not everything. There are four critical components of expectations. Each expectation element is important to the success of the project and is subject to the natural push and pull between project reality and stakeholder perceptions. This relationship is portrayed in Figure 18.2.

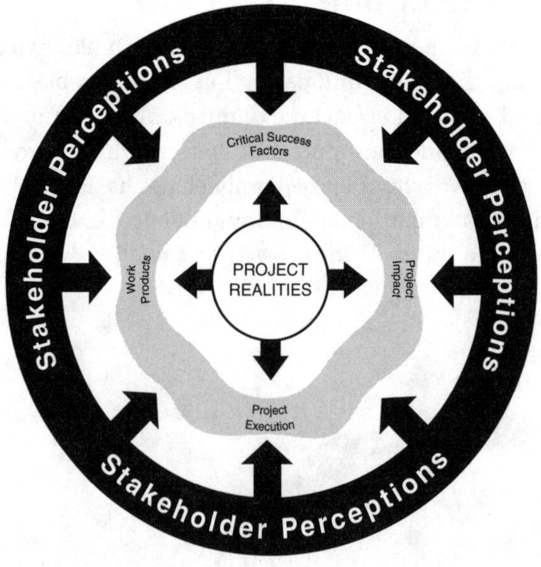

FIGURE 18.2
Aspects of expectations management.

Let's review each expectation component in greater detail, explain the specific elements included in each group, and discuss some of the tools and techniques that we can use to help us manage each part.

- **Critical Success Factors**—This aspect includes the traditional measuring rods of scope, schedule, and budget. In addition, it includes any additional acceptance criteria that you established with your key stakeholders during project definition and planning. The heart of project management (and nearly this entire book) is focused on managing expectations around these elements, but the key tools are a solid project definition document, a realistic schedule, a baseline budget, early detection of performance variances, and disciplined change control.
- **Project Impact—**This component highlights the "change" impact of the project output (results, solution, work products). It accounts for any work, process, or organizational change experienced by any stakeholder as a result of the project outcome. This aspect is commonly neglected by less experienced organizations and project managers. As Dr. Stephen Covey (a world famous personal development coach and author of *The 7 Habits* book series) always says, the key here is to think (and plan) with the end in mind. With this clarity, you can better communicate a common vision of the project outcome and help stakeholders prepare for the changes that will affect them.
- **Work Products—**This category covers things such as "that's not what I asked for," "that's not what I meant," and "oh no, you gave me exactly what I asked for." This could be considered a part of project scope, but

depending on the level of detail in your scope statement, it may not be adequately addressed. This category deals with the detailed expectations surrounding the individual work products that each stakeholder has. At a minimum, it focuses on requirements management, quality management, and overall project approach. We discuss key requirements management techniques that greatly improve your effectiveness here.

- **Project Execution**—This final component deals with the day-to-day execution of the project. While not as critical as the other aspects, a lack of attention to these elements will certainly create situations that can easily lead to underperforming projects, and then to major expectation management activities. This category deals with the efficiency and effectiveness of the project team, and with the confidence the stakeholders have in them to successfully deliver the targeted solution and in you to lead them there. Common elements in this group include interactions between team and client stakeholders, clarity of roles, responsibilities, work processes, and work assignments.

We will review many of these elements in greater detail in Chapter 19, "Keys to Better Project Team Performance." In addition, many of the communication and leadership techniques we reviewed in Chapters 16, "Leading a Project," and 17, "Managing Project Communications," come into play here. Important principles to remember here: Make sure team members are prepared for their interactions with stakeholders; do not assume stakeholders have a clear understanding of project processes and their work assignments; always look at the project from their perspective; and proactively review (with a gentle touch) key tasks and targeted completion dates.

While we have broken down expectations into various components, which are summarized in Table 18.1, it's important to remember: Effective expectation management is not complicated. The success formula for each aspect of expectation management is relatively straightforward:

The expectation component classifications are academic in nature and are there to serve discussion and review. Many expectation elements could be placed in more than one of these categories.

A common mistake made in expectation management is to sell or commit to requirements that cannot be met given the project constraints. This is often done in efforts to get business, make the customer happy, or instill confidence in the team's abilities. The "under-promise, over-deliver" principle is one that reminds us that it is much better in regard to expectation management to promise less and deliver more.

- **Get real**—Set realistic expectations; get initial agreement (buy-in) from affected stakeholders; review assumptions and constraints; talk about it; address it; get clarity and understanding.
- **Keep it balanced**—Manage changes; align project reality with stakeholder perceptions; proactively communicate; educate; constantly validate and affirm perceptions; regularly assess performance; reset expectations as needed.
- **Follow-through**—Deliver; honor the agreements; get the work done; "under-promise, over-deliver."

Table 18.1 Summary of Critical Expectation Components

Expectation Area	Elements	Key Tools and Techniques	Notes
Critical Success Factors	Scope statement. Project budget. Target dates. Performance versus cost versus time. Acceptance criteria. Agreement on what defines success.	Project definition document. Project plan. Change control. Performance reporting. Realistic schedule. Kickoff meetings. Milestone reviews.	Be proactive. No surprises. Ensure right people are informed of changes. Forecast missed deadlines.
Project Impact	ROI. Key Performance Indicators (KPIs). Individual work task changes. Business process flow changes. Organizational change impact.	Acceptance criteria. Stakeholder analysis. Prototypes, simulations. Future workflow models. Pilots. Phased implementations.	Often neglected. May need separate deployment project. Organizational change management plan needed.
Work Products	Requirements. Deliverables. Interim deliverables.	Requirements management. Quality management. Iterative development. Prototypes, scenarios, simulations. Pilot implementations. Product reviews and signoffs.	Get something tangible early. Heavy customer. Involvement. Use internal team QA reviews.

Expectation Area	Elements	Key Tools and Techniques	Notes
Project Execution	Decision making process. Roles and responsibilities. Work assignments. Project processes. Common goals. Personal credibility. Avoids issues. Team interactions with stakeholders. Leadership confidence.	Responsibility matrix. Realistic schedule. Resource plan. Team charter. Kickoff meetings. Walkthrough schedule, processes. Coaching team members. Internal reviews.	Take other perspective. Don't assume understanding/clarity. Be aware of "busy" team members. Use gentle touch to proactively remind team of key tasks, responsibilities, dates. Always set context to improve understanding. Educate along the way.

Seven Master Principles of Expectation Management

Now that we have a good feel for the breadth of managing expectations, you can understand the value of many key project planning and project control fundamentals we reviewed in prior chapters. Before we do a quick capsulation of those items and then delve into two other powerful tools for managing expectations—requirements management and kickoff meetings—let's look at the seven master principles that drive all expectation management activity:

1. **Get buy-in**—Whether it's the critical success criteria, resource and time commitments, or individual work assignments, invest the time and energy to gain their trust and to make sure you have genuine buy-in from the affected parties. This is why effective planning is a must.
2. **Take care of business**—This is the "blocking and tackling" fundamentals of project management. Set your baselines, manage to them, and properly handle and communicate any variances.

Most of the principles depend greatly on the effectiveness of your communication and interpersonal skills. Your ability to manage the perceptions of each individual associated with the project is the key to managing expectations.

3. **Communicate the "big picture"**—With the end goal in mind, clearly sell the vision on where the project is going, what the targeted solution will be like, and why each work assignment is important. People want to know "why" and understand the importance of their role.
4. **Listen and be alert**—If stakeholders are not "on the same page" or have "unstated expectations," there are always cues and signals. Look and listen for them and make it a priority to deal with them quickly. When we discuss managing requirements, probing for unstated expectations will be a key focus.
5. **Take their perspective**—We discussed leadership in Chapter 16, but its importance is worth re-emphasizing. This ability is a mainstay for effective expectation management, and it empowers you to anticipate the needs and concerns of your project stakeholders. It also drives a "flexible" mindset that allows you to adapt approaches, plans, and specifications to best meet the situation at hand.
6. **Never assume**—A key principle that needs constant attention. Many don't realize the assumptions they are working under until it is too late. To help you avoid assumptions, keep the following in mind:
   - Err on the side of over-communication
   - Always set context for all your communications
   - Constantly confirm understanding
   - Clearly communicate what is expected from each team member
   - Continuously reset expectations
   - Verify that you have the correct solution to meet the project's objectives (rather than just validating documented requirements)
7. **Understand priorities**—There are always many stakeholders, often with their own distinct views of the world and sets of priorities. While you always aim to find compromises that appeal to entire group, it is important to understand the decision-making process and whose voices have greater influence and priority. In particular, always be very clear on who controls the budget for your project.

Essential Elements of Managing Expectations

Let's take a look at the essential tools and techniques that are available to the project manager to effectively manage stakeholder expectations.

Project Planning and Control Elements—A Quick Review

At many times during our chapters on defining, planning, and controlling a project, we referenced managing expectations as a key reason or benefit of specific project management tools and techniques. Table 18.2 and Table 18.3 summarize the most important project management tools, techniques, and actions to manage stakeholder expectations.

Table 18.2 Summary of Essential Planning Elements to Manage Project Expectations

Element	Impact on Expectations
Project Definition Document	Defines why we are doing this Defines what organizational level goal(s) is supported Defines how this project fits/aligns with the other projects Defines expected benefits from this project Defines what will be done Defines who is impacted Defines how success will be measured
Scope Statement	Sets boundaries for what will be done, and what will *not* be done
WBS	Allows stakeholders to see the work that must be done
Project Budget	Sets cost and ROI expectations
Estimates	Foundation for budget and schedule
Assumptions and Constraints	Key for better expectations around estimates, scope, budget, and schedule
Project Schedule	Sets time expectations
Project Plan	Sets expectations for how project will be managed
Project Organization Chart	Identifies and communicates who is involved and how team is structured
Stakeholder Analysis	Defines who is impacted and what their needs are
Communications Plan	Defines how the communications needs of project stakeholders will be addressed
Responsibility Matrix	Sets expectations regarding role and work tasks
Project Approach	Stakeholders need to know what is going to happen and why Approach needs to be tailored to best manage stakeholder expectations

Table 18.3 Summary of Essential Control and Execution Elements to Manage Project Expectations

Element	Impact on Expectations
Kickoff meetings	Notification project is underway Facilitates "expectation setting" for the group
Status reports	Regular, consistent performance monitoring and reporting keeps everyone informed
Change control	Allows scope, time, and budget expectations to be reset and controlled along the way
Quality management	Focused on satisfying real customer needs and ensuring solution does the right thing
Risk management	Anticipates, forecasts, and attempts to avoid impacts to the critical success factors
Issue management	Communicates issues to the right people
Requirements management	Drives expectations on the product of the project (more on this later in this chapter)
Completion criteria	Clarifies expectations for any work package
Formal signoffs	Documents acceptance of work products at points in time Used in conjunction with milestone and work product reviews
Reviews	Validates expectations of work products along the way
Milestones and checkpoints	Validates expectations of project performance along the way
Requirements traceability matrix	Keeps visibility of targeted requirements throughout the project process
Team charter	Communicates team rules and procedures (more on this in Chapter 19)

Leveraging Kickoff Meetings

Kickoff meetings are a simple but powerful tool to help manage expectations. We could have discussed these in our chapter on project communications (Chapter 17), as is typically done, but they are such an instrumental tool in managing expectations, I felt it was better to do it here.

In general, a kickoff meeting is simple. Get all the targeted stakeholders together to officially review the project and get it underway. So why focus on this technique? Kickoff meetings are invaluable for accomplishing certain things related to expectation management, and many people either do not do them properly or under-utilize them.

Primary Goals

The three primary goals for any kickoff meeting should include the following:

- Give official notification that the project (or project phase) is underway
- Achieve a common expectation baseline for all stakeholders
- Start the relationship-building process between project team, customers, and other stakeholders

The main factor impacting the nature of kickoff meetings is "where are you in the planning process?" If detailed planning is complete, the kickoff meeting is more of an informational session. If not, the kickoff meeting can be used as a detail planning workshop.

Key Recommendations

With these goals in mind, here are some key recommendations for better kickoff meetings:

- The meeting size, length, and logistics will vary depending on organizational culture, project size, number of stakeholders, project methodology, and project importance. Plan your kickoff meetings accordingly.
- As a rule, don't try to do too much or cover everything. Use follow-up, mini-kickoff meetings with focused groups or specific individuals to cover the details.
- For general kickoffs, get everyone there if possible, especially the executive sponsors.
- Set context for everyone. Focus on the "why." Review project purpose, objectives, and value to the business.
- Clarify the priorities, target goals, and the critical success factors.
- Paint the picture. Enable everyone to visualize how the final solution will look, how it will impact them, and how all the pieces fit together.
- Get to know each other. Start the relationship-building and teamwork processes. Introduce everyone.
- Review roles and responsibilities and project team organization. Emphasize each person's role, expected time commitment, and value.
- Establish your leadership and the energy for the project. Set the tone; generate enthusiasm and motivation.

- Review important project plan items:
  - Scope and major deliverables
  - General approach (methodology)
  - Critical milestones
  - WBS
  - Schedule
  - Estimated effort and budget
  - Review key assumptions, risks, and constraints
  - Review key project communications processes
  - Review process/procedures for monitoring project performance
- Whenever possible, hand out team keepsakes (or promotions) at the beginning of the project. It helps to build team unity and project awareness.
- Ask for feedback. Clarify any confusion now.
- Ensure people know what to do first/next (short-term). They should be clear on their next steps.

tip

Utilize mini-kickoff meetings at the beginning of each project phase, not just the start of the entire project, to reset expectations.

Requirements Management—The Difference Maker

A large percentage of expectation misunderstandings have their origins in the requirements gathering and requirements management processes. The frustrating thing about these situations is that most of these can or could be avoided. While the subject of requirements definition is a field of study itself, we will leverage the Pareto principle here. We will focus our attention on addressing the common requirements-related problems and the key principles and guidelines that make the most difference in your future requirements definition and management efforts.

Common Problems to Avoid

To better understand the value of the recommended principles and guidelines, let's take a quick review of the common problems with gathering and defining requirements:

- **Not well-written**—Requirements are ambiguous, inconsistent, too high-level, or not clear.
- **Incomplete**—List of requirements is not complete to properly define the solution.
- **Unstated expectations**—The list of requirements does not accurately reflect all the expectations held by the stakeholders for the targeted solution.

- **Inflexible process**—While specifications do need to be agreed to and finalized at certain points, defining requirements is an evolutionary process and things do change. The system for managing requirements must anticipate this reality.
- **Lack of verification**—The age-old problem with language. Using statements to describe a targeted solution creates many opportunities for misunderstandings and misperceptions. In most cases, you need to employ other techniques and methods to verify that you are defining the "right" solution.
- **Lack of education**—Often, the stakeholders who are defining the solution requirements don't fully understand the entire requirements process and the significance or impact of their decisions.

Appropriate stakeholders should be educated on the following points at a minimum:

- Requirements serve as the primary target for the project and as the foundation for detailed project planning
  - Walk them through the various techniques and methods to be employed in the requirements definition process
  - Changes to requirements impact cost and schedule, and they cost more the later in the project they are made
  - Requirements can serve as provisions in the contract

Principles to Remember for Better Requirements Management

To help you develop better requirements and to improve your ability to manage both requirements and expectations throughout the project, let's review the following principles:

- Requirements definition is an evolutionary process. Plan your project approach and requirements management tools accordingly.
- The requirements definition process should consist of a combination of gathering techniques. The specific techniques chosen should be based on risks and characteristics of the project.
- Requirements should describe *what*, not *how*.
- Requirements should avoid any unnecessary constraints.

tip

Understanding the process flow will help you identify stakeholders, scope boundaries, change impact issues, and better requirements.

- Requirements should be complete, explicit, realistic, and understandable by all parties.
- Requirements should be linked to the intended solution.
- Requirements should be prioritized.
- Listen. Do not pre-judge or draw conclusions too quickly.
- Strive to convert expectations into requirements.
- Educate appropriate stakeholders on the requirements process.

caution

Expectations that cannot be quantified should be identified as project risks. Make sure your project assumptions are consistent with your final requirements.

tip

Translate performance and quality expectations into tangible, documented requirements.

Guidelines for Better Requirements

To avoid the common problems identified earlier and to greatly increase your requirements definition prowess, note these guidelines:

- Focus on user "experience." Understand how the user interacts with the targeted solution.
- Understand the user's workflow.
- Understand the user's work environment.
- Always ask "why?"
- Include other non-language exhibits/models as part of the requirements definition.
- To drive out unstated expectations, understand the following from each user representative:
  - What are biggest problems now, and why?
  - What functions or features will be the most useful, and why?
  - What aspect of the new solution are you most anticipating, and why?
  - What are your quality and performance expectations for the final solution, and why?
- To help make better design decisions, define requirements in both present and future needs whenever possible.
- Identify each requirement with a unique ID.
- Document any accompanying assumptions.

- Use a quality checklist to improve the effectiveness of your requirements.
- Monitor and control changes to requirements.
- Use a requirements traceability matrix (RTM) to link each requirement to one or more aspects of the final solution. This is a powerful tool to ensure that every requirement is accounted for and to better control "gold-plating."

The Absolute Minimum

At this point, you should have a solid understanding of the following:

- The goal of managing expectations is to have a common set of expectations shared by all stakeholders in terms of what is being delivered, what it will accomplish, when, and at what cost.
- Managing expectations is more than managing project scope.
- The master principles of expectation management are
    1. Get buy-in
    2. Take care of business
    3. Communicate the big picture
    4. Listen and be alert
    5. Take their perspective
    6. Never assume
- Two key tools for managing expectations are kickoff meetings and requirements management.
- Requirements management mistakes to avoid:
    - Poorly written requirements
    - Incomplete set of requirements
    - Unstated expectations
    - Inflexible process
    - Lack of verification
    - Lack of stakeholder education
- Other key expectation management tips include
    - Avoid surprises
    - Keep people informed of status (project health)
    - Avoid last minute communications
    - Clearly communicate what is expected by team members

Figure 18.3 summarizes the main points we reviewed in this chapter.

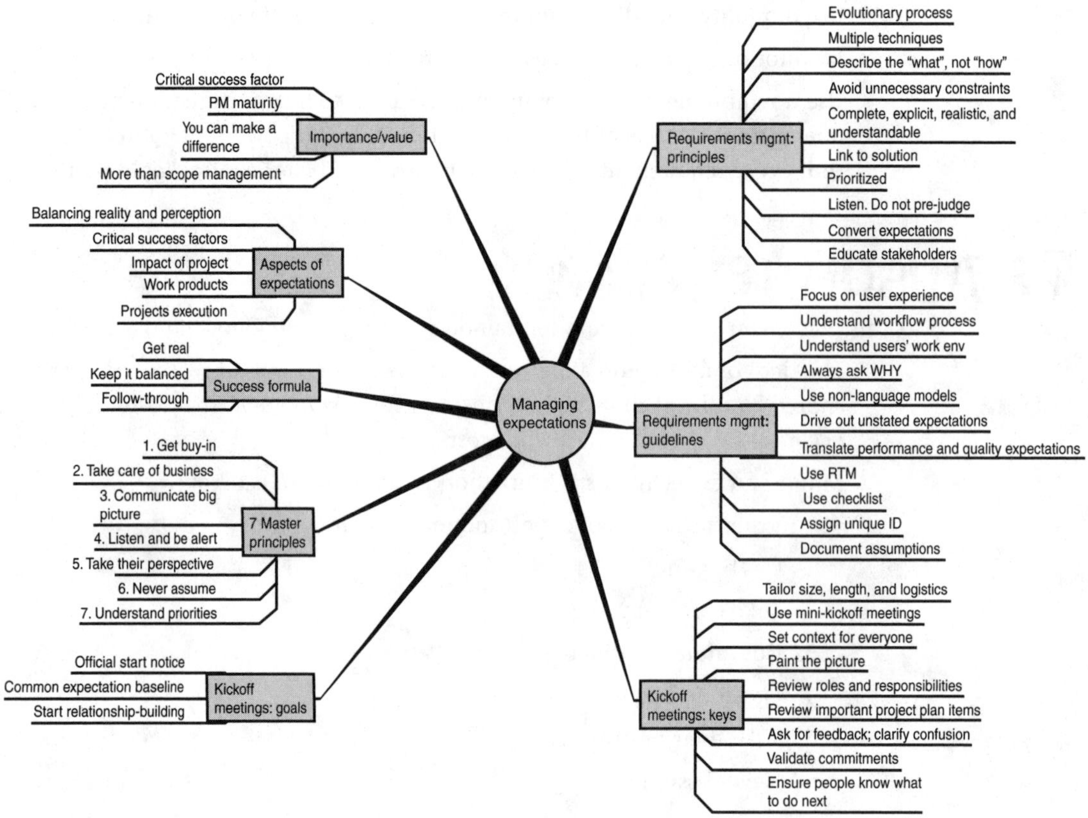

FIGURE 18.3

Overview of managing expectations.

IN THIS CHAPTER

- Review the primary traits of high-performing teams
- Understand the key principles that lead to better project team performance
- Review proven techniques to improve project team performance
- Learn effective responses to special situations, including poor performers, high maintenance team members, and team conflicts

19

KEYS TO BETTER PROJECT TEAM PERFORMANCE

When it comes right down to it, you've got to deliver. And the key to doing this is having a high-performing project team. You can have the greatest plan in the world, but if your core project team can't get the work done as expected, it really doesn't matter. Conversely, a high performing project team can go a long way to compensate for inadequate planning and other "less than ideal" project environments. While effective leadership and communication skills are key ingredients of a successful project team environment (and we reviewed these important facets in Chapters 16, "Leading a Project," and 17, "Managing Project Communications," respectively), there is tremendous value in understanding the specific principles and techniques that we can apply to maximize the performance of our project team.

In this chapter, we will review the common characteristics of high-performing project teams, explore the management principles and techniques that foster better team performance, and offer key advice on how to best handle challenging project team situations frequently encountered by project managers.

High-Performing Teams

Before we delve into the management principles and techniques that can lead to better project team performance, let's get clear on the goal. In other words, what do high-performing teams look like? What do they have in common? Do they all look and act the same? While no two teams ever perform in precisely the same manner, and every team will have their particular strengths, I have found a core set of traits that are shared by high-performing teams.

- **Clarity**—This trait is likely the most important. High-performing teams know where they are going, what they are doing, and why they are doing it. They understand the project goals and priorities, they have clear roles and responsibilities, and they understand their assigned work tasks and how their piece fits in with the rest.
- **Commitment**—Members of high-performing teams are committed to the success of the project. They demonstrate a persistence and determination to get the job done. The source of the commitment is not always the same. It may be personal, to the team, to the customer, or to the organization.
- **Professional**—High-performing teams are professional about their work. Members take individual responsibility for the quality of assigned work, personal communications, and interactions with all stakeholders.
- **Synergy**—High-performing teams develop a synergistic force about them that allows them to accomplish more as a combined team than they could do collectively as individuals. This synergy is developed over time, but generally results when the team has the right mix of skills and experiences, has a healthy team-orientation, and has clearly defined roles and responsibilities.
- **Trust**—High-performing teams display a high level of trust in each other and in their project leader. Trust is earned over time, too, and demonstrating effective leadership and creating a collaborative team environment with an open exchange of ideas are keys to building this trust level.

Ten Key Principles

Now that we have a better sense for what a high-performing team looks like, let's review ten key management principles that are paramount to our efforts to guide our team's performance.

1. **Adapt management style**—While as a rule, a collaborative, servant-leadership management approach to leading project teams will be the most effective in most situations, you may need to adjust your style depending on the project phase, the needs of your particular team, and the project environment.
2. **Get the right people**—Whenever possible, personally select the members of your core team. You should have the best understanding of the skills, abilities, and behaviors that are needed for project success. In particular, get people who have a track record of success. As any successful project manager will attest, having the right people is 80% of the battle. Of course, in the real world, you don't always have this luxury, and we'll talk about that in the "Special Situations" section.
3. **Plan as a team**—A major component of modern-day project management is the idea that planning is a team activity. This was a heavy emphasis in our planning chapters. Why is this key? If the team develops the project plan, it becomes "their" plan and "their" schedule. With this, comes a much higher level of commitment, buy-in, and accountability, and much less time spent battling the issues you get when this is not present.
4. **Keep the team focused**—One of the most important things a project manager can do is to make sure each team member is simultaneously crystal clear on the "big picture" of the project (mission, objectives, and priorities) on one hand and focused on his/her immediate task on the other. To focus, not only must each team member have clear work assignments and roles, but the project manager needs to be an "umbrella." As an umbrella, you protect the team from the politics, noise, and other factors that distract them and slow their progress.
5. **Set clear expectations**—To encourage maximum team productivity, nothing is more important than making sure each team member understands what is expected from him or her in advance. This applies to both work assignments and team protocols. A key aspect of this expectation setting activity is to review the completion criteria for any work assignment up front. This step alone goes a long way to avoiding rework and increasing productivity.
6. **Facilitate productivity**—Continuing our productivity theme, the focus of the project manager should be on doing everything he/she can to enable each team member to be as productive as he/she can possibly be. What does this mean? It means the following:
    - Ensure work assignments are clear and understood
    - Provide all resources that are needed to accomplish the work in a timely fashion

- Facilitate resolution to any issue impeding work assignment completion
- Anticipate issues that may impact work productivity and take action to mitigate or prevent them (risk management at the work task level)

7. **Improve marketability**—A key goal I have for every person on my team is to improve their marketability through their experiences on the project. In the end, the only real job security we have is to always be "marketable"—and to continuously improve our marketability. Look for ways to improve skills, build résumés, and to help each person make progress on their career goals. This mindset is key to both how you assign and "sell" work tasks. Personally, I like to find out who desires to become project managers or gain project management skills, and then assign roles and responsibilities throughout the project to facilitate this marketable growth.
8. **Leverage individual strengths**—An extension of the previous principle, this one has three primary components:
   - Look for the strengths that each person brings to the table, but understand their weaknesses. This approach will keep you positive and is especially important when you have not personally selected your team or when you have given a team member with a "reputation."
   - Understand what drives each person, their motivators, and what they care about. Not only will this help you position people to do better, but it will also enable you to reward and recognize them more effectively.
   - Align project roles and responsibilities with each team member's "sweet spot" as much as possible. The sweet spot is the combination of natural strengths and personal motivators.
9. **Recognize and reward**—This principle has three primary aspects:
   - **PR agent**—Pretend you are the public relations agent for each one of your team members. In addition to providing timely feedback and appreciation to each person personally, make sure the "right people" (especially the people who influence their career advancements and compensation) know about the excellent work your team members are doing throughout the project. Don't wait to do all this at the end of the project or at annual review time; it will be much more effective and meaningful if it is communicated as it happens.
   - **Celebrate**—Take the time and make plans to celebrate interim milestones along the way. This forces you to acknowledge the efforts to-date and helps to build team momentum.

- **Rewards**—Two key items here: One, look for ways during initial project planning and throughout the project that will allow the team members to share in the rewards (profits) if the project accomplishes certain goals. Two, if the project team or specific team members are asked to perform heroic efforts, set up an incentive that will both reward and acknowledge the special efforts.

10. **Facilitate team synergy**—Especially early on in the project, use methods to help build the cohesiveness of the team. Most teams naturally go through the traditional "forming, norming, storming, and performing" stages, but there are things you can do to be a positive influence on this process. Depending on how much the given project team has worked together before and where they are physically located, the specifics will differ, but as a guide, you want to focus on the following:
    - **Build relationships**—Set up team-building outings, team lunches, team meetings, and so on that will enable relationships to begin and grow.
    - **Setup team procedures**—Determine what rules, guidelines, and protocols are needed to help establish team productivity (such as modes of communication, core hours, standard meeting times, work standards, work processes, and administrative procedures).
    - **See progress**—Structure the project approach so that the team can get some early, visible progress. Not only will this create enthusiasm for the stakeholders, but it will do the same for the core team's efforts too. In addition, track the team's progress and accomplishments in a very visible fashion. This helps build enthusiasm, but also encourages pride and accountability in project efforts.

tip

Utilize mini-kickoff meetings at the beginning of each project phase, not just the start of the entire project, to reset expectations.

Proven Techniques

With these principles as our foundation, let's take a look at a few proven techniques that generally lead to better project team performance:

- **Conduct team kickoffs**—Conduct separate kickoff meetings with your core team at the beginning of each phase. This is an excellent way to reset expectations on project context, project goals and priorities, team member roles and responsibilities, team member assignments, project schedule, and team procedures.

- **Collocate**—This is not always possible, and it is becoming more uncommon as project work becomes increasingly distributed. However, results speak for themselves. When project team members are physically located in the same area, it is much easier to build relationships, share ideas and experiences, develop answers to problems, and increase team synergy.
- **Use meeting time wisely**—To communicate both respect and value for individual's time, and to help team productivity, have a definite purpose or need for any team meeting and confirm that this purpose is understood by all team members. At a minimum, conduct a general team status meeting each week to share knowledge and lessons learned, and to provide gentle peer pressure accountability. The need for formal meetings will vary depending on how the team is naturally collaborating, the composition of the team, team productivity, and on the list of outstanding issues.
- **Develop team charter**—To align individual expectations with desired team behaviors, develop a team charter that defines the guidelines, procedures, and principles by which the team will operate. The emphasis point here is not whether or not you take the time to document this, but it is the act of working with the team to develop these guidelines and procedures. This way, much like the overall project plan and schedule, it becomes theirs.
- **Set standards**—Especially on projects where multiple individuals may be doing the same type of work or when work will be outsourced, develop and communicate the standards the work must meet to be accepted. This helps clarify expectations, reduces rework activity, improves quality, and leverages expert knowledge.
- **Leverage expertise**—This is an invaluable method to improve team performance and to improve the skills of multiple individuals. Especially in cases where the project involves newer technologies, the primary resource pools do not have adequate skill levels, or the organization needs to avoid allocating their most senior, sought-after talent on a single project.
- **Resolve conflicts right away**—High-performing teams do not let intra-team conflicts or project issues linger, because if they do, they can adversely effect team productivity. As the project manager, you need to facilitate resolutions quickly. This does not mean that you do not listen and make rash judgments. It means that you "deal with it"—don't avoid it. In all cases, it is very important that you stay objective, treat all sides with respect, place your focus on potential solutions, and seek out win-win scenarios.

- **Prepare for client interactions**—To better manage client expectations and to avoid unproductive issues, prepare the team for direct client interactions. Make sure they understand the project from the client's perspective, the expectation the client has of the team's abilities, specific actions to take if they need assistance when they are with the client, and any talking points to either avoid or emphasize.
- **Set up project repository**—To help facilitate team productivity, share knowledge, and protect project assets, set up a common repository that is accessible by all core team members to store project work products and project management deliverables. We discussed this in greater detail in Chapter 12, "Managing Project Deliverables."
- **Develop team rituals**—To help build team unity, develop specific rituals that engage the entire team. Examples include going out to lunch together on a certain day each week, sharing breakfast together on a certain day each week, celebrating individual birthdays or anniversaries, and so forth.
- **Effective task assignments**—We've talked about this one in various ways many times already, but the point I want to emphasize here is that you can't just assume a task assignment is understood and will be done because it appears on the schedule and there is a person's name beside it. The keys here are the following:
    - Instill a sense of ownership on assigned tasks. Look for modules or domains that specific people can have lead responsibility over.
    - Verify that the person assigned the work is clear on task completion criteria. This will avoid the need to micro-manage your team. (Because I'm naturally lazy, this is an important one for me.)
    - Ensure that one person is primarily responsible for a task and that you have buy-in on that responsibility.
    - Ensure that the level of schedule detail is appropriate to effectively assign and monitor work.
- **Plan for orientation**—For any new team member joining your project, there is an introductory orientation period. Your goal is to streamline this period and to have each team member at maximum productivity as soon as possible. The four specific actions I employ are
    - **Protect your schedule**—Do not assume the new team member will be 100% productive on day one. The length of the ramp-up period will be specific to project, work assignments, and previous work experiences.

  - **Prepare an orientation packet**—Put yourself in the new team member's shoes and think about what you need to know in order to get a solid understanding of the project environment.
  - **Setup work environment in advance**—In any project environment, where team members need specific equipment, tools, access privileges to do their work, do whatever you can to get this set up before the team member starts. If you can't, account for this in your schedule.
  - **Invest the time up-front**—Plan on spending time with any new team member up front. By investing focused attention with any new team member, you can better communicate your energy for the project and the expectations for the project, their role, and their contributions. As an avid follower of the Pareto principle, this is a clear case where spending a little extra time up-front avoids the need to spend a lot more time on down the road on team productivity issues.

The Pareto principle is also known as the "80-20" rule. It's a common rule-of-thumb and an effective management tool that states, "20 percent of something always are responsible for 80 percent of the results."

- **Plug-in**—To help facilitate the performance team, you must stay connected with the team. Keys here are to stay visible, use the same communication channels the team is using, take time to meet with each team member one-on-one, and make sure the team knows you are there to help them be productive.
- **Share leadership responsibilities**—To help team members develop leadership skills and to help build commitment to the project, look for opportunities to share leadership responsibilities. This is natural on larger and cross-functional projects.

tip

Performance feedback should be timely, discreet, and specific.

Special Situations

There are going to be project situations where you won't have a stellar, high-performing team. There may be times where you have just the opposite situation to deal with. In either case, you still need to get the work done. It's in these situations where your goal is to get "better" team performance. While we could spend an entire chapter on all the problem situations you may encounter, I at least want to spend a section looking at some special situations related to project team performance that you are likely to encounter and offer a few helpful recommendations in each case.

- **Poor performers**—Poor performers generally fall into two categories: unacceptable work results or unacceptable behaviors. In many cases, the poor performance is a result of unclear expectations. If faced with this situation, keep these action items in mind:
  - **Verify expectations**—On first occurrences, don't overreact—verify the expectations that they had and take responsibility for any lack of clarity.
  - **Provide feedback**—After you have proper information, provide specific feedback to the team member as soon as possible in a private setting. Focus on the behavior or result, not the person.
  - **Enable success**—Do everything that you can do to enable each team member's success. Provide resources. Knock down obstacles. Provide every opportunity for their performance to improve.
  - **Initiate backup plans**—At the same time, you cannot assume their performance will get better. At the first signs of performance issues, start thinking about what you can do to mitigate the impact to the project, if you do need to replace the team member or if the performance does not improve.
  - **Cut your losses**—Assuming you've done everything we've mentioned so far, there comes a time when you've got to cut your losses. The main reason why a poor performer needs to be removed is the effect it can have on the performance and morale of the rest of the team.

tip

Keep in mind: The rest of the team is watching how you deal with these situations. Your challenge is to strike the balance between handling the person fairly and not letting the poor performance become a drag on the team.

- **High-maintenance staff**—This group of team members includes those individuals who have a reputation of either being difficult to work with or possessing unusual personalities. In most cases, these are the people you need for your key critical path tasks—of course. From experience, here are my two key recommendations for these situations:
  - **Check for yourself**—Don't assume the reputation (the perception) is totally true. Verify for yourself. I have found that in many cases, these individuals are unfairly labeled. These labels often say more about the people who are uncomfortable working with individuals who are different from them than anything else.
  - **Treat them the same**—Use the same approach with them as you would any other team member. Work to understand their motivators, clarify expectations, avoid surprises, and help them to be successful.
- **Schedule developed without team**—I know we emphasize the importance and the value in developing the detail project plan and schedule with the team. I also realize this does not always occur in the real-world (shocking I know). If you find yourself in a situation where either you or your team is asked to take responsibility for a schedule that they did not help develop, you must take the time to review the schedule. You need to get a buy-in from the team members before continuing. Two important items for consideration here:
  - **Understand the schedule assumptions**—In many of these situations, team members totally dismiss the merits of a schedule because they are not aware of the assumptions that serve as the foundation for the schedule. Key assumptions include those about resource ability and quality level of work product (completion criteria).
  - **Identify risks**—If there are gaps between the schedule assumptions and project reality, or if you cannot get commitment from the team, you have some new project risks if not outright issues. Follow your designated risk and issue management procedures to handle it.

THE ABSOLUTE MINIMUM

At this point, you should have a solid understanding of the following:

- The core set of traits for high-performing teams are clarity, commitment, professionalism, synergy, and trust.
- In most situations, a participative approach to project management, decision-making, conflict resolution, and brainstorming leads to better project team performance.
- The key project management skills that are needed to lead better project team performance include leadership, communication, facilitation, interpersonal, and team-building skills.
- The ten key management principles that lead to better project team performance are
    1. Adapt management style to best meet the needs of the project.
    2. Select your project team yourself whenever possible.
    3. Develop the project plan and schedule with the team.
    4. Keep the team focused on both their immediate tasks and on the project's "big picture."
    5. Set clear expectations.
    6. Enable each team member to be as productive as possible.
    7. Strive to improve the marketability of each person on your team.
    8. Leverage the individual strengths to best accomplish the project goals.
    9. Constantly look to recognize and reward the accomplishments and good work of your team members.
    10. Use team-building methods and procedures to help develop team synergy.

Figure 19.1 summarizes the main points we reviewed in this chapter.

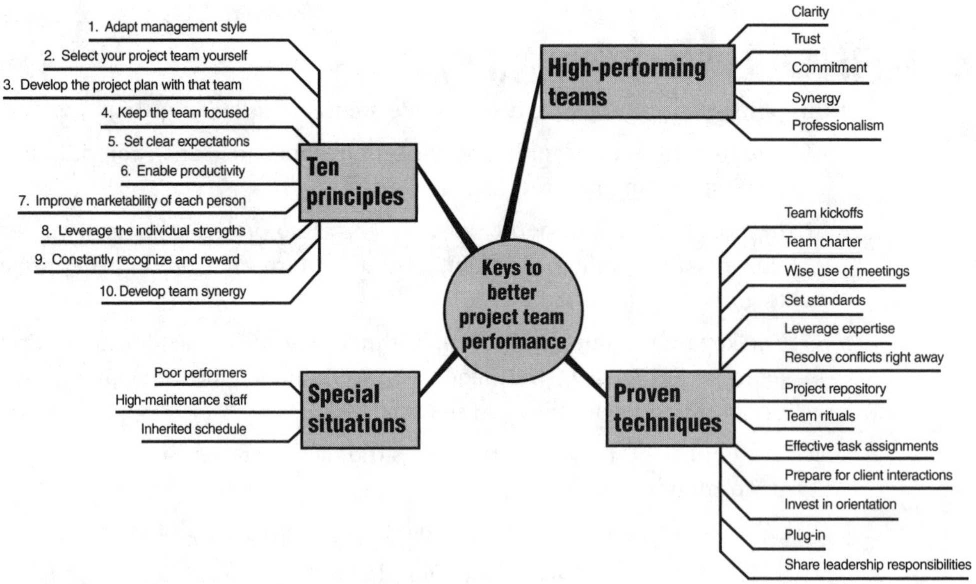

FIGURE 19.1

Overview of keys to better project team performance.

IN THIS CHAPTER

- Review the key management principles for cross-functional, cross-cultural, or virtual project environments
- Learn tips and techniques to better lead cross-functional projects
- Learn tips and techniques to better lead cross-cultural projects
- Learn tips and techniques to better lead virtual projects
- Gain awareness of the common problems that can arise in these project environments

20

MANAGING DIFFERENCES

With the current trends in business and technology, the odds that you will manage a project consisting of stakeholders from the same culture, located in the same environment, and representing a common business function decrease as each day passes. In the past, these more complex project situations were assigned to proven, experienced project managers. Today, you are likely to deal with cross-functional, cross-cultural, or virtual environments (or combinations of these three) in your initial project management opportunity. This is why I feel it is important to review key aspects of managing differences in project environments.

In this chapter, I want to accomplish two primary goals. One, I want to share with you the unique aspects of each of these project situations, the common problems to watch out for, and most importantly, the key principles and lessons that I have learned managing these types of projects. Two, I want to emphasize how these special situations do not require any additional project management techniques—just disciplined application of the principles and techniques we have reviewed in earlier chapters. With this knowledge and awareness, you will be more confident and better prepared to manage these aspects of your project environment.

Five Key Principles

No matter the situation, there is a common set of principles that you can apply to better manage any project where there are significant differences in the composition of the team. The differences can include location, business function, or cultural aspects. Let's take a look at the five fundamental principles that will guide our efforts in any of these situations:

caution

These project environments can, and usually do, create risks around work productivity and communication effectiveness, because there is often a greater chance for misunderstandings.

1. **It's the same, but more**—The first principle to understand is that it does not take additional or new management techniques to be effective at leading these types of projects. These project situations just place more emphasis and importance on the project management fundamentals we have reviewed in earlier chapters. In particular, these aspects of project management become essential:
   - Well-defined and properly planned project
   - Effective project sponsorship
   - Buy-in and commitment on success criteria
   - Well-managed expectations
   - Clear roles and responsibilities
   - Effective communications
   - Effective risk management

   In addition, the discipline to properly document plans, meeting minutes, decisions, and issues is generally more important due to the need to ensure proper and clear communications.

2. **The right leadership approach**—The best project leaders in these situations are ones who possess the right mix of communication, facilitative, interpersonal, and expectation management skills to accomplish the following:
   - Instill confidence in the stakeholders that he/she can lead them to the accomplishment of the project objectives
   - Take the perspective of each stakeholder group to ensure each group believes they are included, understood, valued, and "heard" in the project process
   - Create alignment around the project goals and concentrates the team's focus on what unifies them (the common ground)
   - Help each stakeholder group understand how their piece (work process, interests, and needs) fits into the overall puzzle
   - Takes flexible approach by maintaining focus on the major project priorities and an understanding that everything else is just a means for getting there

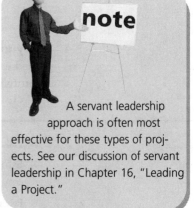

A servant leadership approach is often most effective for these types of projects. See our discussion of servant leadership in Chapter 16, "Leading a Project."

3. **Communication is king**—As we reviewed in Chapter 17, "Managing Project Communications," effective project communications are a bedrock aspect of project management. Specifically, in these types of project situations, here are the key points to keep in mind:
   - Use communication mechanisms that are accessible to everyone.
   - Develop a project vocabulary. Be willing to use their terms and terms they understand. Be mindful of any confusion over terminology being used.
   - Plan on frequent touchpoints to compensate for the lack of face time, especially in virtual project team settings.
   - Document project communications, especially anything discussed verbally, to ensure mutual understanding and agreement.
   - Ensure each team member is clear on the following at all times:
     - Project context
     - Project goals

   - Team members' roles and responsibilities
   - Team members' assignments
   - Project schedule
   - Chain of command and reporting relationships

4. **Verify understanding**—In these project situations, more time will be needed to verify that you are being understood and that you (your team) accurately understood the other stakeholders. A few specific things to be mindful of:
   - Be wary of any assumptions
   - Ask the extra question to make sure
   - Establish and clarify team norms and procedures
   - Explain project processes and the value they serve
   - The larger the project, the more effort to get through requirements definition and review cycles
   - Requirements gathering needs to use multiple methods to ensure completeness and understanding
   - Take the time to walk through their current processes

5. **More project management effort**—This is somewhat implied by the first principle in this list, but it is important to understand that the project management component of these type of environments is more significant (as a rule). There can be a misperception that the effort to leverage these latest technologies and business trends to gain efficiency and to accomplish projects faster also means less project management effort. Incorrect. The effort to lead, facilitate, ensure understanding, and build teamwork in these situations is at least equal, and in most cases much greater, than the effort to do the same with a collocated team.

caution

A prime cause for issues on cross-functional projects is neglect of a specific functional area or group. Make sure each affected stakeholder group is properly represented, consulted, respected, and kept informed.

Another prime cause for issues on cross-functional projects is poor performance by a functional leader. Common performance issues include:

- Not fulfilling role responsibilities
- Lack of functional knowledge or experience
- Misalignment of priorities; unable to meet time commitments for role
- Not consulting other members of his/her functional group
- Not keeping other members of his/her functional group informed
- Unable to complete reviews in a timely fashion

Reminder: To help build the sense of ownership, work with the designated functional leaders to perform the detail planning for the project.

Proven Techniques for Leading Cross-Functional Projects

With the prior principles understood, let's review a few proven tips and techniques specific to leading cross-functional projects that I have either confirmed or realized over the years:

- **Ensure proper project sponsorship and governance**—Any time a project's scope addresses more than a single business function, it is critical that the project sponsor have jurisdiction over all the business functions affected. If the sponsor does not have this jurisdiction, then a process (often by a senior level committee—steering committee, change control board) needs to be established up-front to deal with any territorial issue or change request that impacts the cross-functional environment.
- **Designate functional leaders**—As part of your project organization and your role-responsibility matrix, include functional leader positions as the primary representatives from each distinct group. These roles will be instrumental to facilitating the project process and to reducing your workload.
- **Acknowledge the importance and value of each group**—While you may serve as the ringmaster and steadfastly communicate the vision and process approach for the project, you should be quick to acknowledge the importance, value, and role that each group contributes to the success of the project. You don't have all the answers, so you need to facilitate the execution of the project and instill a sense of ownership into each of your functional leaders.
- **Get commitments from respective resource managers**—As part of the collaborative approach that is needed for these types of projects, make sure to work closely with the various resource managers who are responsible for assigning the appropriate personnel to the project. In many cases, the resource managers are the bosses of the individuals who will serve as your designated functional leads. Invest the time with them. Review project definition with them. Include them on the review and acceptance of the project plan, especially the resource plan and project schedule.
- **Ensure project alignment**—In case you were not involved in the project definition process, make sure your cross-functional project is aligned with the other projects underway or planned in the enterprise. There is nothing worse for team spirit and commitment than to start a project that has an obvious conflict with other initiatives.

- **Focus on workflow process**—To add more value to the project, to better serve your role as facilitator, and to help you make better decisions, invest the effort early to understand the complete workflow process that is affected by the project. In many cases, your functional leaders will have silo outlooks and will not fully understand how they get the inputs they do or how their outputs affect the rest of the operation.
- **Kickoff meetings are essential**—Kickoff meetings are always excellent tools for setting expectations and communicating the same message to the key stakeholders. On cross-functional projects, where multiple departments or business units are involved, this type of event is critical to getting the project started correctly and to improving the chances for success.

tip

Make sure to include the resource managers, and if not the same person, the bosses of the functional leaders in your project communications.

- **Resolve issues aggressively**—On cross-functional projects, you are likely to see issues occur that do not have a clear owner. As we discussed in detail in Chapter 13, "Managing Project Issues," it is imperative that you take an aggressive attitude toward finding resolutions to any issue to protect the project's critical success factors.
- **Lookout for dysfunctional relations**—Now, you would think that since the various functional areas are all members of the same, common organization that it would be one big happy family. Well, people are people, families are families, and dysfunction is always close by. Just understand that in many organizations, there can be historical disputes between functional groups or individuals within the group that affect your project's performance.

Cross-functional projects are excellent candidates for conducting project and requirements definitions as a project by itself, as we discussed in Chapter 4, "Defining a Project," due to the number of stakeholders that need to be consulted and due to the potential change impact.

- **Invest time on communications planning**—As we've iterated many times in many different ways, communication is key to project success. For cross-functional projects, you need to invest additional time in planning your project communications due to the heightened importance they will have in this setting and to the increased number of stakeholders that need to be included.

- **Invest time on requirements definition**—As we discussed in Chapter 18, "Managing Expectations," the requirements definition process is often the source for missed expectations. This is especially true with cross-functional projects due to the increased breadth of scope, the number of stakeholders, and the team dynamics that can come into play. In addition, as we mentioned in the fourth principle in managing these types of projects, more effort is needed to verify understanding. The key is to plan adequate time and effort for a thorough requirements definition phase, so you can avoid the common problems that contribute to insufficient requirements definition, including:
  - **Reluctant signatures**—Stakeholders who approve requirements without a real understanding or buy-in. Be especially cognizant of stakeholders who are quiet, susceptible to peer pressure, or who offer no non-verbal signs that the light bulb has gone on.
  - **Misunderstandings, assumptions, and unstated expectations**—Use multiple requirements gathering methods, leverage visual models, ask extra questions, and focus on change impact.

caution

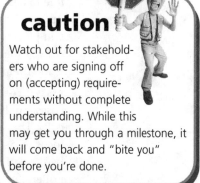

Watch out for stakeholders who are signing off on (accepting) requirements without complete understanding. While this may get you through a milestone, it will come back and "bite you" before you're done.

Proven Techniques for Leading Cross-Cultural Projects

With the prior principles understood, let's review a few proven tips and techniques specific to leading cross-cultural projects that I have either confirmed or realized over the years. Keep in mind that a project does not need to be global in nature to be a cross-cultural project. Many times, projects with stakeholders from different parts of the U.S. can qualify as cross-cultural projects too, especially if the project touches a combination of the distinct regions (such as Northeast, Midwest, South, Texas, and West Coast).

- **Be respectful**—Take time to consider the impact that the different cultures, time zones, holiday schedules, and work day schedules will have on the project. Common impact areas are terminology, risk management, communications planning (including best times for status meetings), and the project schedule.

- **Potential culture impacts**—Understand potential culture impacts on project communications and team interactions. Specifically, be aware that due to cultural differences, others may not be as assertive or willing to speak up to the degree you would expect. In addition, review any conventions that you plan to use for status reporting. Make sure the conventions do not convey some unintended meaning and that everyone is comfortable using them.
- **Listen for understanding**—Even with a common language (in most cases, English), the use and the sound of the language can vary dramatically. The key here is to kick your active listening skills into high gear and focus in on understanding. Don't let yourself get distracted or tune out because of accents or the irregular use of certain words. Stay engaged, be patient, ask questions, clarify terms, and don't stop until you are comfortable that you're on the same wavelength with your cross-cultural partners.
- **Plan on more formality**—To reduce the impact of cultural differences and to ensure mutual understanding, cross-cultural projects are more mechanical, formal, and by-the-book. You just need to plan on this and realize that project management shortcuts are not as likely in these environments.

Proven Techniques for Leading Virtual Projects

Any project that consists of team members not collocated in the same physical location is a virtual project to some degree. The more geographically dispersed the team members and the more interaction that is done with non–face-to-face communications, the more virtual the project is.

With the continued advances in communications and information technology, and the common everyday use now of mobile phones, remote network access, email, Web mail, pagers, and instant messaging, the ability of people to productively collaborate on common work is increased dramatically. And, of course, the reduced office costs and the increased ability to leverage outsourcing options are very attractive to most organizations.

However, these potential productivity gains and cost reductions do not happen automatically—especially in the demanding environment of most projects. There is a tremendous amount of energy needed to plan, coordinate, and manage a virtual project team. Let's review a few key tips and techniques specific to leading virtual project teams that I have either confirmed or realized over the years that will help you take advantage of virtual project team situations:

- **Get some face-to-face time, especially early**—If there is any way possible to get face time with your virtual team members, do it. It has been my experience that face-to-face interaction is instrumental in building trust, developing relationships, and jump-starting project momentum. I would recommend the following scenarios for your consideration:

- Get everyone together for the project kickoff meeting.
- Try to collocate the team for the first stage (or as long as you can), then let team members return to their remote locations.
- If none of these are possible, try a mini-kickoff session that focuses on the work planning and identifying risks.
- Depending on the project phase and the nature of the work, look at split work environments (such as two days on-site, three days remote or one week on-site every month).
- We'll mention this later too, but if available, look to leverage video conferencing as much as possible. If not, consider creative use of digital pictures.

- **Establish team norms**—Facilitate the rules and procedures that will guide team interactions and productivity with the team. Key items include
  - Core hours everyone needs to be available (online)
  - Access to team members during non-core hours
  - Preferred team communication mechanisms
  - Preferred meeting times, especially important when members are in different time zones
  - Reporting status
  - Project repository
  - Contingency plans for network or phone outages
  - Team directory
- **Responsiveness is the difference-maker**—The key to successful virtual project teams is responsiveness. If people are easily accessible and respond quickly, most organizations could care less where people are working. These environments do require team members to be professional and mature.
- **Set up protocols for virtual meetings**—Virtual meetings will be the lifeblood of a virtual project team. Here are some key reminders to make these meetings more productive:
  - Use technologies that are available to everyone.
  - Use technologies that are reliable for everyone.
  - Ensure everyone understands how to use the technologies.
  - Make sure to send agenda and reference materials in advance of the meeting (or just post to the project repository and send a link to it).
  - Review protocols for asking questions.

    - Keep discussions focused on items that pertain to all participants. For other items, take them offline. Stop the discussion and assign an action item to schedule a separate meeting with those involved.
    - Instant messaging conferences may be appropriate for core team meetings.
- **Establish clear time zone references**—This may not be as much of an issue for you, but in this age of multiple time zones and daylight savings time, take the time to review and clarify time zone designations and conventions. This goes a long way to avoiding meeting time conflicts. Two recommendations here:
    - Use the newer time zone references, such as Eastern Time (ET) to refer to whatever time it is on the East Coast rather than Eastern Standard Time (EST) or Eastern Daylight Savings Time (EDST).
    - Reference city or state to clarify the intended time, such as Arizona time, Chicago time, or London time.
- **Verify productivity early**—To ensure that the virtual work environment will generate the expected level of productivity needed for project success, pay close attention to initial work efforts. The fundamentals of work assignments apply the same here, just even more important:
    - Invest time to clarify work expectations and completion criteria.
    - Provide all necessary resources.
    - Keep work packages small—less than the standard reporting period.
- **Use preferred communication methods of customer and sponsor**—Either as part of your initial communications planning or as an observation you make during the project, make sure to communicate with your sponsor and your key customers in the manner they prefer and in the manner that best fits their learning style. If this is in person, meet them in person. If it is via phone at 7:30 a.m., call them at 7:30 a.m. If it is email at the end of the day, email them. The two important things to note here are
    - The communication mechanisms you use for the core project team may likely be different than what you use for sponsor and customer communications.
    - Use the methods they prefer, not what you prefer. This approach will lead to less miscommunication and expectation management issues.

The Absolute Minimum

At this point, you should have a solid understanding of the following:

- The key principles to note in leading cross-functional, cross-cultural, or virtual project environments include the following:
    1. The same project management fundamentals apply.
    2. A leadership approach that emphasizes effective communication, collaboration, interpersonal, and expectation management skills tend to work the best.
    3. Communication, communication, communication.
    4. Invest more time to ensure understanding.
    5. More project management effort is needed.
- Proven tips and techniques for leading cross-functional projects include:
    1. Ensure the project has the proper sponsorship and governance procedures.
    2. Designate functional leaders to represent each distinct group.
    3. Consistently acknowledge the importance, value, and role that each group contributes to the success of the project.
    4. Get buy-in and commitment from resource managers.
    5. Ensure that the project is aligned properly with other organizational initiatives.
    6. Invest the effort early to understand the complete workflow process that is affected by the project.
    7. Kickoff meetings are essential.
    8. Resolve issues aggressively.
    9. Look out for dysfunctional interactions.
    10. Invest time on communications planning.
    11. Invest time in requirements definition.
- Proven tips and techniques for leading cross-cultural projects include:
    1. Be respectful of cultures, customs, time zones, and holiday schedules.
    2. Recognize the potential culture impacts on project communications and team interactions.
    3. Turn your active listening skills into hyperdrive.
    4. Plan on more formality.

continues

- Proven tips and techniques for leading virtual projects include:
    1. Get some face-to-face time, especially early in the project.
    2. Establish team rules and procedures.
    3. Focus everyone on the importance of responsiveness.
    4. Set up protocols for virtual meetings.
    5. Establish clear time zone designations.
    6. Verify productivity levels early.
    7. Use the communication methods preferred by the customer and the sponsor.

The map in Figure 20.1 summarizes the main points we reviewed in this chapter.

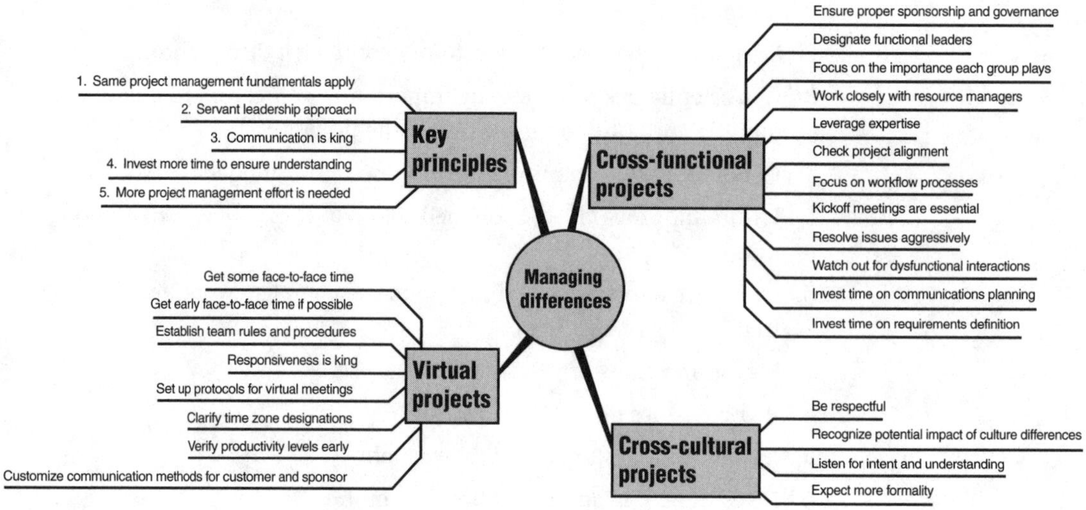

FIGURE 20.1

Overview of managing differences.

In This Chapter

- Understand why managing vendors is important to even first-time project managers
- Understand the key principles that lead to better vendor management
- Learn to avoid the common mistakes made on outsourced projects (they are not all due to the vendor)
- Review tips and techniques for both the client (buyer) and vendor (seller) organization and project manager
- Understand the key skills that have the greatest impact on managing vendor situations
- Learn contract fundamentals, and how different contract types impact your approach

21

Managing Vendors

As more and more organizations look to focus on their core competencies and reduce their fixed operating costs, while simultaneously attempt to execute more projects, it is very likely that your project, even your first one, will involve collaboration with other organizations.

While the specific process for establishing working relationships with other organizations depends largely on the industry you work in, many project managers lack considerable exposure to procurement and vendor management. Often, this is due to organizational structures and the common use of procurement specialists due to the legal and contractual nature of this activity.

For these reasons, I felt it was important to include this chapter, so you would be better prepared for whatever you face on your initial project assignment.

This chapter is not meant to be a comprehensive overview of procurement or vendor management, and I encourage you to study these areas further. Rather, this chapter intends to focus on the outsourcing of project work (as opposed to outsourcing entire departments or other operational work), and on the key fundamentals and frontline tips that make the greatest difference in your ability to manage these project relationships and to avoid the mistakes made by both first time and experienced project managers.

Specifically, we review what activities are actually included in vendor management, the core principles that should drive your work, and helpful advice for both the buyer and seller project manager. In addition, we'll touch on the important basics of contracts, including the impact certain types of contracts have on the project manager, and we will highlight the skills that make the greatest impact on your ability to effectively manage outsourced projects.

First, Let's Clarify a Few Terms

For the sake of clarity and brevity, let's review a few terms and touch on the focus on this chapter. By *vendor*, I mean the seller organization—the organization that is contracted to provide product or services. I will generally refer to the client organization—the organization purchasing the services—as the buyer. The use of buyer and seller terms here is consistent with the current PMI standards on procurement management.

In addition, we focus on arrangements that involve the outsourcing of entire projects, project phases, or specific project deliverables to external entities. Thus, this excludes "staff augmentation" arrangements where a vendor is contracted to provide a resource to fill a role on your project team.

With these clarifications, we're now ready to take a look at the principles that provide the foundation for effective management of the buyer-seller project relationship.

Ten Proven Principles of Vendor Management

The following ten fundamental principles will guide our efforts in managing vendor relationships.

1. **Solid project management goes a long way**—Outsourced projects place more importance on the project management fundamentals we have reviewed throughout this book. While you may be able to "get by" with less on internal projects, outsourced projects bring a visibility and accountability (both financially and legally) that make solid project management and leadership a requirement to make the relationship work. In particular, these aspects of project management become essential:

- Well-defined and properly planned project
- Effective project sponsorship
- Buy-in and commitment on success criteria
- Well-managed expectations
- Clear roles and responsibilities
- Effective communications
- Formal change control management
- Effective issue management

tip

The principles and techniques in managing virtual and cross-cultural teams in Chapter 20, "Managing Differences," are valuable in outsourced project arrangements.

2. **Vendor management is multifaceted**—Effective vendor management has four distinct elements that need attention:
   - Evaluation and selection
   - Contract development
   - Relationship management
   - Delivery management

Just because procurement and vendor management require formal communications and processes, it does not mean that only formal communication methods are used. In fact, the formal communications should just follow (and document) what has already been discussed and agreed to.

3. **"See" the contract, "be" the contract**—Borrowing an expression from the sports world, you need to be fully aware of what the contract states. Ideally, you are involved in the development of the contract, or at the very least, the project definition document that is referenced by the contract. In either case, you need to have full knowledge of what the contract states for three reasons:
   - To ensure you clearly understand what the vendor is responsible for
   - To ensure you are managing the project and vendor consistent with the contract
   - To understand what incentives are motivating your seller
4. **Formality rules**—Due to the legal implications of the work relationship, all changes must be in writing and formally controlled, no matter who originates the change. In addition, all project communications dealing with procurement management should always be formal and written.

5. **Contract complexity should be consistent with project risk**—Both the procurement process and the level of contract detail should be consistent with project risk. The same due diligence process needed for a multimillion dollar project should not be used for a $50,000 project.
6. **If it is important, put it in**—Any aspect of an outsourced project that is important to either party should be in the contract. This includes, but is not limited to, deliverable specifications, the methodology used to create the deliverable, specific resources, roles and responsibilities, planned communications, deliverable acceptance criteria, and project success criteria. Do not rely on assumptions.
7. **Management commitment is key**—Partnerships between organizations are the result of demonstrated management commitment. More important than what the contract says or doesn't say, the commitment level and flexibility demonstrated by senior management (from each party) to make the relationship work will be the determining factor.

In many organizations, a natural conflict exists between the contract administrator and the project manager. There are three reasons for this:

- The contract administrator is the only one authorized to change the contract.
- The contract includes or references the project definition document and/or project plan.
- The project manager owns and manages the project definition document and project plan.

8. **Focus on "win-win"**—This principle is a cultural shock to many organizations, but both parties should focus on building win-win relationships throughout the project. When issues and tensions occur (and they will), actions should be focused on mutually beneficial resolutions and on easing tensions—not escalation and provocation.
9. **Clarify terms and processes**—Take the time to review, explain, and clarify all terms and processes involved in the project. More conflicts results from misunderstandings than anything else.
10. **Clarify internal roles and responsibilities**—Make sure to clarify the roles and responsibilities for the procurement (purchasing) department versus the project team, especially between the contract administrator and the project manager. Conversely, the seller project manager needs to clarify his role and responsibilities in this arrangement with his/her sales, accounting and legal departments.

Twelve Tips for Buyers

The following tips and techniques have been picked up from the front line of project management and may be helpful to buyer organizations and project managers in their efforts to get the most from their outsourced project arrangements:

The motivation behind incentives is to align the seller's objectives with the buyer's.

1. **Align seller's goals with yours**—This could be a principle of managing vendors. To get the most from your vendors, make sure their goals are aligned with your goals (which should be in sync with the project goals). The terms of the contract should be set up so that all parties win together. The use of incentives, risk-reward scenarios, and requiring accepted deliverables for payment approval are popular techniques here.
2. **Ensure WBS is appropriate**—Make sure the work to be outsourced is clearly defined, complete, and appropriate for the given environment. A few questions to consider:
   - If the vendor is off-shore, can the work be done with limited interaction with your organization?
   - Do you expect the vendor to help with training?
   - What documentation do you need or expect?
   - How will you transition the final deliverable(s) to your organization?
3. **Tie acceptance of deliverables to payments**—A key condition to associate with any payment is formal acceptance of the targeted deliverable(s). This works better when clear acceptance criteria are established in advance.
4. **Use phases to reduce risk**—An excellent way to manage the natural risk involved in outsourcing project work is to limit the commitment length by project phases. By limiting the scope of the contract to one or two project phases (specifics will depend on project risk and methodology used), you minimize your dependency on a vendor that may be underperforming, and you force a systematic review of vendor performance before committing to additional work.
5. **Understand resource and process dependencies**—Get a clear understanding of the resources that the vendor needs from your organization to effectively perform their work and when those resources are needed, and then proactively manage those dependencies. Use the same approach on project processes—especially deliverable reviews and testing stages.

6. **Use project management fundamentals to reduce risk and improve quality**—Besides the tips already mentioned, focus on these other solid project management fundamentals to reduce risk, improve quality, and meet expectations:
   - Request and review interim deliverables
   - Request tangible results early in the process
   - Focus on clear specifications
   - Establish clear acceptance criteria for each deliverable
   - Leverage requirements traceability matrix
   - Establish frequent status reporting cycles
7. **Integrate vendor teams whenever possible**—Whenever the nature of project work allows it, always look for opportunities to integrate the vendor's project team with yours. Besides creating better teams and working relationships, this technique is effective for knowledge transfer and more proactive risk and issue management.
8. **Use a third party to QA vendor's activities**—If the risk of the project warrants, consider using a third-party resource as a quality auditor on your primary vendor, including another vendor. This can be an additional project expense, and you are adding potential complexity to your management efforts, but if there is not an in-house quality department or there is lack of experience with this type of project, it is an investment that can pay considerable dividends. This arrangement helps protect the interest of the client and helps keeps everyone accountable to the contractual arrangement.
9. **Evaluate vendor estimates**—Determine how you will validate the integrity and reasonableness of the vendor's cost and time estimates. Common methods include use of multiple vendor bids, requesting a WBS to support estimate, and review by subject matter experts.
10. **Look for "go to" partners**—Encourage your organization to seek true vendor partners rather than just view them as disposable, interchangeable suppliers. Vendors that have demonstrated the ability to get the job done, the management commitment to meet your expectations, the flexibility to resolve conflicts and honor the spirit of contractual agreements, and the ability to establish synergy and trust with your enterprise give your enterprise a strong operational advantage.
11. **Tryout a new vendor**—To reduce the risk of going with a new vendor, consider giving any new vendor a tryout. Use a new vendor for a smaller project or piece of larger project first before making a commitment on a higher profile engagement. There's nothing like seeing a vendor in action to determine whether they are a good fit for your enterprise.

12. **Beware of certifications**—As the advantages of organizational process maturity are understood by more and more industries and enterprises, more organizations are placing a higher priority on process maturity certifications such as CMMi and ISO. Three questions to consider in regard to these certifications:
    - When did they earn the certification and who performed the audit?
    - Does the certification apply to the entire organization or only to a specific project or department?
    - What evidence exists that proves the organization is still operating at the certified level?

Seven Tips for Sellers

The following tips and techniques have been picked up from the front lines of project management and may be helpful to seller organizations and project managers in their efforts to get the most from their contracted project work and business relationships.

1. **Get formal acceptance**—Make sure to get some form of formal verification or sign-off from the client to document acceptance of the targeted deliverable(s).
2. **Clarify standards and acceptance criteria**—Make sure to understand what standards you are expected to adhere to before you begin your work (put in the contract) and document what criteria will be used by the client to officially accept each deliverable.
3. **Define review process**—Make sure to clarify with the client what process will be used to review and accept each deliverable. In particular, specify who will be involved in the review process, how much time will be allowed for the review, and how many iterations (for refinements) should be expected and included as part of the scope.
4. **Control invoicing process**—There is nothing worse than visiting with the client project manager or project sponsor after they have received an inaccurate project invoice that you did not know had been sent or had never seen. To avoid these situations and to manage the credibility of your organization, ask to have review-and-approve powers on any project invoices before they are issued.
5. **Keep a close eye on resource dependencies**—From the start, understand what elements of the WBS need collaboration with resources from the client (or other) organization and make sure these dependencies are clearly understood by the client and that they realize the impact (time, cost, quality) of not having them when needed.

6. **Manage communications**—This goes without saying: Take control and ownership of all communications between your team and the client organization and communications with your senior management.
7. **Be transparent**—The more open, transparent, and visible that you are regarding your team's activities and progress, the more trust and confidence you build with your client. If you happen to find yourself in a crisis, your "truth and nothing but the truth" approach and the relationship you have established may be the only things that get you through these times.

Twelve Key Project Management Skills for Better Vendor Management

To better help you prepare for responsibilities of vendor and procurement management, let's review the type of skills and knowledge a project manager should possess to be effective in these areas. The key project management skills needed for procurement and vendor management include the following:

1. Managing expectations
2. Effective verbal and written communications
3. Managing virtual and cross-cultural teams
4. Defining a project
5. Proficient negotiating
6. Vendor selection and evaluation
7. Strong interpersonal skills
8. The ability to identify risks and develop appropriate responses (managing risks)
9. Contract knowledge
10. The ability to manage to a contract
11. Understanding when and how to use legal assistance
12. Managing changes

Stuff You Need to Know About Contracts

We mentioned earlier that contract knowledge is a key project management skill for procurement and vendor management. So, what exactly do we mean by *contract knowledge*? Although there is no substitution for actual experience, in-depth study, and formal training, here is a quick synopsis of the key contract facts that you need to understand to improve your effectiveness in this area of project management.

Conditions for a Legal Contract

The four conditions that make a contract a legally binding agreement are

- It must be voluntarily entered into.
- It must contain mutual considerations.
- It must be created for legal purposes.
- It must be signed by authorized parties.

Key Contract Elements

Not every contract is the same, and not every contract will contain all these sections (they may not apply), but the common contract components include the following:

- Scope statement—Including deliverables, requirements, out-of-scope items, and assumptions
- Timetable and milestone dates
- Acceptance criteria
- Responsibilities of each party
- Financial arrangements—Including payment schedule, invoicing arrangements, and incentives
- Identification of the person authorized to make changes
- Change control procedures
- Issue resolution and escalation procedures
- Performance measurement and reporting
- Communications plan—Status reporting, senior management meetings
- Procedures and/or penalties for ending the contract prematurely
- Liability for failure to perform
- Ownership and property rights of project deliverables
- Security agreements
- Non-disclosure agreements

Primary Contract Types

The three common contract types are as follows:

- Time and materials (T&M)
- Fixed price (FP)
- Cost reimbursable (CR)

The three variations of cost-reimbursable contracts are as follows:

- Cost Plus Fixed Fee (CPFF)
- Cost Plus Percent of Cost (CPPC)
- Cost Plus Incentive Fee (CPIF)

A common variation of T&M contracts is to cap the top end.

- T&M with a Cap

The Impact of Each Contract Type

In the previous section, we mentioned the three key contract types. In this section, we will review the points you need to understand about each type. The key categories include the following:

- Its advantages and disadvantages
- What situation is best for its use
- Who owns the risk
- The required project management tasks

Table 21.1 summarizes these key facts about each contract type.

Table 21.1 Summary of Contract Types

	T&M	FP	CR
Advantages	Quick to create. Brief duration. Good choice when hiring people to augment your staff.	Less work for buyer to manage. Seller has strong incentive to control costs. Buyer knows total project price. Companies are familiar with this type. Can include incentives.	Simpler scope of work. SOW is easier than an FP one. Lower cost than FP because the seller does not need to add as much for the risk. Can include incentives.

	T&M	FP	CR
Disadvantages	Profit in every hour billed. Seller has no incentive to control costs. Good only for small projects. Requires most day-to-day oversight by the buyer.	Seller may underquote and make up profits with change orders. Seller may reduce work scope if it is losing money. More work for the buyer to write the SOW. Can be more costly than CR if the SOW is incomplete. Seller will increase the price to cover risk.	Must audit seller's invoices. More work for buyer to manage. Seller has only moderate incentive to control costs. Total project price is unknown.
Best to use when...	You need work to begin right away. You need to augment staff.	You know exactly what needs to be done. You don't have time to audit invoices.	You want to buy expertise in determining what needs to be done.
Who has the risk?	The buyer.	The seller (cost), or both the buyer and seller if not well defined.	The buyer.

Table 21.2 summarizes these key facts about each contract type.

Table 21.2 Summary of Contract Types

	T&M	FP	CR
Scope of work detail	Brief. Limited functional, performance, or design requirements.	Extremely complete. Seller needs to know *all* the work. "Do it."	Describes only performance or requirements. "How to do it."
Project management tasks	Providing daily direction to seller. Striving for concrete deliverables. Close monitoring of project schedule. Looking for a situation to switch the contract type.	Establish clear acceptance criteria of deliverables. Managing change requests. Monitoring project task dependencies. Managing risks. Monitoring project assumptions.	Auditing seller's costs. Monitoring seller work progress. Ensuring added resources add value to the project. Watching for shifting resources. Watching for unplanned seller charges. Rebudgeting.

The Absolute Minimum

At this point, you should have a solid understanding of the following:

- Solid project management is essential to reducing risk and improving quality on outsourced projects.
- Vendor management is composed of four distinct elements:
  - Evaluation and selection
  - Contract development
  - Relationship management
  - Delivery management
- Effective vendor management requires more formality in regard to communications and change control.
- Do not assume anything. If it is important to you or your organization, put it in the contract.
- Focus on "win-win" to build better vendor relationships.
- Make sure the vendor has the same goals that you do. Use incentives to align their goals with yours.
- Make sure the WBS (work breakdown structure) is appropriate for effective outsourcing.

The map in Figure 21.1 summarizes the main points we reviewed in this chapter.

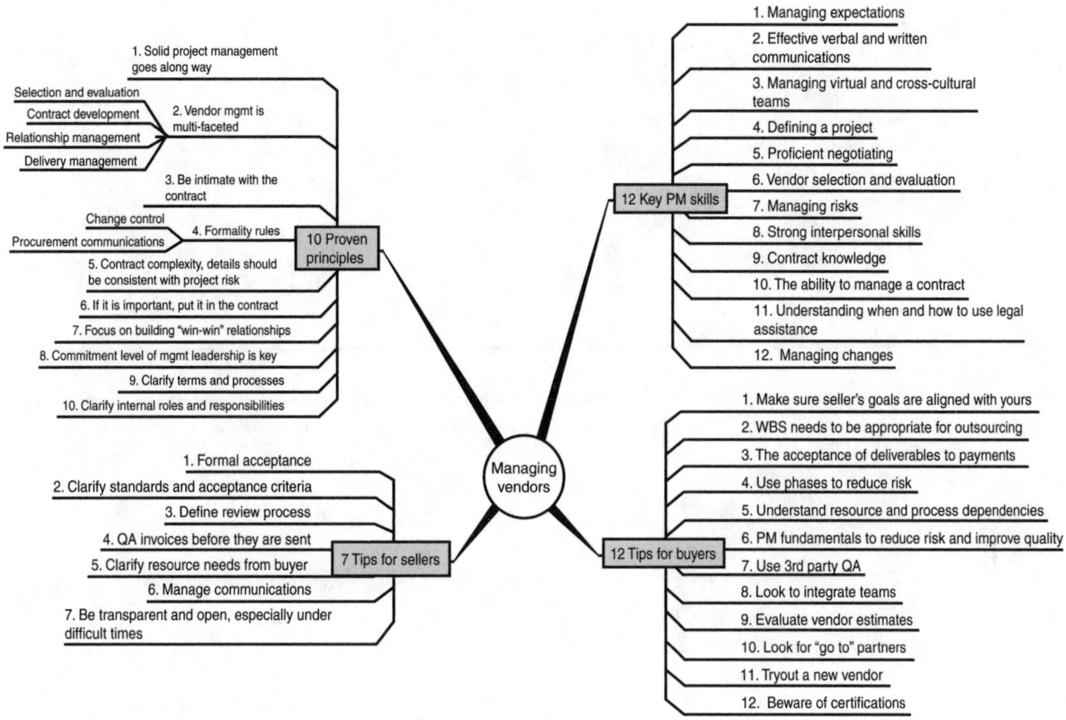

FIGURE 21.1

Overview of managing vendors.

In This Chapter

- Learn how to properly bring closure to your project
- Use the Project End Checklist to make sure your projects end in style
- Understand the common challenges to overcome when ending your project
- Review the different reasons a contract and project can end

22

Ending a Project

As in most personal interactions, how we begin and end the process can make all the difference. The same can be said for projects. Continuing to use the personal interaction analogy, we know how initial impressions and the relationship we establish can make our "goodbye" extremely awkward, or very exciting for the promise of what is yet to come. In addition, there is nothing more frustrating in personal relationships than a lack of closure. Our goal, as a project manager, is to bring proper closure to our project for all parties involved and to make sure the last impression everyone has of your work is professional and positive.

In this chapter, we review the key principles that drive successful project closures, the different ways a project can end, the challenges many organizations have in ending a project properly, and of course, the invaluable checklist for ending a project in style.

Three Key Principles

Before we review the checklist items that will drive our project ending efforts, let's touch on the key principles that drive a successful project close:

- **It is earned along the way**—The main purpose of project management is to achieve the success criteria set forth at the beginning of the project and to meet stakeholder expectations throughout the project. If this is done, a successful project close is almost guaranteed. If not, this is generally why unofficial games like "activate the spin machine," "pick the fall guy," and "bring in the lawyers" were invented.
- **Think end from the start**—A key part of the project plan must focus on how this will look when we are done, who will own and operate the deliverables, and how to transition those deliverables to them. Many projects have difficulty ending because this process is not clear or understood.
- **Bring closure**—To avoid the emptiness and frustration that is frequently experienced when there is not proper closure, make sure to properly acknowledge the contributions of all project participants, close out the legal and accounting elements, and officially signal that the project is complete.

tip

Develop a Project End QA Checklist to improve both your and your organization's performance.

Leverage a standard form to document client acceptance and approval of project deliverables. This streamlines the process and helps condition the stakeholders to perform this important activity.

Requirements for formal contract closeout procedures should be defined in the contract's term and conditions.

Project End Checklist—13 Important Steps

With these principles in mind, the 13 steps included in the Project End Checklist will ensure that we perform a complete project close and leave the stakeholders with a positive lasting impression of our project management abilities.

1. **Gain client acceptance**—Personally, I would make sure you have this completed before you attempt to close the project. This is most often handled as exit criteria for user acceptance, post-implementation walkthrough, or a final tollgate meeting (or a combination of these). The key here is to make sure the client has formally verified and accepted the project deliverables. You need to have this documented.

2. **Transition deliverables to owner**—Complete the necessary steps to properly hand off the project deliverables to their intended owner.
3. **Close out contract obligations**—Work with your procurement advisors to make sure that all obligations of the contractual relationship have been met and that all exit criteria has been satisfied.
4. **Capture lessons learned**—Both the positive and negative aspects of the project should be recorded. Ideally, this allows future projects to duplicate the constructive aspects of your project and avoid similar downfalls or mistakes. Of course, this is easier said than done. See the section "Common Project Closing Challenges" later in this chapter for more on this.
5. **Update organization's central information repository**—Archive all project management records and as many project deliverables as possible to the organization's central information repository (or knowledge management system). Assuming the repository is easily accessible, searchable, and the contents are protected by a configuration management process, this is a powerful way to reduce learning curves and gain efficiency on future projects.
6. **Issue final financials**—Depending on the nature of the project, work with accounting and procurement to make sure that all financial transactions have taken place, such as invoice generation and final payments. In addition, you should develop the final project financial reports, such as budget summary and variance analysis.
7. **Close accounts and charge codes**—While working with the accounting department, make sure that the process for closing all associated accounts and charge codes is completed.
8. **Update resource schedules**—This is a step that should occur throughout the project. Make sure that the resource scheduling arm of your organization knows well in advance when your project team members will be completed with their assignments on your project and will be available for other opportunities.

Lessons learned should be documented throughout the project lifecycle and include both positive and negative aspects of the project. This allows future projects to duplicate the constructive aspects of your project and avoid similar downfalls or mistakes.

A common approach for creating an organizational résumé is to develop a *white paper* that summarizes the business challenge, goals, approach, key deliverables, and value achieved by the project and organization.

9. **Conduct performance evaluations**—While you should offer performance feedback to team members throughout the project, make sure to complete the formal performance evaluation forms and process when their work assignment is completed. This formal documentation is often key to the individual's career and compensation growth.
10. **Update résumé** —Make sure to update your personal résumé to accurately reflect your project experience, including your roles, responsibilities, accomplishments, and impact. Encourage your other team members to do the same.
11. **Market project accomplishments**—The organizational résumé is a trademark of professional services organizations, but one that can be employed by all organizations and departments. Capture the project highlights and accomplishments in a format that enables the organization to effectively communicate its successes and the value it has offered.

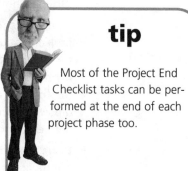

> **tip**
>
> Most of the Project End Checklist tasks can be performed at the end of each project phase too.

12. **Ask for referrals/references**—Of course, the best testament to client satisfaction is whether the sponsoring individuals (organization) will officially endorse your work. At both a personal and organizational level, this should be the goal from the start. Make sure to ask for it, if the goal has been achieved.
13. **Celebrate!**—Nothing helps bring closure to a project better than an official celebration that recognizes the team's contributions and the accomplishment of the project goals. Make sure to plan the celebration event from the start.

Common Project Closing Challenges

The proper ending of a project is the most neglected project management process. To understand why and to better prepare yourself for this important activity, let's review the common challenges that project managers and organizations have here:

- **Rush to the next project**—Due to the pace of business in today's times, there is often zero downtime between project assignments, and in many cases, the next project is getting started before you have completely ended your previous one. This mode of operation often results in an incomplete project close, especially if the project is completely in-house.

- **No accountability**—If there is no one (or department) making sure the project close activities occur or if it is not part of your evaluation, it is very easy to let this go. After all, you've delivered the goods, the client is happy...you're done...right?
- **Not seen as "value-add" activity**—As a project manager, if you do not see your organization putting a priority on project close activities, you are going to be much less likely to follow through here. By *priority*, I mean does the organization include this as part of your evaluation? Does it leverage lessons learned from past projects? Does it value the support, development, and use of a knowledge management system?
- **Lack of transition plan**—Quite simply, there was not enough attention paid at a detailed level to how the project would end and how the deliverables would be handed off to the eventual owners. In some environments, separate *deployment* projects are established to deal with the logistical and detail issues that come into play here.
- **Sanitization of lessons learned**—The most valuable lessons to be learned are often "what not to do." But who wants their faults or bad decisions to be recorded for posterity's sake? It takes strong executive management support and a "politician's touch" to record useful lessons learned for an organization.

Contract duration does not always equal project duration.

Methods for Ending a Contract or a Project

To simplify the coverage of this process, I have assumed that our project completed as planned, and that any contracts involved also ended at the same time the project completed. In reality, many of these ending a project steps could and should be done at the end of each project phase and not just the end of the project. These are part of the closing project management process described in the PMI PMBOK Guide®.

Also, there are other scenarios that can occur to either your project or contractual relationships, and we will quickly review these next. In each of these cases, you should review the Project End Checklist to see how many of these you can perform.

Terminating a Contract

In many cases, the duration of your contract will be shorter than the duration of the project, especially if you have only outsourced a specific phase or a portion of the project work. In these cases, your work to bring closure to the contract and vendor relationship will be separate from the steps to end the project.

In other cases, the contract may end early because of mutual agreement between the parties or because of a breach of the contract terms. To clarify, a contract can end in one of three ways:

- Successful performance
- Mutual agreement
- Breach

Successful performance is what we think of as "getting the work done." All the work specified in the contract was performed by the seller and formally accepted by the buyer. The term *contract termination* refers to the other two ways a contract can end: mutual agreement or breach.

If there is *mutual agreement*, the contract is terminated because both the buyer and seller involved in the project agree that the project work should not continue. However, if a project contract is terminated due to *breach*, a party involved in the project work has failed to obey its side of the contract.

Terminating a Project

In the preceding section, we reviewed how a contract can be completed or terminated, and we mentioned that a contract closeout does not always signify the end of a project. However, the end of a project almost always forces a related contract to end. For your reference, Table 22.1 lists the various ways a project can be terminated—all of these would trigger some or all aspects of our Project End Checklist.

Table 22.1 Methods of Project Termination

Method	Description
Completion	Successful performance; getting the work done.
Cancelled	Portfolio management decision due to either poor performance, better resource utilization, or realignment with organizational goals.
Displacement	Project becomes obsolete due to another project.
Collapse	Project ends due to external factors, such as natural disasters, corporate mergers, and so on.
Absorption	The project becomes a permanent part of the sponsoring organization (a new department or division).
Deterioration	A "slow death." Neglect. The sponsoring organization gradually reduces its support and budget for the project.

THE ABSOLUTE MINIMUM

At this point, you should have a solid understanding of the following:

- Many of the steps involved with ending a project may need to be performed at the end of each project phase.
- Client acceptance of project deliverables should be formal and documented.
- Ensure that the transition plan of project deliverables is performed.
- Capture lessons from the project (both positive and negative) to help the organization in the future.
- Take care of your project team members—give them official performance feedback, offer to serve as a reference (if appropriate), and help them transition to their next assignment.
- Archive all project management items and all project deliverables (if permitted) to your organization's knowledge management system for future use and reference.
- Ensure that contractual obligations have been met and that all contracts are finalized properly.
- Tie up the financials, including final transactions, reports, and closing of associated charge and accounting codes.
- Capture and market the accomplishments of the project.
- Make sure to celebrate and recognize the achievements of the project.
- Another good source of project management information and articles can be found at http://www.niwotridge.com/.

The map in Figure 22.1 summarizes the main points we reviewed in this chapter.

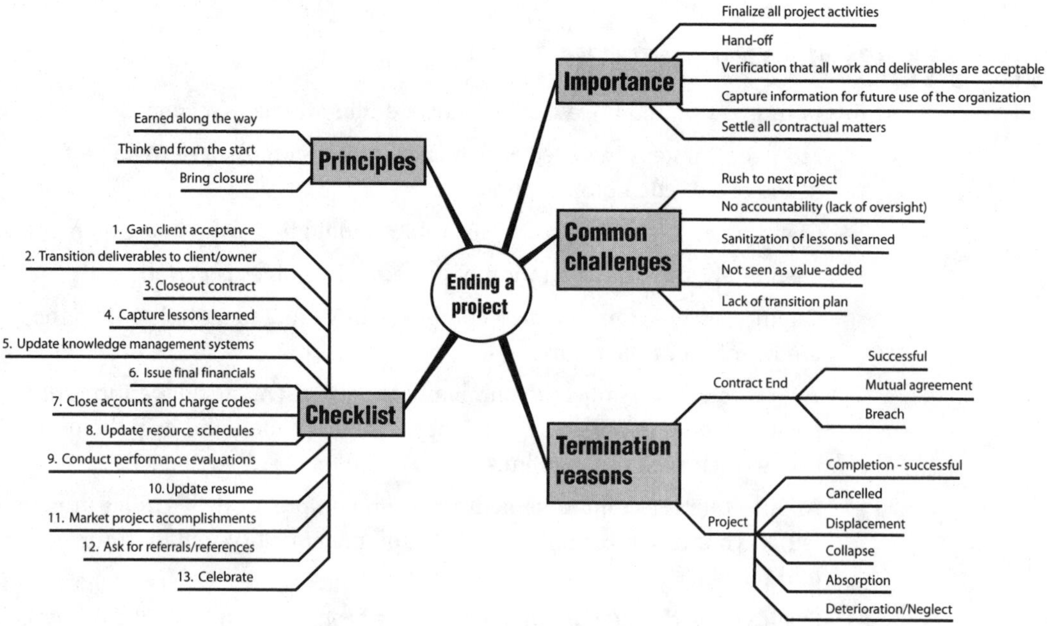

FIGURE 22.1

Overview of ending a project.

PART V

Accelerating the Learning Curve...Even More

IN THIS CHAPTER

- Accelerate your Microsoft Project learning curve
- Learn how to make Microsoft Project work for you, instead of the other way around
- Understand why Microsoft Project is more flexible than you think
- Learn how to avoid the common frustrations with Microsoft Project
- Learn what to do first when you start any new Microsoft Project file
- Review insights to quickly improve your reports
- Understand how to make resource leveling work

23

MAKING BETTER USE OF MICROSOFT PROJECT

It's not perfect. It has limitations. It can be frustrating. But, with a little experienced insight, you can quickly learn how to make Microsoft Project your friend, and more importantly, how to use Microsoft Project to be a better project manager.

This chapter is not a comprehensive instruction manual on Microsoft Project. This chapter is focused on accelerating your learning curve. It assumes you have some working knowledge of Microsoft Project already and that you are using Microsoft Project to manage an isolated, single project that does not include Microsoft Project Server.

Specifically, this chapter reviews the key design elements that drive how Microsoft Project behaves, the best practice for starting any new project, ten "must-know" features of Microsoft Project, tips for avoiding common frustrations, and powerful techniques for effectively reporting from Microsoft Project.

It's important to understand that while I have acquired a great deal of experience with Microsoft Project over the last 18 years, received consistent, positive feedback for my use of the tool from my circle of peers (of course, this may more be a reflection of my peers), and I know I can share lessons, tips, and insights that will greatly reduce your learning curve—I am still learning too. The continuous learning is due to three primary factors: Microsoft Project is a feature-packed application, new versions bring additional and revised features, and you learn what you need to know to accomplish the task at hand.

Understand This ...and It All Becomes Easier

As is the case when we are learning any new concept, skill, or tool, if you are taught the supporting principles first, it makes everything else that follows much easier. Why? Because you have a framework, a context, to organize the details and to explain the specific behaviors. It's no different here. Let's review the key design fundamentals behind Microsoft Project that will help you better understand how the tool works and help you avoid many frustrations that others commonly experience.

- **It's a database**—This is an important one. Microsoft Project is not like most other Office products. There is a relational database engine behind it. Why is this good to know?
  - First, it helps explain all the View, Display, and Table options from which you have to choose. These are all just different slices (views) of the same set of core database tables.
  - Second, you can include any of these standard fields in any view you want. Do not limit yourself to what you first see. You are not limited to the default column displays that you are first presented, and you can easily insert new columns at any time.

Take the time to review the available tables in Microsoft Project. It reinforces the idea that Microsoft Project is indeed a database, accelerates your awareness of all the data points that are available, and opens your mind to new ways to leverage the tool.

The tables can be accessed from the View, Table menu. In addition, a complete description of the available tables is available from the Project Help system (Help, Microsoft Project Help).

- **Dates are serious business**—Two of the most powerful and useful aspects of Project are its ability to develop an accurate calendar-based schedule based on the tasks, effort estimates, and assigned resources, and its ability to provide "what if" impact analysis based on any proposed change to those elements. However, these can both be neutralized by doing one simple thing: Manually entering values for either the Start Date or Finish Date for a task. When a Start or Finish Date is manually entered, a constraint is established for this task, either a "Start No Earlier Than" or "Finish No Later Than" constraint. Either prevents Project from scheduling the task, and the task will not respond to changes to predecessor tasks or resource assignments as you would expect due to this fixed constraint. We'll cover the best practice for entering tasks on new projects later in this chapter. To be clear, I'm not saying that you will *never* enter a fixed date for a task, because there are times it will be appropriate. However, it should be the exception.

caution

Avoid entering a Start or Finish date when adding new tasks.

- **Task Duration = Work Effort * Resource Units**—When you understand the fundamentals behind a schedule development, as we reviewed in Chapters 6–8, this one is easy to understand; however, if you do not, it can frustrate you. What does this formula mean? It means that the amount of time it takes to complete a given task is a product of the total work effort involved and the number of resources applied to the task, not to mention the availability of those resources. So, why does it cause confusion at times?
    - Many people assume Duration is the same as Work Effort and Duration is a default column displayed by Microsoft Project on many popular views.
    - When you update/change any of those three components, Project updates the other values accordingly. This routinely occurs when resources are assigned to tasks.
- **Multiple calendars**—Although most people are aware that there is a calendar for the project—after all, it is the ability to easily capture the time dimension for our WBS and task lists that makes Project an attractive work tool option—many people do not leverage the project calendar properly nor realize that each resource can have its own calendar too. This provides a great deal of flexibility and accuracy when scheduling resources and evaluating impact to your overall project timeline. In addition, a specific task can even have its own calendar (which overrides the calendars of any resources assigned to that task). Calendars are available from the Tools, Change Working Time menu item, and they are summarized in Table 23.1.

Table 23.1 Summary of Microsoft Project Calendar Types

Calendar Type	Description	Notes
Project	The calendar applied as default for all project tasks	Standard is the default. Apply organizational calendar and any non-standard productivity levels here.
Resource	The calendar for specific resource	Project creates one for each resource. Apply resource specific schedule constraints (vacations) and availability levels here. Overrides project calendar.
Task	Calendar applied to specific task	Ignores project calendar. You control whether this ignores resource calendars.

- **Planned versus Actual versus Baseline**—Microsoft could have avoided a lot of confusion by simply adding one word to two fields in the Project database. If the Start Date field was named "Planned" Start Date, and the Finish Date field was named "Planned" Finish Date, most users would have a quicker understanding what the fields actually represent and a quicker understanding how these fields relate to their Actual and Baseline versions.
- **Default settings**—Like any software application, Project has default settings. The key is to understand what they are, what they impact and how you can change them to make Project work the way you want it to. The default settings are found primarily on the Tools, Options dialog. We'll review the key default settings to consider as part of our New Project Best Practices later in this chapter.

Need-to-Know Features

With those fundamentals in mind, let's review specific features of Project that will help you make better use of the tool. Four complaints often heard about Project include "it's hard to develop schedules that reflect reality," "it's difficult to show all the information to others," "it's tough to read/understand a Project schedule," and "it's good for planning, but not very helpful as a tool to manage the project." These features address those complaints. They will help you develop a more accurate schedule, communicate more effectively, or make it easier to use as a management tool. Most importantly, these features are *not* obvious to new users.

- **Calendars**—By default, Project uses a calendar that recognizes no holidays and assumes all resources work five days a week, eight hours a day. This can result in a schedule that is not as realistic as it should be. All Project calendars are found (and can be adjusted) from the Tools, Change Working Time... menu option, including the individual resource calendars. Normally, you want to adjust the default project calendar to account for organization-wide resource availability factors, such as standard holidays and standard productivity levels. For availability factors that apply only to a specific resource, you want to adjust the respective resource calendars. The common reasons to do this would be to accurately account for days the resource is not available to the project effort (planned vacation days, planned paid time off, planned conferences, etc.) and to account for non-full-time availability levels.
- **Custom fields**—A powerful and useful feature of Project is the availability of custom fields. Custom fields can be added to any view, and they can be used to store or display any data item. They can be used to help you better manage the project or to help you better communicate project status to others. In a custom field, you can store any type of data, you can define a value list, and you can even incorporate visual indicators (graphic symbols).

  Personally, I use custom fields for visual indicators (I cover this next), to capture resource notes (especially if I want to show assigned resources at the summary task level), to save a previous set of baseline (or target) dates, or to show which deliverable is associated with the task. You can leverage custom fields by first defining your custom field (via the Tools, Customize, Fields menu option or by selecting Customize Fields from the right mouse-click pop-up menu) and then inserting the field into your desired table or view.

There are a couple ways to accurately account for part-time resources in your schedule. You can adjust their resource calendar to show how many hours a day they are available. This is best when the availability level is constant for the duration of the project. You also can indicate the availability level at the task level when the resource is assigned (i.e., Horine [50%]). This is best when the availability level is not constant or is unique for this specific task.

It is also the best approach if you need to clearly and explicitly communicate the part-time level of the given resource for the task.

- **Visual indicators**—As hinted earlier, the custom field can incorporate visual (graphical) indicators into your project file. Project provides a set of visual symbols that can be used to provide better reporting and better communication. You can define the field to change the graphical indicator (symbol) displayed based on the value associated with the field. The value could be a value you manually enter (and control) or the value could be automatically determined by a formula you define. See Figure 23.1, Figure 23.2, and Figure 23.3 for examples of using a formula with a custom field (Baseline Check) to automatically display a visual status for each task when comparing against the Baseline Finish date. You can refer to Table 23.2 for a summary of the logic and parameters used. Graphical indicators are defined by selecting Customize Fields, Values to Display, Graphical Indicators....

  The most popular indicators are the three-dimensional color symbols, the three-dimensional arrows, the colored flags, the emoticons, and the light bulb icon. See Figure 23.4 for a partial list of the available symbols.

FIGURE 23.1
Formula assigned to custom field (Baseline Check).

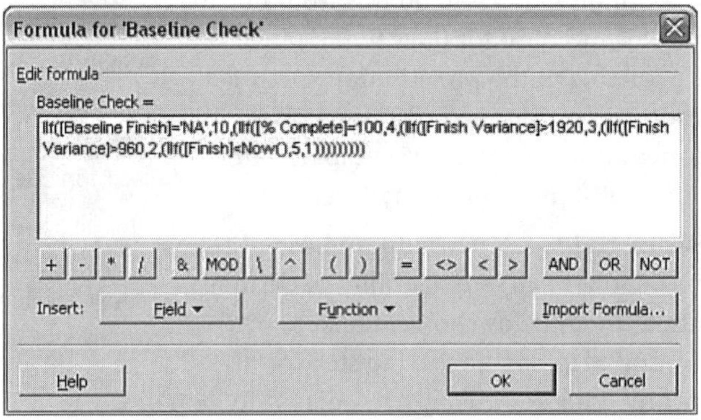

FIGURE 23.2
Assigning formula values for Baseline Check to graphical symbols, part 1.

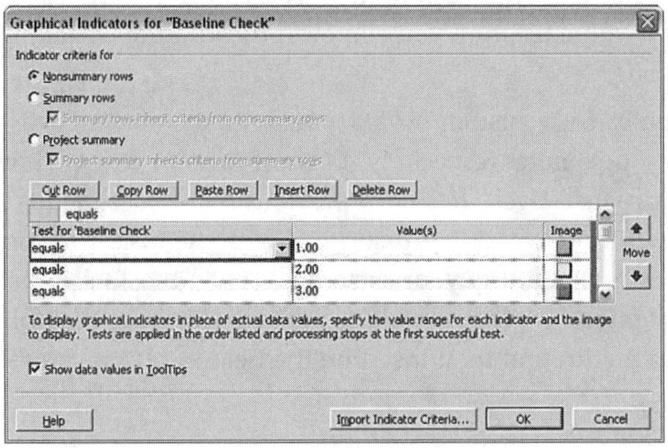

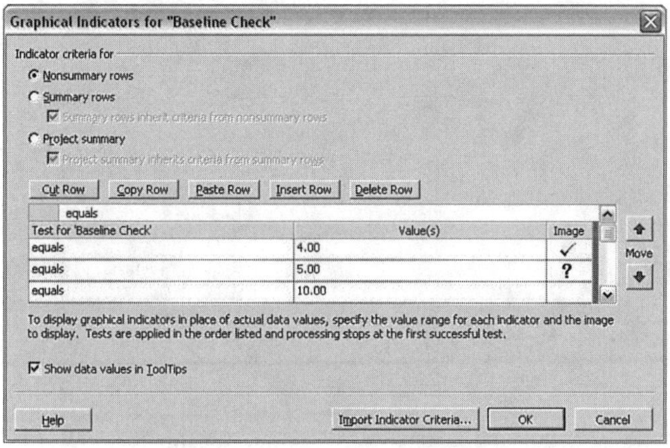

FIGURE 23.3
Assigning formula values for Baseline Check to graphical symbols, part 2.

Table 23.2 Summary of Parameters Used for Baseline Check Example

Test	Value	Action	Notes
If no baseline finish date for task	10	Do not display anything	Baseline Finish has NA value
If task is not completed and variance cannot be determined	5	Display question mark symbol	
If task is completed	4	Display checkmark symbol	
Finish variance more than 4 days	3	Display RED three-dimensional square	Formula uses 480 minutes to represent an 8 hour day. 4 days = 1920 minutes
Finish variance between 2–4 days	2	Display YELLOW three-dimensional square	2 days = 960 minutes
Finish variance less than 2 days	1	Display GREEN three-dimensional square	Formula returns this value if none of the other conditions are satisfied

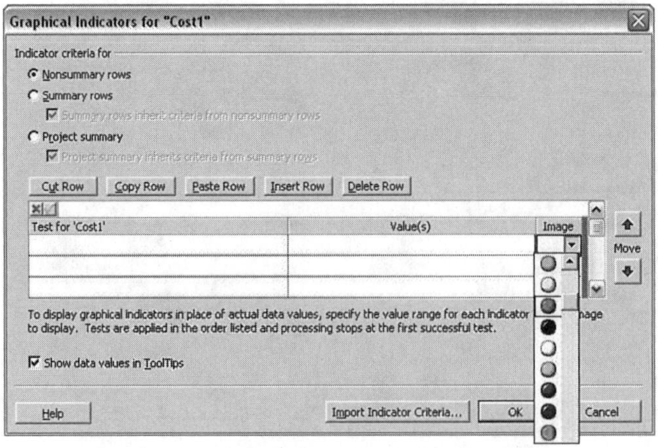

FIGURE 23.4
Partial list of available graphical indicators.

- **Gantt Bar Format**—Another default setting that contributes to the perception that Project is difficult to use for status reporting is the Gantt Bar default format. Many users of Project do not realize that the format of the Gantt Bar can be changed. You can change the size, the color, and the end point symbols used. You can have different task types automatically use different Gantt Bar format settings (Bar Styles), and you can determine what field values (if any) that you want to display alongside the bar. Gantt Bar format can be modified by right-clicking directly on the displayed Gantt Bar or by selecting Format, Bar or Format, Bar Styles.
- **Task Format**—Closely related to the Gantt Bar formatting feature, you can also control the textual display format of each task. Many new users of Project get frustrated with the default task displays, especially if they attempt to use their Project file for communication or reporting purposes. You can have different task types automatically use different display format settings, and you can change the size, font, and color of any task.

  It's worth noting that once you have a format you like, you can quickly apply the same format to other selected tasks by using the Format Painter function. Task Display format can be modified by right-clicking directly on the highlighted task and selecting Font or Text Styles or by selecting Format, Font or Format, Text Styles.

tip

Use the standard Microsoft Office Format Painter function to quickly apply a desired display format to other tasks.

- **Timescale**—Another feature that greatly improves reporting and communicating from Project is the ability to adjust the timescale that is displayed.

Many new users of Project do not realize this can be modified. By altering the timescale displayed, you can better control how much of your project timeline (Gantt Bar) can be seen on one page (or screen). In other words, you can make the Gantt Bar fit. The timescale can be modified by right-clicking directly on the displayed timescale in the Gantt Bar view or by selecting Format, Timescale.

- **Copy Picture**—Here's another powerful reporting feature that even many experienced Project users do not know how to leverage properly. Rather than trying to insert an entire project (.mpp file) object into a Word document or PowerPoint presentation and then spending time attempting to get it to display in a semi-legible manner, you can use the Copy Picture function to take a snapshot directly from your Project file and then "paste" the resulting image into your target Word file or PowerPoint presentation slide. In addition, you do not have to copy all the currently displayed tasks. If you only want to copy certain tasks, you can select those targeted tasks before you choose the Copy Picture function. You can access the Copy Picture function from the standard tool bar or from Edit, Copy Picture....

tip

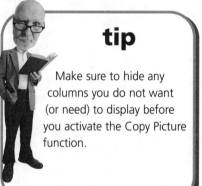

Make sure to hide any columns you do not want (or need) to display before you activate the Copy Picture function.

- **WBS**—Another common complaint with Project files, especially for files that have a large number of tasks, files that have a lot of detail, or files that have multiple levels of task detail, is that it can be very challenging to see the organization (the context) of the work tasks. It can be difficult to see how one task relates to another task.

  A simple, but powerful, way to enhance the organization and readability of your schedule is to display the Work Breakdown Structure (WBS) field. This provides a numeric identification for each task that quickly communicates how it relates to the other tasks. There are two methods for displaying the WBS value. If you want the WBS value to appear in its own column, then you need to add the column by selecting Insert Column... and choosing the WBS field from the list. If you want the WBS value to appear as a prefix to the task name, then you need to enable "Show Outline Number" from the Tools, Options, View tab - Outline Options section.

- **Detecting Resource Over-allocation**—Another common issue with schedules created with Project is that users do not check for over-allocated resources, often because they do not know how to do this. This is actually an easy aspect to check. If you select View, Resource Allocation or View, Resource Usage, Project displays any over-allocated resource in red text. In addition, it shows you in which time period(s) the resource is over-allocated. Knowing this, you can decide what action to take to resolve each over-allocation situation. Of course, you may simply need to perform *resource leveling*, and we'll discuss this in more detail later in this chapter.

- **Displaying Tasks**—Many new users do not realize that you can easily control what level of task detail is displayed, which tasks are displayed and even how the tasks are organized when they are displayed. With this control, you create much more flexibility with how you communicate and report using your Project file. These task display control features are readily available from the standard Project toolbar (and from the Project menu), but they are frequently under utilized. See Figure 23.5 for the toolbar references.
    - **Show Outline**—Allows you to display the tasks by WBS hierarchical level. It allows you to control how much detail is displayed. In many cases, I'll use this feature to reset my display to base level. Then I'll selectively expand certain tasks to show the associated detail.
    - **Filters**—Allows you to display only the tasks that meet certain criteria. This is commonly used to show only tasks assigned to specific resource(s) or to show only tasks within a certain time period. Project provides a comprehensive set of predefined filters, but it also allows you to define custom filters, including filters based on your own custom fields. In addition, you have the same auto-filtering capability you are accustomed to using in Excel.
    - **Group By**—Allows you to categorize and report project information in a variety of ways. Grouping also allows you to view rolled-up summary information for tasks, resources, or assignments on each field in the group. Like filters, Project provides a solid predefined list of groups, but also allows you to define your own groups, including ones based on your own custom fields.

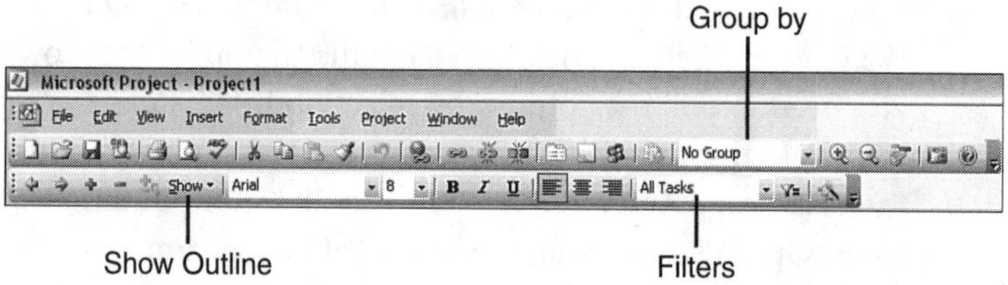

FIGURE 23.5
Task selection functions on toolbars.

- **Baselining**—A closing step in the schedule development process and an essential tool for proactively controlling project performance is to establish a baseline (see Chapters 8 and 10 for more detail on this). The baseline captures the data entered to-date (estimates, tasks, resources, assignments, and even actual work) as permanent reference points that can be used as a point of comparison. You save a schedule baseline by selecting Tools, Tracking, Save Baseline...(or Set Baseline...). Project stores up to ten different baselines for you (in case you need to re-baseline). Project provides several ways to compare actual performance against the baseline, including the Tracking Gantt view (View, Tracking Gantt). In addition, if I do need to re-baseline the project schedule, I like to do three things to link the schedule with the project change control system:

1. Update the baseline version number (and display the baseline version somewhere in the footer or header).
2. Capture the event that is responsible for the re-baseline as a new task/milestone (if you have not already done so) and link this to the tasks that were impacted.
3. Capture the associated Change Request Number that documents the schedule change in the Project file—either on the task mentioned in #2 or as a project note.

tip

When re-baselining a schedule, capture the event (issue, delay, decision) that is responsible for change and link this to impacted tasks rather than directly modifying the date fields.

New Project Best Practices

Now that we've reviewed the key fundamentals and need-to-know features of Project, let's run down the best practices for setting up a new file. Many of the frustrations experienced by new Project users originate from the start in part because they do not build their schedule file with these practices in mind. By following this approach, you can build a schedule file that allows for "what-if" analysis, a file that becomes a useful management tool throughout the project. In addition, these practices are consistent with the schedule development process we covered in Chapters 6–8. Here are my recommendations for starting a new project:

- **Set Project Start Date**—Control the date Project uses as the beginning date for your schedule by setting the Project Start Date. This is done in the Project, Project Information dialog shown in Figure 23.6.
- **Set Project Summary Task (Row Zero)**—Go to Tools, Options, View, and in the Outline options area, select the Show Project Summary task checkbox. With this set, Project adds a row zero to the top of your schedule that summarizes all your project information. This is a tremendous timesaver for identifying the planned finish date and the total work effort.

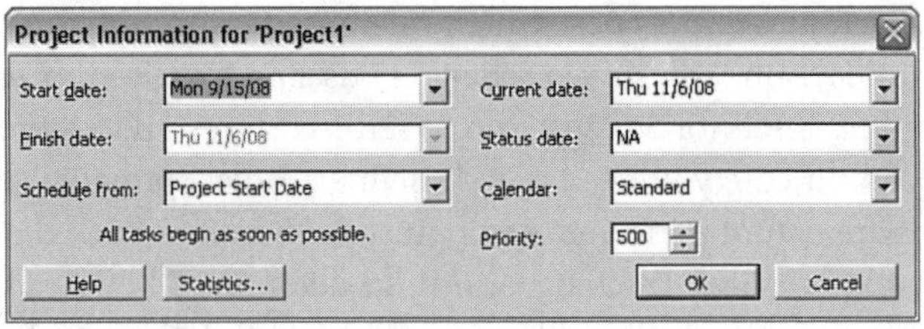

FIGURE 23.6
Dialog used to set Project Start Date.

- **Review Default Settings**—There are a handful of default settings under Tools, Options that can be troublesome if you're not aware of what is going on (see Figure 23.7).

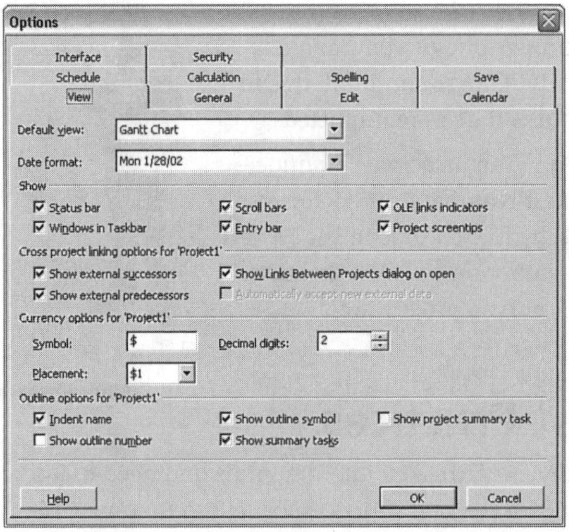

FIGURE 23.7
Use Tools, Options dialog to review settings.

- **Autolink tasks**—On the *Schedule* tab, clear the *Autolink on inserted or moved tasks* checkbox, if you do not want Project to automatically create predecessor links (dependencies) between tasks as you enter them. I turn this off (uncheck, clear), because I want to purposefully set the logical dependencies between my tasks.
- **Tasks honoring constraint dates**—On the *Schedule* tab, clear the "Tasks will always honor their constraint dates" checkbox. This causes a warning indicator to constantly appear in the Indicators column whenever the given task is violating a constraint date. Otherwise, you only receive an initial warning. You want to be sure you are aware of these constraint violations.
- **Multiple critical paths**—Most users only want to deal with one critical path at a time. You want Project to clearly identify the single critical path driving your planned completion date. To be sure this

happens, go to *Calculation* tab and clear the Calculate multiple critical paths checkbox.

- **Adding new resources**—This is personal preference. By default, Project automatically adds resources for you as you assign them to tasks. This sounds great, and it can be a timesaver. However, it does not perform any validation on your resource entries. You can end up with a lot of typos as resources and a lot of multiple references to the same resource. Both are problematic. On the other hand, if you turn off this feature, you will need to enter your resources in advance (on the Resource Sheet) before you can assign them to tasks. If you want to turn off this, go to the *General* tab and clear the Automatically add new resources and tasks checkbox.

tip

To help ensure that any future project file you create has the desired default setting, select the Set as Default button on the General tab before closing the Tools, Options dialog.

- **Set Project Calendar**—Go to Tools, Change Working Time to modify the standard calendar that should be used for the project.
- **Set Header and Footer**—To better prepare your Project file for reporting and distribution, set up the header and the footer sections. I like to add the project name to the header section, and I like to add the following to the footer section: filename, baseline version number, and page x of y. You can access the header and footer under File, Page Setup.
- **Enter and Organize Tasks**—If we followed our schedule development process, we'll enter the tasks using our deliverable-based WBS. Besides the reminder to *not* enter a Start or Finish date for the task, I strongly encourage use of the Notes field to capture any assumptions that will be important to reference. In addition, it is easy to see these notes, because Project includes a notes icon in the Indicators column, and it automatically displays the note when you put your cursor over the icon.
- **Set milestones**—If there are any milestone or fixed target dates that must be honored, enter those dates for the respective tasks. You may want to change the constraint to Must Start On or Must Finish On. To the extent possible, I would avoid doing this on the initial planning iterations.
- **Set external dependencies**—I would also enter placeholder tasks for any external dependencies that your project has, and I would establish a link (predecessor relationship) to those tasks. This way, you can clearly communicate these dependencies so that they are not just assumptions that get lost in

other planning documents. And if the completion dates for those dependencies change, you can clearly identify the impact to your project.

- **Capture Logical Dependencies**—After your tasks are entered and organized, you want to purposefully capture the logical dependencies between your tasks. Do not consider any resource dependencies. Again, if you have followed the schedule development process discussed in Chapters 6–8, you will have this information from your team work sessions.

tip

After you setup a project file ("*.mpp") with the custom columns, formats, and settings you like, you can use this file as a template for future projects.

- **Setup Custom fields**—Insert and setup any custom columns you want/need for this project.
- **Enter estimated durations or work efforts**—For each task, enter the estimated duration or work efforts by resource. Until a resource is assigned, no work effort is calculated for the task.
- **Assign resources to each task**—Now you are ready to assign resources to the tasks and continue the schedule development process.

Keys to Making Resource Leveling Work

One of the key need-to-know features of Project mentioned earlier was the ability to detect resource over-allocation. A step that you can take to be sure your resources are not over-allocated is to perform resource leveling on your schedule. If used correctly, resource leveling is a powerful tool to help you identify and remove resource allocations, especially with large, detailed schedules. Often, these over-allocations identify the tasks that might benefit from additional resources. However, in my experience, many project management professionals under-utilize this feature. One of the main reasons for this is the "lack-of-control" feeling that many people experience when attempting to use it. I can't promise to alleviate all your frustrations, but here are some keys to making resource leveling work for you rather than against you:

- **Use manual resource leveling**—The resource leveling function is sensitive and may give you some unanticipated schedule changes if Project does this automatically. If you want to control when resource leveling occurs, select the Manual radio button in the Leveling Calculations area on the Tools, Level Resources… dialog.
- **Capture task dependencies**—Make sure to follow the schedule development best practices and capture the logical dependencies between your tasks.

This goes a long way to getting logical results from the resource leveling process.

- **Assigning resources to summary tasks**—This issue applies to several behaviors of Project, and resource leveling is one of them. For summary tasks, make sure a resource is *not* assigned to both the summary task and to one or more of the detailed tasks. It's okay to assign a resource to a summary task, if all the detail tasks apply to them. Often this situation occurs when a task is further detailed (sub-tasks added) after the initial resource assignment is made.
- **Use Priority column**—In my experience, this is the least understood key to making resource leveling work for you. Often, when all tasks have the same default priority value, Project does some "funny" things when leveling resources. A common result is Project bounces a resource between two separate summary tasks for no logical reason, or it will assign a resource to a "less important" task first. But, if we have not told Project which tasks are more important (by adjusting the task priority level), then how will it know? Again, this is an issue for tasks that do not have logical dependencies established, but that have the same priority level. To do this, insert/display the Priority column and adjust the priority values for each task accordingly. Then when you execute resource leveling (Tools, Resource Leveling), be sure that the Leveling Order is set for "Priority, Standard" (see Figure 23.8).
- **Set "Level Only with Available Slack"**—When you prepare to execute resource leveling (Tools, Resource Leveling), make sure the Level Only with Available Slack checkbox is selected. This prevents Project from moving the Finish Date and forces the over-allocations to be identified. Once you feel most of your over-allocations that are due to a lack of resources have been resolved and you want Project to give you a more realistic Finish date, then clear this checkbox.

tip

For better control of resource leveling, set the priority level of your tasks (Priority field).

caution

Remember, resource leveling does not guarantee you the best plan, it only guarantees to remove resource over-allocations.

One way to check the results of the resource leveling process is to use the Filters view to show only the tasks for a selected resource (Project, Filtered For, Using Resource...). With this view, you can quickly check whether the resource has been logically assigned to tasks and that his/her availability has been maximized. For individuals that are new to resource leveling, this can be an educational exercise—and it can help build confidence in the resource leveling engine.

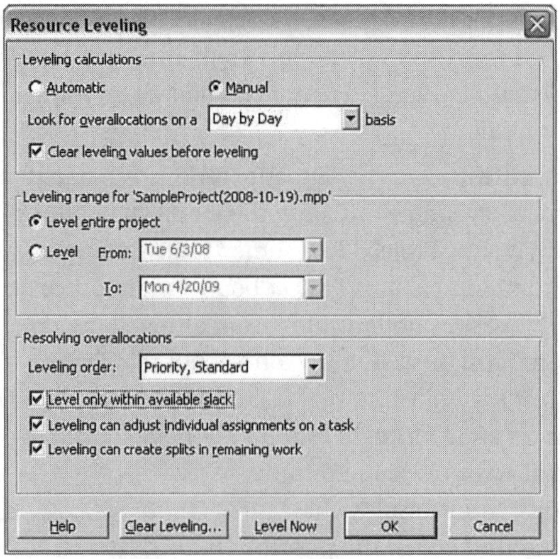

FIGURE 23.8
Set the leveling order in the Tools, Resource Leveling dialog.

Powerful Reporting Secrets

What do we frequently hear when it comes to generating Project reports or when other stakeholders attempt to read a Project schedule: "I can't show all the data I need," "I can't get the Gantt Bar to fit on one page," "I don't like the appearance of the schedule," "The reports are boring," "There's too much detail—I can't tell what where I'm at," "It's too hard to read," "It takes a lot of effort," "I can't share my project file with anyone because they don't have Project." Yeah, that's a fair sampling. Does it have to be this way? No, it does not—and by now, you likely have a good feeling for how you can address many of these complaints.

The three primary keys to better reporting with Project are awareness of capabilities, clarity of audience needs, and creativity. A significant portion of this chapter has focused on "raising awareness" of Project capabilities and options, and we'll revisit the ones that deal with reporting. Next, the more you understand about what your audience wants, the better. It will help you focus on where to invest your effort. What do they need to see? What level of detail are they concerned with? How will they read your report? If you combine the answers to these questions with your knowledge of what Project can do, you can develop a targeted approach to best share your Project schedule information. Let's review the keys to improving your reporting efforts:

- **Take care of the basics**—How many times have you seen a Project printout and you have no idea what project it is from, when it was printed, when it was last updated, what page number you are looking at, or what baseline it is from? A simple, yet often overlooked, step you can take to improve the readability of your Project file is to use a Header and Footer. At a minimum, I like to show the Project Name in the Header section, and the file name, baseline version, and page number X of Y in the Footer section.

> **tip**
>
> Include an organizational logo picture in the Header section of your Project file to further personalize for your targeted audience.

- **Control the fields you are displaying**—Often, users have a difficult time getting everything to fit, because they are showing fields/columns they do not need. Remember to hide any columns that are not essential for your given audience. In addition, you can adjust the width of any of your columns.
- **Tailor with custom fields**—As we've discussed earlier with Custom Fields, you can show practically any type of information alongside each task row. You are not limited to the standard columns that Project shows in a given view. On past projects, I've used Custom Fields to show information like Status Comments, Resource Notes and Deliverable Notes. In addition, I've used a custom field like Resource Notes to show resource assignments at the summary task level without impacting the actual work effort calculations in Project.
- **Control the tasks you are displaying**—Use the outlining, filtering, and grouping features (discussed earlier) to control which tasks are actually displayed. In most cases, showing summary tasks at a given level is sufficient for reporting purposes. This step can go a long way to providing reports that are understandable and useful for your audience. In my experience, I find that the level of detail I need to show is not consistent for the entire schedule. For example, phases that have already been completed can easily be shown at a high summary level, while activity for the current phase will be displayed at a lower level of detail.
- **Modify formats**—As mentioned before, you have the power to change the format of the displayed text. I often develop a style for tasks at a certain hierarchical level. They have the same font, size (normally larger), and color. This way it is even easier to see and understand the organization of the project.

■ **Determine whether you need to show the Gantt Bar**—This may sound like heresy, but check to see whether your audience wants to see the Gantt Bar. If they do, you need to decide what data to show with the task Gantt Bar, what format to use for the Gantt Bar at each level, and which data to show in the table columns. If they do not, you end up with a table and with space to show much more information. I have found the Gantt Bar to offer the most value in high-level summary presentations of your schedule. For conveying detailed schedule information, I rarely use the Gantt Bar.

■ **Modify timescale**—This is important if you are displaying the Gantt Bar, and we talked about this feature earlier too. In many cases, to show the entire Gantt Bar on one page, you need to adjust the default timescale that Project is using.

■ **Add "attention getting" visuals**—Use custom fields with graphical indicators to add stoplight status to each task or to visually highlight other aspects about the task such as risk level, task has associated issue, task is in-progress, or importance level of task. See Figure 23.9 for an example of a schedule that uses two custom graphical indicator columns.

FIGURE 23.9

Example of "attention getting" visuals.

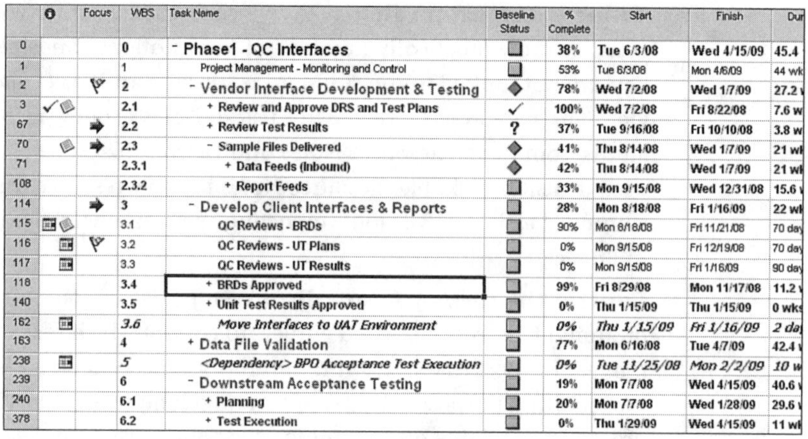

	ⓘ	Focus	WBS	Task Name	Baseline Status	% Complete	Start	Finish	Dur
0			0	⁻ Phase1 - QC Interfaces	☐	38%	Tue 6/3/08	Wed 4/15/09	45.4
1			1	Project Management - Monitoring and Control	☐	53%	Tue 6/3/08	Mon 4/6/09	44 wk
2		▽	2	⁻ Vendor Interface Development & Testing	◆	78%	Wed 7/2/08	Wed 1/7/09	27.2
3	✓		2.1	+ Review and Approve DRS and Test Plans	✓	100%	Wed 7/2/08	Fri 8/22/08	7.6 w
67		➡	2.2	+ Review Test Results	?	37%	Tue 9/16/08	Fri 10/10/08	3.8 w
70		➡	2.3	⁻ Sample Files Delivered	◆	41%	Thu 8/14/08	Wed 1/7/09	21 wk
71			2.3.1	+ Data Feeds (Inbound)	◆	42%	Thu 8/14/08	Wed 1/7/09	21 wk
108			2.3.2	+ Report Feeds	☐	33%	Mon 9/15/08	Wed 12/31/08	15.6
114		➡	3	⁻ Develop Client Interfaces & Reports	☐	28%	Mon 8/18/08	Fri 1/16/09	22 wk
115	▦		3.1	QC Reviews - BRDs	☐	90%	Mon 8/18/08	Fri 11/21/08	70 day
116	▦	▽	3.2	QC Reviews - UT Plans	☐	0%	Mon 9/15/08	Fri 12/19/08	70 day
117	▦		3.3	QC Reviews - UT Results	☐	0%	Mon 9/15/08	Fri 1/16/09	90 day
118			3.4	+ BRDs Approved	☐	99%	Fri 8/29/08	Mon 11/17/08	11.2
140			3.5	+ Unit Test Results Approved	☐	0%	Thu 1/15/09	Thu 1/15/09	0 wks
162	▦		3.6	*Move Interfaces to UAT Environment*	☐	*0%*	*Thu 1/15/09*	*Fri 1/16/09*	*2 day*
163			4	+ Data File Validation	☐	77%	Mon 6/16/08	Tue 4/7/09	42.4
238	▦		*5*	*<Dependency> BPO Acceptance Test Execution*	☐	*0%*	*Tue 11/25/08*	*Mon 2/2/09*	*10 w*
239			6	⁻ Downstream Acceptance Testing	☐	19%	Mon 7/7/08	Wed 4/15/09	40.6
240			6.1	+ Planning	☐	20%	Mon 7/7/08	Wed 1/28/09	29.6
378			6.2	+ Test Execution	☐	0%	Thu 1/29/09	Wed 4/15/09	11 wk

■ **Leverage Copy Picture**—Leverage the Copy Picture function to include your Project information in other document format types like PowerPoint and Word. Just be sure to tailor the columns and tasks you want to display first.

■ **Use the Power of Page Setup**—The page setup options are certainly not unique to Project, but it seems like many users forget about the flexibility that can be found here. In my experience, the most useful Page Setup features are scaling adjustments (just like in Excel), margin adjustments, and on the View tab, fit timescale, and print the first X columns on each page. See Figure 23.10 for a reference to the Page Setup, View dialog.

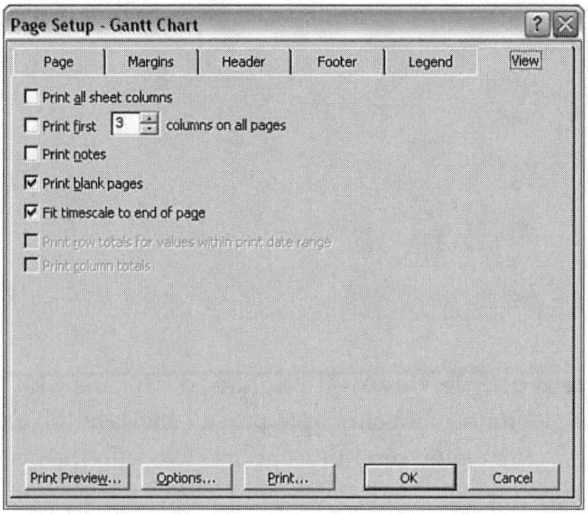

FIGURE 23.10
Page setup options are set in the Page Setup, View dialog.

- **Determine how users will read it**—This goes hand-in-hand with "controlling the tasks you display." You need to know how your audience will read your report (or schedule view). Do they have Project or Project Viewer? Do they want to see it as a part of another report or presentation? Do they want it online or just hard copy? The answers to these questions tell you whether you need to create snapshots and if you need to develop snapshots, what format you'll need to target.

tip

If your stakeholders do not have Project, distribute your report (schedule views) as PDF files.

- **Leverage canned "Reports"**—Project provides a significant list of canned reports that most people never look at it. (See Figure 23.11 for the Reports main menu.) There are three reasons why.
    - The standard views end up meeting 80–90% of the information needs
    - Users have not invested time to become aware of what reports are there.
    - Users do not like the standard information or appearance of the reports. This area is an untapped resource for most people.

Nearly all the canned reports that are available under View, Reports can be customized. At a minimum, you can adjust appearance details like color, font style, and font size and this is often by row or data category. However, in many instances, you can change the data that is used and the data that is presented.

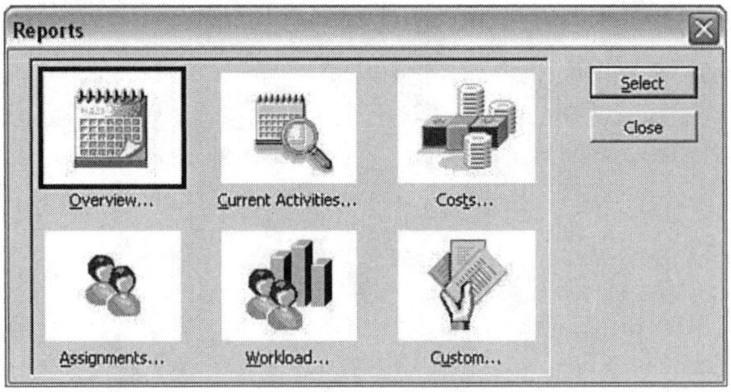

FIGURE 23.11
Project's Reports main menu dialog.

- **Distribute multiple views**—If you have a schedule with multiple levels of work detail, it can be challenging to provide views at the detail level while also ensuring the reader maintains perspective with the overall schedule. This challenge increases with additional levels of work detail and with stakeholders who do not have Project. In these cases, I do not hesitate to provide multiple views (or snapshots) of the schedule. One view, a higher level summary view, to provide overall schedule context and additional detail views for each "current" or "hot" area of the schedule.
- **Use callout features**—This is one feature I wish Microsoft would incorporate directly into Project. If you find yourself having to use PowerPoint or Word to deliver your schedule updates, consider the use of callouts to highlight key risks, dependencies, assumptions, and target dates (see Figure 23.12). I normally use Copy Picture to get the base Gantt chart view from Project, then access the callout object from the Drawing toolbar (AutoShapes, Callouts).

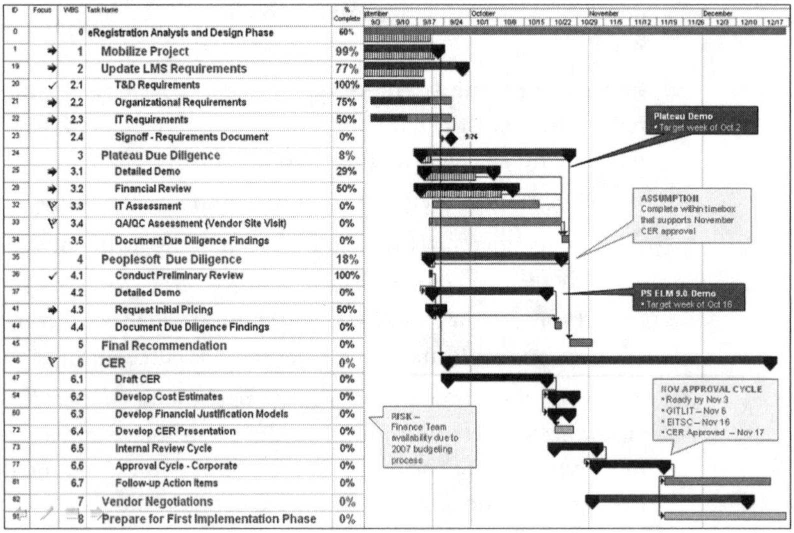

FIGURE 23.12
Example of the using callout feature.

- **Two can be better than one**—In many situations, it may be simpler and less time-consuming to work with two versions of your Project schedule. You can use one version for managing the project, and another version for reporting status. This approach can free you to capture all the details you want and need in your day-to-day working schedule without impacting the clarity and conciseness of your reporting process.

More Insights to a Better Project Schedule

Here's a list of additional tips and insights from my experience that can help you build a better schedule with Project.

- **Managing timeline expectations**—Often, people avoid using Project to communicate during the project definition or project planning stage, because Project incorporates the calendar aspect and when stakeholders see real calendar dates even in preliminary, high-level schedules, their expectations can be influenced. A simple way to manage these expectations is to change the timescale labels that Project displays. As we mentioned before, the timescale can be modified by right-clicking directly on the displayed timescale in the Gantt Bar view or by selecting the Format, Timescale menu option. After the Timescale dialog is displayed, you will want to change the Label format used. Simply select an option that does not use an actual calendar date, such as "Week 1, Week 2...Week N".

tip

If you use any other calendar for the main project calendar besides the Standard calendar, be sure you also update Gantt chart timescale format to use this calendar by going to Format, Timescale, Non-working time tab and select your non-standard calendar as the one to use.

- **Assigning resources to summary tasks**—If you are using Project to estimate, schedule, or manage resource work hours, be wary of assigning resources to summary tasks. In Project, the resource assignment to a summary task is separate from the resource assignments to the detail tasks belonging to the summary task. In many cases, the resource is assigned to the summary task either for display purposes or before the detail tasks were added. I am not saying that you cannot assign resources to a summary task, there are times it is very appropriate. I am saying be sure you understand how this works and review any resource assignment that has the same resource assigned at both the summary and detail level.

■ **Displaying assigned resources**—If you have a task that happens to have a few resources assigned, or you have resources with long names or you are assigning resources at less than 100% availability, it can be very challenging to fully display the assigned resources along with the task, especially if you are using the Gantt Bar view. Here are a few suggestions to better manage this display situation:

- Use a Custom text field, such as Resource Notes, to display what you want for the resource names
- Use the Resource Initials instead of the default Resources field/column
- Assign the list of resources to a "group," then assign the group resource to the task
- Further decompose the task, so you can assign each resource to his/her own task
- If the task cannot be broken down, consider duplicating the task, then assign a different resource to each instance of the task

tip

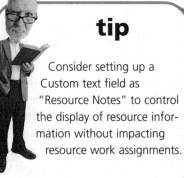

Consider setting up a Custom text field as "Resource Notes" to control the display of resource information without impacting resource work assignments.

■ **Capture impact of issues and delays**—Rather than simply updating the start date for a given task when a new baseline needs to be set, capture the reason for the schedule impact (event, issue, delay, change request) as a new task in your schedule. This way, the source of the impact has visibility and you do not forget why the schedule change was made (see Figure 23.13).

FIGURE 23.13

Example of "showing impact."

	❶	Focus	WorkStatus	WBS	Task Name	% Complete	Work
606		😊	◆	6.3	⁻ User Acceptance Testing (UAT)	98%	294 hrs
607	✓			6.3.1	Setup Test Environment	100%	16 hrs
608	✓	😊		6.3.2	«Delay - Security Migration Issues, 8.8 Infrastructure»	100%	0 hrs
609	✓			6.3.3	Execute UAT Test Plan	100%	88 hrs
610	✓			6.3.4	Address Issues	100%	84 hrs
611	✓	⚑		6.3.5	«Additional Test Cycle Needed»	100%	100 hrs
612		➡	◯	6.3.6	+ UAT Summary Report	0%	6 hrs

■ **Once progress is recorded, it changes**—Remember, once progress is recorded against a task, it does not automatically calculate planned dates. I often see people get frustrated because they assign resources to a task and the planned finish dates do not change. In most cases, the task already has a percentage complete amount recorded against it.

■ **Saving baseline dates**—Until you get comfortable with how Project manages baselines, you can always save your own copy of your baseline dates and duration by using custom fields.

- **If whacked, do over**—If all else fails and you cannot get the values of a resource assignment to make sense to you (dates, hours, resource allocation), simply enter a new task and rebuild the resource assignment. After the assignment is rebuilt, you can delete the one that was giving you fits. This technique seems to work 99.9% of the time.

tip

If defining a new work process that will be repeated, nail down the process first before you propagate the detail. It will save you a lot of re-do or editing.

THE ABSOLUTE MINIMUM

At this point, you should have a solid understanding of the following:

- Project is a database application.
- Task Duration = Work Effort * Resource Units
- Project utilizes multiple calendar types—project, resource, and task.
- The three main date types that Project uses are Planned, Actual, and Baseline.
- Custom fields can be added to any view and can be used for visual indicators, too.
- The best practices for starting a new project schedule file.
- The keys for making resource leveling work.
- The techniques for effective reporting from Project.

Figure 23.14 summarizes the main points reviewed in this chapter.

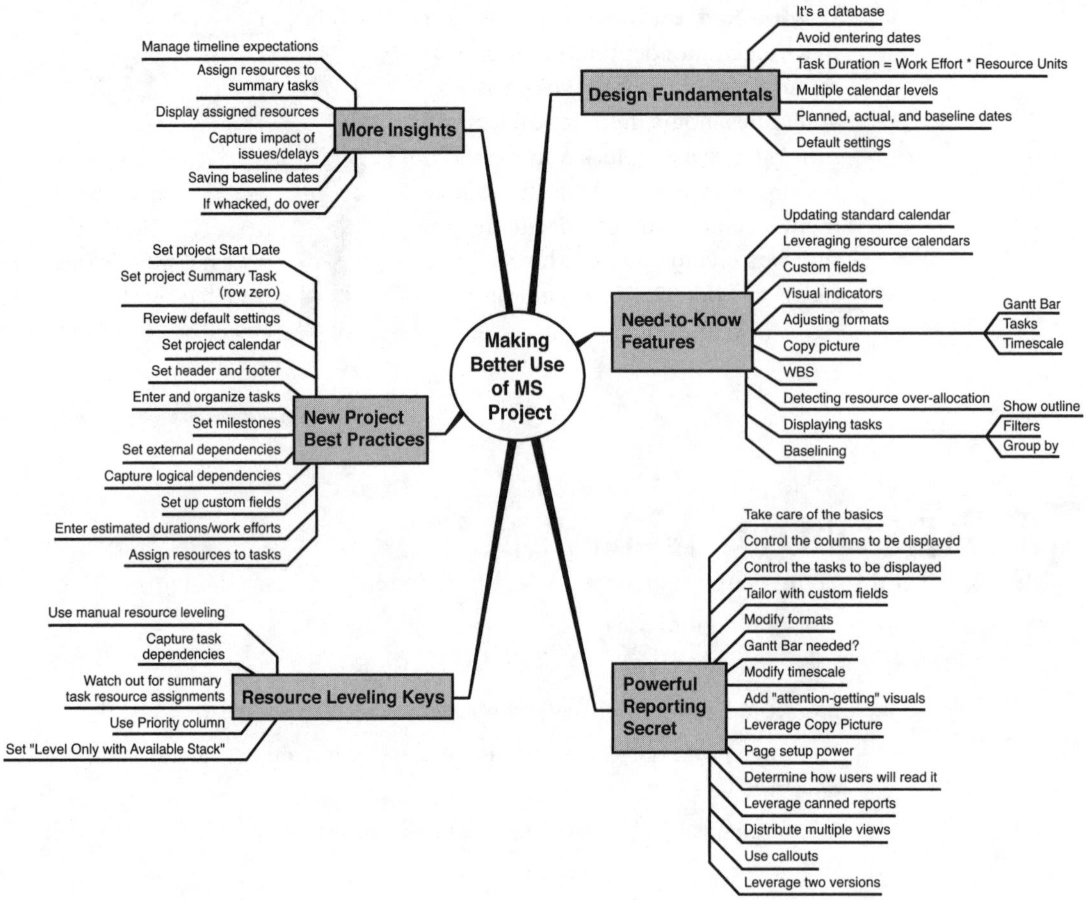

FIGURE 23.14

Overview of making better use of MS Project.

In This Chapter

- Understand how to manage a project in a project management "lite" culture
- Learn what to do when a detailed schedule cannot be developed
- Review insights for managing a project with a hard milestone date
- Learn how to deal with difficult resources
- Review steps to better prepare for and manage turnover
- Learn powerful tips for managing a selection process
- Learn how to improve any testing process

24

When Reality Happens

While the last chapter focused on accelerating your knowledge and use of Microsoft Project, this chapter focuses on accelerating your project management effectiveness by taking a closer look at common scenarios and challenges you are likely to encounter—even on a first assignment.

The first four sections of this book addressed the fundamental project management concepts and processes. With this knowledge, you have a solid foundation for handling any project situation. However, there is nothing like "real life" project scenarios to make us question all of this. In this chapter, we review a few of those common challenging situations. Each review emphasizes the fundamentals that apply and provides additional recommendations to better prepare you for when these "realities" happen in your work life.

What If I'm in a Project Management "Lite" Culture?

Let's face it. There are environments, situations, and organizations that are not supportive of ideal project management practices. The reasons for these project management "lite" cultures can vary. The organization or industry may be new to project management. The organization may have been burned by ineffective Project Management Office (PMO) experiments or frustrated by past project managers who emphasized administrative details at the expense of critical success factors. In some organizations, the project manager is responsible for several projects simultaneously. In other situations, the project manager is serving multiple roles on the team. Whatever the reason, you may find yourself in an environment where you cannot implement the full arsenal of project management best practices. Yet, you are still accountable for successfully managing the project. What can you do?

First, take confidence in knowing that many successful projects have been managed using project management "lite" approaches. You can do it too. In many cases, it is in these environments where a project manager must use all their skills and leverage their creativity. In most project management lite environments, the "lite" pertains more to the level of documentation, planning detail, and tracking administration (project control detail) that is generated. Let's review the keys to thriving in a project management "lite" culture.

- **Focus on the core**—No matter the project situation, you (and your team) must have clarity on the following:
  - Project context—Why are we doing this project?
  - Project scope—What are we doing on this project?
  - Success factors—How will we be measured?
  - Approach—How will we get the work done?
  - Roles and responsibilities—What are these for each team member?
  - Timeline—When does work need to be completed?
  - Management approach—At the minimum, what meetings/tools/reports will be used to check and facilitate team progress?
- **Focus on communication, relationships, and managing expectations**—These are always important, but in these environments, you must be very effective in all three areas to successfully lead and manage a project.

tip

No matter the environment, you need to document and communicate these core project definition items. See Chapter 4, "Defining a Project," for additional details.

- **Lead the project**—In these environments, you cannot be successful by simply "managing" the project. You need to lead it. See Chapter 16, "Leading a Project," for a review of these principles and skills, especially servant leadership.
- **Emphasize personal contact and relationships**—Especially in these environments, you need to get to know your team, the key expert resources you will need, and anyone else who will need to provide work to your project. Take the time to learn what drives them, how they work, and what other priorities they are managing. Look for ways to help make them successful, and always show your appreciation for their willingness to help you.
- **Emphasize "value-added" deliverables only**—You should only require a deliverable (work product) that is "value-added' to the overall process, especially if you are asking others to generate effort that is not directly related to their targeted work products (such as project administration or management items). Look for opportunities to right-size or combine your list of required deliverables.
- **Tailor your scheduling approach**—In environments like this, you may not be able to develop a detail work schedule, and we'll discuss how to manage this in more detail in the next section. At the minimum, what is important is that everyone is clear on what they are working on (responsible for), the quality level that is expected or the process that needs to be followed, and when the work product is due.
- **Right size your monitoring and tracking procedures**—This is closely related to the emphasis on value-added deliverables. For both yourself and your team, be sure all project monitoring and tracking procedures are streamlined, necessary, and not duplicated.
- **Generate work products as early as possible**—In environments where it is either difficult or impractical to perform detail planning or detail requirements definition, an approach that generates tangible results early can be invaluable. This approach is one of the tenets of iterative, agile methodologies that I will talk more about in Chapter 25, "Intriguing Project Management Concepts and Topics." The approach is invaluable, because until stakeholders are able to experience the targeted concepts or products, they are not able to consider all their requirements.

tip

Leverage iterative, agile approaches in project management "lite" environments.

- **Plan on multiple iterations**—For the same reasons as above, you should plan on multiple iterations of your process. To assume that any work product will be correct on one iteration is not practical. This applies to definition, design, development, testing, and deployment approaches.

tip

No matter the environment, always emphasize effective communication, positive relationships, and clear expectations with all project stakeholders.

What If I Can't Develop a Detailed Schedule?

In spite of all the logical and practical benefits we reviewed in Chapters 5–8 for leveraging a detailed schedule development process, you may actually find yourself in an organization or in a project situation where you cannot build a project schedule to the level of detail or completeness that you would ideally like. In other cases, you cannot develop a detailed multi-phase schedule, because there is too much "unknown", too much "uncertainty" in the early stages of the project. What can we do in these cases? The best approaches are to leverage one or more aspects of quality schedule. Here are techniques to consider:

- **Detail what you can**—Include as much WBS detail as you can. This is one of the advantages of building a schedule using a WBS. At a minimum, you should always know the first few levels of your WBS. Do what you can.
- **Manage to milestones**—Set target dates for key deliverables, events, and decision points, then monitor progress against these dates. The key with this approach is target the right milestones and to include enough interim checkpoint milestones, so you can identify any major issues and variances early enough to take corrective action.
- **Manage to deliverables**—A similar approach to "managing to milestones" except the emphasis is on the targeted work products. The work details are delegated to the respective deliverable owner, but they are accountable to the target completion. The key with this approach is to ask for enough interim deliverables, so you can identify any major issues and variances early enough to take corrective action.
- **Manage to project phases**—In this approach, you organize the project into phases with a defined checkpoint (gates, review session, go/no-go decision point) at the end. The appropriate stakeholders review the health of the project and determine whether the project should proceed to the next phase. The keys here are to clarify what the project health evaluation criteria will be and which stakeholders will participate in the evaluation process.

- **Manage to 30/60/90 day detail plans**—This is a common technique with iterative, agile projects, troubled projects that are in recovery mode, projects with a lot of uncertainty and scheduler risk, and with projects that are managed by phases. In this approach, your focus is on the next milestone. What are we getting done in the next 30, 60, or 90 days? By ensuring that the work details (process, assignments, roles, expectations) are clear to your team, they stay focused and productive. This helps the team experience accomplishment more often, and it is essential to building overall project momentum.

A quality schedule leverages combinations of these techniques.

What If I Must Manage to a Hard Milestone Date?

If you have not already, you will soon find yourself managing a project that absolutely, positively must be completed by a certain date, a project in which being late or saying, "it can't be done," is not an option. What do you do in these cases? What do you need to focus on? Here are my recommendations for managing a project that has a hard milestone date:

- **Clarify the real driver for the milestone date**—As with any project goal, you need to be clear what is behind it, what is driving it. In the case of milestone dates that are imposed on a project, there are several common sources:
  - External event
  - Business/organizational goal
  - Business/organizational budgeting cycle
  - "Stretch" goal from Project Sponsor to make sure the project is completed by the actual/real target date
- **Give yourself a contingency buffer**—For any project that has a true hard milestone date, the project's target completion date should be set well in

tip

For any project that has a true hard milestone date, the project's milestone completion date should be set well in advance of this date whenever possible. Give yourself a contingency buffer whenever possible.

advance of this date whenever possible in order to provide a contingency buffer and to increase the probability that you will be ready for the actual, hard milestone event.

- **Competing project demands**—Remember the classic project management triangle we discussed in Chapter 1, if time is fixed, then our management focus turns to the other factors. The common responses are increasing resources and decreasing scope/quality.
- **Clarify what "done" looks like**—Especially for these situations, you need to make sure your vision of the solution is the same as your project sponsor. This is the core of your expectations and scope management efforts, and includes a detailed review of project success factors, assumptions, priority requirements, and implementation/deployment strategies.
- **Get crystal clear on "must have" functionality**—As mentioned previously, you need to have clear priority on your solution requirements, including quality standards. This clarity helps drive and focus your team's work efforts and provides a basis for a staged (or incremental) delivery approach.
- **Manage scope diligently**—When you must hit a specific date, you must be diligent about scope management. Invest the time upfront to get buy-in on requirement priority levels and common understanding of final solution. From there, use your change request process to manage any requests (or decisions) to modify scope, approach, priorities, assumptions, etc. See Chapter 11, "Managing Project Changes," for a review of this process.
- **Focus team's work effort**—Focus on the productivity level of your team and any key resources. Review Chapter 19, "Keys to Better Project Team Performance," for a reminder of powerful techniques you can leverage here. Here is a quick summary to keep in mind:
    - Get dedicated resources whenever possible
    - Co-locate your team whenever possible
    - Conduct frequent touchpoints with your team
    - Remove any overhead or non-value added tasks from their plate
    - Avoid downtimes and delays. Be sure your team has the information, deliverables, and resources they need to stay productive each day
    - Resolve issues quickly
- **Prioritize testing efforts**—Often in a fixed time project, the work effort that is squeezed—asked to do their work in less time—is testing. It is always important to prioritize testing efforts based on two primary factors: requirement priorities and risk levels. If you have limited time, you want to get the biggest bang for your buck in your testing efforts. Focus on your high-risk items and set these expectations with your stakeholders.

- **Strongly consider phased implementations**—Leveraging a phased implementation (incremental delivery, multiple releases) approach for deploying the project solution is not only invaluable for change management and risk management reasons, but it can also be a powerful mechanism for balancing the needs of the project sponsors with the capacity of the project to get work done within a given timeframe. This technique can be considered as a response (corrective action) to a project issue, even if it was not part of the original plan.

tip

Scope management is critical if the milestone date cannot be moved.

What If I Have Difficult Resources?

On occasion, you may have resources that do not seem to be concerned about the success of your project. Their lack of concern can come in various forms, from subtle or passive on one end to more direct, aggressive actions on the other end. These situations can be tough, and the best response can be less than obvious. Here are a few observations and recommendations for your consideration if you happen to find yourself in this situation:

- **It's not about you**—Remember 99.9% of the time the source of their "less than cooperative" attitude has nothing to do with you personally, so stay calm, stay detached; be the "eye of the storm" and don't react emotionally.
- **Difficult or different**—Many people confuse difficult with different, especially those that are new to an organization. There is a wide range of personality types out there. Some people just naturally have "more challenging" styles. I always check with other people, people who have more experience with the given resource, before determining whether the observed behavior is normal.
- **Diamonds in the rough**—In many cases, resources are difficult when they are frustrated, especially if they feel they are not being heard or if they are not clear on the project context and purpose. Take the time to meet with them and listen purposefully. They can often provide early insights to risks you need to manage. In addition, people generally appreciate the opportunity to vent and offer counsel.
- **Don't avoid**—Remember, good project managers do not avoid risks and issues. You need to proactively manage any potential resource issue. You need to clarify whether you have a real difficult resource issue as soon as possible.

- **Focus on results**—In most cases, after my initial investigation, I flag any difficult resource situation as a risk. It only becomes an issue, if the resource is not delivering quality work on time, or if they are impacting the work of other team members. This helps to take the emotion out of things and helps make sure you are not overreacting to a "different personality" situation.
- **Look for "win-win"**—While most people want to do their best and to be part of successful endeavors, it may take more incentive for others. This occurs more frequently with shared resources, resources that are not 100% dedicated to your specific project. Continue to build relationships with these people and look for opportunities to help them recognize them and to make them care about your request/need.
- **Avoid silos**—If you have a resource with a difficult work history or is a known turnover risk, you want them to work on tasks where their knowledge and skills it takes to generate their deliverables does not reside solely with them.
- **Assign noncritical tasks**—If you have a quality of work concern from a resource that you have to keep, reduce your risk by assigning them non-critical, less visible tasks.
- **Outsource the role**—If you have known organizational resource difficulties, you should give strong consideration to a risk avoidance strategy—outsource the roles.
- **Meet with supervisor**—If you have not had any success in changing the resource's behavior on your own, or learn that the real problem is a matter of priorities, reach out to the appropriate supervisor and discuss your situation. Often, immediate supervisors are much better equipped to change behavior.

What Can I Do About Turnover?

Nothing can put a project schedule more at risk than the sudden loss of key resources. As a project manager, you hope you are aware of these potential events well in advance, but this is not always the case. Let's take a look at a few observations and recommendations that might help you prepare for and manage a turnover situation:

- **The longer the project, the more likely turnover will occur**—If you manage a project that is scheduled to last more than six months, you should assume that you have resource turnover risks, especially with your core team members. Circumstances change: People receive other opportunities, their personal/family situations change, their career interests shift, and they can lose interest. To the extent possible, leverage compensation packages, project incentives, and quality of work assignments to minimize this risk.

- **Prepare for turnover**—A benefit of documenting the definition of the project, your management plans, and your detailed work schedule is that it makes it much easier for a new resource to come up to speed on the context of his work. I think about how I would quickly orient any new person to the project. If you don't have these materials, develop them.
- **Avoid silos**—To the extent that you can build in mentoring arrangements to your project teams, the better. Not only does it build work satisfaction, it also reduces impact if a resource leaves. In addition, encourage work processes that encourage openness and sharing of all work products.
- **Increase visibility**—If you are concerned about a key resource leaving, consider increasing the visibility and importance this person has on the project. This is generally done by a combination of the roles and work tasks assigned. Common examples include providing more exposure to senior management, more exposure to customers, assigning leadership roles, assigning mentoring roles, and assigning quality assurance tasks.
- **Assign non-critical tasks**—If you are concerned about a resource leaving, you can take the opposite approach to reduce your risk. You can assign them noncritical, less visible tasks. If resource is part of an organization, this should be a decision made in collaboration with other impacted managers.
- **Outsource to transfer the risk**—If you have a known organizational resource turnover risks, you should give strong consideration to a risk avoidance strategy—outsource the roles.
- **Transition period or not?**—What do you do if you actually lose a resource? First, determine whether you want a transition period. In some cases, it may be better to make a sudden, no-notice change. In most cases, especially if replacement resources cannot be found quickly, a transition period is helpful, the longer the better.
- **Promote from within, backfill less senior positions**—Next, you need to determine how to replace the departing resource. There are various strategies available, but the one I encourage you to consider whenever possible is to fill the position by promoting from within, and then backfill the promotee's former position.

Tips for Managing a Selection Process

In Chapter 21,"Managing Vendors," we mentioned that the evaluation and selection process is a core aspect of effective vendor management. Because outsourcing continues to grow as a business management selection process, the odds are very good that you will direct a selection process, in one form or another, early in your project management career. Given the importance that this process has to your project success criteria, funding efforts, and your ability to establish valuable vendor partnerships—not to mention the visibility you have to senior management and the market place—it is critical that you handle these endeavors well. To help you with this, consider these tips and observations from my experience as you plan your next evaluation or selection process:

- **Understand *why* you are doing this**—Due to the number of stakeholders and accompanying agendas to be managed, the logistical details involved, and the effort it takes, it can be easy to forget why we do evaluation and selection processes in the first place. The main reason that organizations perform selection processes is to reduce risk. There can be other, closely related, reasons including gaining consensus, developing business case, and satisfying due diligence requirements.

Selection processes are all about managing risk.

- **What are the *real* goals?**—One of the common complaints of these processes is that the organization ends up selecting the option, which was not recommended by the evaluation team. This generally happens because the real purpose of the selection process or the actual decision criteria was not clear to the evaluation team. In addition, what is your organization really after? The answer can guide the focus and the specific approach you take. Do you just need competitive bids? Are you performing market research? Do you need to satisfy procurement requirements? Do you need to satisfy due diligence requirements?
- **Clarify the driving strategies**—It helps to design your selection process, if you have agreement and clarity on answers to the following questions:
  - Which is more important—partner relationships or lowest price?
  - Do we want a custom solution?
  - Are we willing to adapt the best practices of available market solutions?
  - Which is more important—the best solution or the best "working relationship" fit?
- **Scale process to risk level**—Selection processes can range greatly in activities, stages, time, cost, and effort. The important principle is to scale the

process to the level of risk involved. For high-risk decisions, the process can include steps such as:

- Current state assessment
- Future state analysis
- Develop Long List of Candidates
- Develop Evaluation Criteria (Knockout)
- Develop Scoring Process
- Request for Information (RFI)
- Request for Quote (RFQ)
- Request for Proposal (RFP)
- Bidders Conferences
- Information Gathering Sessions by Candidate Vendors
- Demonstrations (onsite, online)
- Reference Checks
- Client Site Visits
- Vendor Site Visits
- Financial Health Assessments
- Quality Audits
- Executive Relationship Building
- Gap Analysis
- Business Case (Benefit-Cost Analysis)
- Final Rankings/Recommendations
- Contract Negotiations

- **Partner with procurement**—Be sure to involve your procurement representative from the start. Clarify any, and all, procurement requirements and procedures that you need to follow. Clarify who owns vendor communications. Clarify your role versus the role of the Procurement Lead.
- **Establish a clear process**—With your evaluation team, develop a clear game plan for the overall selection that emphasizes objectivity and neutrality. Review approach with your key stakeholders. This goes a long way to build confidence in your direction.

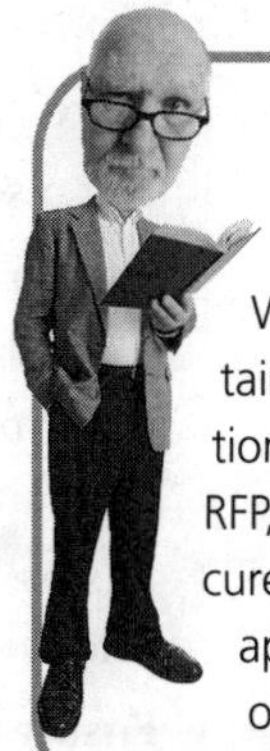

tip

Whenever possible, maintain ownership of all selection documents (RFI, RFQ, RFP, and so on). Assign procurement "review and approval" responsibilities only.

- **Factors to consider**—In addition to aligning with the risk level involved, make sure to consider these other factors before finalizing your selection methodology:
    - How much time do you have?
    - How many vendors/options do you need to evaluate?
    - What is the normal level of investment that vendors are willing to make in an evaluation process?
    - How many evaluators are involved?
    - Where are your evaluators located?
    - How available are your evaluators?
- **Tailor process to evaluators**—As you develop your selection process with your evaluation team, determine what methods would work better for your team. This is closely related to understanding the learning styles and personalities of your team members (and organization). For some, reviewing and scoring a 100 page RFP response is a great fit, for others, not so much. For some, participating in an interactive, online demonstration works great, because they can see something in action, they can ask direct questions, and it's a flexible use of their time. For others, they might lose context perspective or might not fully engage due to multitasking lures.
- **Evaluation criteria**—Determine what criteria will be evaluated. Develop a small set of "must-have" requirements, often referred to as "knockout" criteria, that can be used to quickly narrow your candidate list to a short list. In addition, for your longer list of evaluation criteria, establish a priority level for each criterion. You will need this for your scoring process.
- **Evaluation scoring**—As part of your goal to have an objective process, it is imperative that your scoring process be determined in advance, agreed to by key stakeholders, documented, communicated clearly to all evaluators, and executed as designed. Here is a list of key considerations for your evaluation scoring process:
    - Score against evaluation criteria and requirements "fit"
    - Use a scoring scale with clear differentiators between each score value
    - Use an even number of scoring options whenever possible to avoid a middle-of-the-road, on-the-fence option
    - Determine how non-responses will be handled; make sure they do not skew the final scores
    - Ensure there is a clear method to distinguish between a "poor" score and a "nonapplicable" criteria
    - Ensure stakeholder community is fairly represented

- Determine if scores from specific stakeholder groups will carry greater weight
- Encourage each stakeholder group (department, business unit) to reach a consensus score to ensure that the number of final scores considered remains proportional
- Conduct preview (or readiness) sessions with all evaluation participants
- Ensure all participants are clear on evaluation logistics, the scoring process, and related assumptions
- Archive the original evaluation scores from each participant

tip

To improve the quality of your evaluation scoring process, conduct preview (or readiness) sessions with all stakeholders who will provide feedback to review logistics, scoring process, and related assumptions.

- **Open-book approach**—From my experience, I favor an "open-book" approach with the candidate vendors. You can mitigate your risk with sharing confidential information with non-disclosure agreements (NDA) or confidentiality agreements. The benefits far outweigh the risks. The more open, the more complete, the clearer you are with your candidates about your requirements, your context and your expectations, the better the candidate responses will be and the more efficient your selection process will be.
- **Clarify timing of each process step**—As an essential aspect of managing expectations for both you and your candidate vendors, make sure to communicate the timetable for your overall selection process to the candidate vendors. This helps the candidates plan appropriately, which should help increase the quality of your selection process. In addition, you should clearly communicate the specific timing expectations for any scheduled events or expected responses. If you need to have a documented response by Friday, provide the exact time the response is to be received, such as 12 noon Eastern Time.
- **Control vendor communications**—As part of your efforts to manage expectations and to keep the process objective, clarify who owns what aspects of vendor communications with your own team. In addition, clearly set expectations with your candidate vendors, such as who they are authorized to contact within your organization.
- **Be consistent and fair**—Be diligent that your process is consistent and fair. Be sure each candidate follows the same steps, is given the same opportunities, has access to the same information, and is evaluated using the same criteria.

- **Value your vendor contacts**—Handle all interactions with your candidate vendor contacts with professionalism, candor, and respect. Show appreciation for their interest and investment. Even if you do not select the vendor for this opportunity, you may need their services on down the road. Plus, it never hurts your career to showcase your skills and professionalism with others in your industry and marketplace.
- **Leverage expertise**—There are times, often as a step to further reduce risk, that organizations hire firms (or individuals) to help them with their selection projects. The help can range from background consulting or advising roles to out-in-front leading the project roles.
- **Get to "short list" quickly**—The key to streamlining a selection process is to get to your short list as fast as you can. The short list represents the candidates who have a real opportunity to be selected. Depending on level of due diligence that is required on a final recommendation, you may need to go from a short list to a list of finalists in order to control the effort and cost required to get to a final recommendation.
- **Document gaps**—As part of your evaluation process, make sure to document the gaps between the candidate vendor's solution and your required future state. You need to develop the plan and figure the additional costs to address these gaps. This is a factor when evaluating your options.
- **Focus on partnerships for strategic projects**—When dealing with strategic initiatives, encourage your senior management to focus on partnership relationships versus the lowest cost option.
- **Include negotiation and contract development times**—When developing schedules for selection processes, make sure to allocate sufficient, realistic time blocks for negotiations and contract developments. It is common to underestimate this time, especially in corporate environments. When building your schedule, ask the procurement and legal groups for their input on this, then keep them in your information loop throughout the process.

caution

The nature of negotiations and contract development efforts make them automatic schedule risks.

Tips for Managing a Testing Process

Here's a list of tips and insights from my experience that can help you manage a testing process and avoid many of the common pitfalls:

- **Leverage expertise**—As with any skill or experience that is in low supply on your team, consider procuring testing professionals to assist your effort.

caution

Many testing issues result from a lack of forethought on the management of test data and the detailed logistics of test execution.

- **Trace to requirements**—Think "testing" from the start of the project. Use a requirements traceability matrix to ensure that the final work product(s) satisfy the targeted requirements and all those requirements were properly validated.
- **Develop test plan**—Take the time to plan your testing effort and to document your plan. This is critical when your testing process involves resources that are not dedicated to the project effort. In addition, the test plan should address the "test data" that is needed and how it will be managed, and it should address how the actual test execution will occur.

Review Chapter 15, "Managing Project Quality," for more tips on how to better manage an effective testing process.

- **Types of testing**—Determine what types of testing you will perform. This is generally a factor of risk, schedule, and budget.
- **Think customer experience**—Do not limit your focus to functional testing. Place your focus on the overall customer experience. Key aspects of most customer experience are usability, data, and performance. If the performance risk is sufficient, I strongly recommend the use of load testing tools.
- **Identify high risk items**—Clarify the high risk areas in your solution or in the customer's acceptance of your solution. These should be your priorities. Start testing these as early as possible.
- **Plan on multiple iterations**—When estimating the time for test execution, make sure to include time for multiple iterations. Because it is difficult to know how many iterations it will take, estimates for test execution are often time-blocked and based on historical experiences.
- "**To script or not to script**"—This is often a controversial subject in testing endeavors. Do you need to document (script) how the tester performs each test case? Well, it all depends. If it is a requirement of your organizational methodology, then you'll need to do it. After this, it depends on the

value it would provide. If your testers do not have knowledge or experience with the targeted work product, then you may need to do it. If your testing efforts will be repeated or are a candidate for automated testing, then you may want to do it. Another benefit of test scripts is that it can make it easier to communicate test defects.

- **Don't forget the data**—Data drives organizations. If your project involves data migration, data conversion, or data loading, realize that you need to develop procedures for validating the data is correct and acceptable too.
- **Simulate production**—Closely related to "think customer experience," your test plan should include a testing stage that occurs in an environment that mirrors (or gets as close as possible to) your production environment, the environment that your customer will actually interact with your solution. If you cannot do this, you have a major project risk.
- **Leverage checklists**—Checklists are simple, yet powerful. They clearly capture and communicate the quality standards that must be met by the targeted work package, and they improve project team productivity. They are flexible—separate checklists can be developed for each work product or project management process. They provide a mechanism to capture the lessons learned from past projects. They can also provide a mechanism to document the verification performed on the work package.
- **Completion criteria**—This starts during project definition with defining the acceptance criteria for the project, and it continues for each deliverable and work assignment. Answer this question in advance for each deliverable: "How will we know when it is done?" Understanding the completion criteria up front increases productivity and avoids much of the re-work that can occur when quality requirements are not understood up front.
- **Readiness checkpoints**—To improve the quality of test execution, to better manage expectations of all testing process participants, and to ensure all prerequisite test execution events are completed, schedule testing readiness checkpoints before the start of any new test execution phase.
- **Capture metrics**—To increase the professionalism of the testing process, keep track of the following in your testing process:
    - Traceability to requirements
    - Number of test runs
    - Number of total test cases
    - Number of total defects
    - Number of defects by severity level
    - Number of defects resolved
    - Number of defects closed
- **Determine defect tracking process**—Determine how test defects will be captured, documented, and logged. From there, decide how each defect will be assessed and assigned and who is involved in each step. Once the defect is resolved, determine who needs to verify (re-test) that the corrective action meets expectations.

- **Pre-test customer acceptance**—Here's an excellent expectation management technique. Always test whatever your customer is going to test first; there should be no surprises. This also applies to verifying any resolved defects.
- **Use Defect Tracking/Management system**—Whenever possible, use an online defect management system to capture the defect tracking process you develop. The system helps implement the process, provides visibility, and enforces accountability.

THE ABSOLUTE MINIMUM

At this point, you should have a solid understanding of the following:

- In project management lite environments:
  - Nail the core project definition and planning fundamentals.
  - Focus on communication, relationships, and managing expectations.
  - Emphasize "value-added" deliverables only.
  - Right size your monitoring and tracking procedures.
- If you are unable to develop a detailed schedule, leverage one or more of the following techniques:
  - Manage to milestones, deliverables, and/or project phases.
  - Focus on detail plans for the next 30/60/90 day milestone.
- When your project must hit a hard milestone date, keep these tips in mind:
  - Give yourself a contingency buffer.
  - Manage scope tenaciously.
  - Focus on team productivity.
  - Clarify what the end result looks like and get buy-in from stakeholders.
  - Strongly consider phased implementations.
- If you encounter difficult resources, consider the following pointers:
  - Stay calm and clarify whether your perception is correct.
  - Remember that difficult resources are often passionate, but frustrated, people who can be great assets to your management efforts.
- The longer the project, the more likely that resource turnover will occur.
- Keys to managing a selection process include:
  - Clarify the purpose and goals of the selection process.
  - Scale your process to the risk level involved.
  - Partner with your procurement representative.
  - Establish a clear, objective, fair process.

continues

- Keys to managing a testing process include:
  - Trace back to requirements.
  - Focus on high risk items and on the customer experience.
  - Develop a test plan.
  - Capture testing metrics.
  - Leverage a defect management system whenever possible.

Figure 24.1 summarizes the main points we reviewed in this chapter.

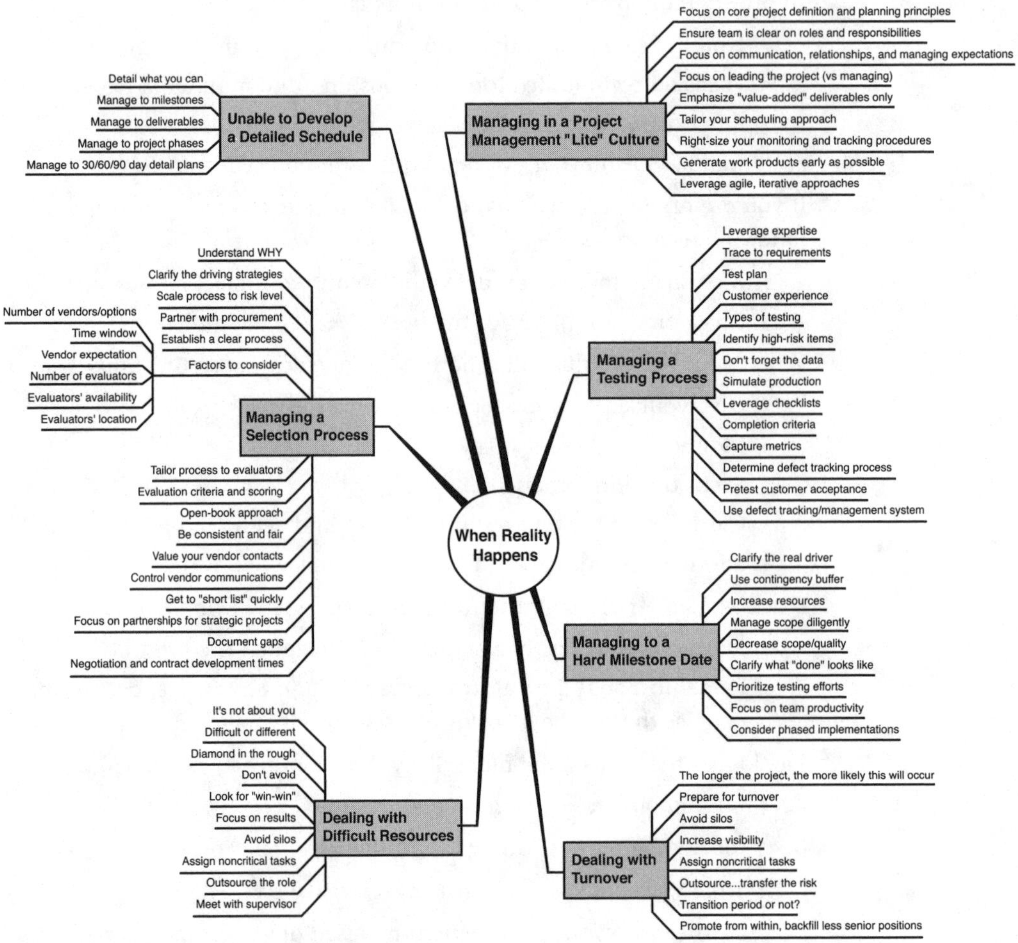

FIGURE 24.1

When reality happens overview.

IN THIS CHAPTER

- Improve your understanding of agile project management approaches
- Learn why there is varied perception on Project Management Offices (PMOs) and what they should do
- Review the common traits of successful PMO implementations
- Improve your understanding of portfolio project management
- Clarify what Critical Chain Project Management is and how it is different
- Increase your awareness of web-based project management software options
- Increase your awareness of mind-mapping tools and how they can help you as a project manager
- Review the value of project management certification
- Review options for additional project management training

25

INTRIGUING PROJECT MANAGEMENT CONCEPTS AND TOPICS

One of the wonderful things about the project management field is there is always more to learn. With this in mind, I want to offer information and insights on additional project management concepts, tools, trends and topics that you are likely to encounter in the workplace to further accelerate your learning curve—or at the very least allow you to discuss these topics with confidence amongst your peers.

Agile Approaches

The term "agile" is used more and more often these days, but I am not sure there is a common understanding of what an agile project approach is and how it is different from more traditional project approaches. I believe this occurs for three primary reasons:

- The agile approach is still relatively new as business practice in many circles
- There are several terms that are used interchangeably with "agile", including iterative, flexible, adaptive, and extreme
- It is rarely implemented as a pure methodology

In most cases, agile techniques are incorporated into more traditional approaches, and in fact, many organizational project methodologies are evolving to adopt the agile practices that work well in their environment.

To help your understanding of agile project management techniques and to increase your confidence in discussing agile methodologies, let's review the common characteristics of agile project management approaches.

- **Iterative development**—Agile approaches take an iterative approach to the development of the targeted solution. It is an excellent technique when the complete set of requirements cannot be gathered, visualized, or agreed to. In some circles, these iterations are called waves, sprints, phases, or even milestones. Other iterative development techniques can include prototypes, pilot projects, and focus groups. The principle behind the approach is to focus on priority requirements, deliver tangible solutions for evaluation as early as possible, and to finish with the desired result.
- **Phased deployment**—In most cases, agile approaches also emphasize an iterative or phased approach to deployment, techniques that we have discussed before as excellent risk management approaches. Any use of test markets, beta releases, pilot projects, phased implementations, or staged rollouts are examples of phased deployments.
- **Detailed, short-term schedules**—Agile approaches focus on detailed schedules for the near-term milestone (current iteration, phase, or wave). The schedule for rest of the project is kept high-level, general, and frequently time-boxed based on historical performances. This is done because the future path of the project is determined (and can be adjusted) based on the actual results and findings of the current iteration. In most cases, an iteration is between 30–60 days.
- **Customer value-driven**—Agile approaches are focused on customer satisfaction. The emphasis is on delivering value, delivering tangible solutions as early as possible. The goal is to get feedback and clarify requirements as

soon as possible. With an iterative approach, the customer stays involved, makes decisions with better data (reviewing tangible results), and remains in control throughout the project.

- **Timeboxing**—Timeboxing is a trademark characteristic of iterative software development methodologies, but has use in many project environments and has grown in popularity as a project scheduling technique. In a pure sense, the work requirements (scope) for a given timebox are set (fixed), and little, to any, change is allowed to occur. The time element is strictly enforced, regardless of work completion status. At the end of the timebox, a customer review is conducted to evaluate the results and to plan the scope of the next iteration. Requirement priority, refinement of requirements and progress to-date all determine the scope of the next iteration. Timeboxing is an effective technique in situations with high uncertainty or situations that need frequent review and evaluation.
- **Change expected**—This is a core differentiator of agile approaches. Agile approaches expect change and are ideal when the unknowns and unpredictability factors are high.
- **Plan-do-review**—Agile approaches emphasize the "plan-do-review" model. Subsequent planning increments are driven by results achieved at the finale of the recently completed iteration, milestone, or timebox.
- **Solution-focused**—Agile approaches focus on the customer experience and on what the customer is after: The targeted solution. There is a strong results-orientation with an emphasis on early value and on clarifying requirements based on experience and evaluating tangible results.
- **People-focused project management**—Agile project management emphasizes the "people" aspect of projects over the bureaucratic, administrative procedures. The focus is on relationships, leading (versus managing), and value. Project management deliverables are limited to the minimal set that offers the most value. Servant leadership principles are a strong fit for agile approaches.
- **Collaborative**—Collaborative development approaches are another common trait of agile methodologies. There is a partnering arrangement between customer and the design-development team, and the normal boundaries are minimized, if not removed. Customers are placed on the core team, and in many cases, collocated with the project team. In addition, the iterative development approach emphasizes frequent feedback loop and continuous focus on the customer's requirements.
- **Risk management focused**—You can argue that the main purpose of an agile project approach is to manage risk. The key risk being that the final solution will not meet the satisfaction of the customer. The agile techniques

of progressive requirement development, short iterations, partnering close to your customers, prototyping, attacking high risk solution aspects early, and people-focused management all contribute to managing this essential risk.

Project Management Offices

The nature, scope, and overall effectiveness of a given Project Management Office (PMO) vary from organization to organization. As a result, there is a wide perception of the value that a PMO offers and a lack of consensus on what it is supposed to do. As a project manager, you need to be clear on the responsibilities that your PMO has, how it can assist you on your project, and how you need to work it during your project. In many situations, your PMO reports are separate and distinct from your status reporting and implemented as an individual line item on your communications plan.

To start, the organizational scope of a PMO can vary tremendously. Some of the first PMOs were developed to manage enterprise projects, such as enterprise resource planning (ERP) implementations. Since then, the scope of PMOs has expanded. In some organizations, the PMO is at the corporate, enterprise level. In others, it is positioned at the business unit or department level. The level is often determined by organizational culture, stage of PMO evolution within the organization, and organizational priority.

In some organizations, the PMO is referred to as the Program Management Office.

In either case, the nature and authority of the PMO falls somewhere on a spectrum. On one end of the spectrum is the support mode. In support mode, a PMO provides project managers with training, guidance, templates, and best practices. On the other end of the spectrum is the central planning, project oversight mode. In this mode, the PMOs provide all the project managers, control the portfolio management process, manage resource allocation, and closely monitor the performance of each project. In addition, the scope of a PMO is not always limited to projects. In some organizations, PMOs are used to monitor and oversee service level agreements with vendors. Specifically, the responsibilities of a given PMO are a combination of the following:

- **Project support**—Provide project management guidance to project managers in business units.
- **Methodology**—Develop and implement a consistent and standardized project management process.

- **Training**—Conduct or outsource project management training.
- **Consulting and mentoring**—Coach employees on best practices.
- **Tools**—Select and administer project management related tools for use by organization.
- **Program management**—Provide management and oversight of multiple, related projects.
- **Portfolio management**—Establish process for requesting, prioritizing, and approving projects. In addition, establish a process for canceling projects that are not meeting portfolio performance standards.
- **Resource management**—Establish and execute processes to ensure resources are allocated effectively based on the portfolio priorities.
- **Monitor SLAs**—Monitor performance of and adherence to service level agreements.

Historically, most PMOs were started by CIOs to provide the needed structure to standardize project management practices, facilitate IT project portfolio management, and develop methodologies for repeatable processes. Today, the best PMOs leverage the organization culture to successfully deliver the project portfolio in a way that satisfies both senior management and the targeted customers. By enabling better resource management, reducing project failures, and supporting projects that offer the biggest return on investment, PMOs can provide the foundation for effectively managing any business.

In most organizations, the PMO is charged with directing the project portfolio management process.

The specific organization and staffing model for a PMO depends on a myriad of organizational factors, including priority organizational pains, targeted goals, natural organizational strengths, strengths of existing resources, and corporate culture.

Traits of Successful PMOs

Now, for all the value that a PMO can provide, there are many organizations that have not experienced success with PMOs. Rather than focus on where many PMO implementations have failed, let's take a more positive tact. Let's review common traits of successful PMO implementations, and you can infer the reasons why some have been less than successful.

- **Aligned with corporate culture**—PMO implementations are "change management" exercises. Developing an effective PMO involves strategy, reviewing industry standards and best practices, process tailoring, patience, and persistence. This can be a challenge and requires some finesse, especially if the culture has not valued disciplined approaches in the past.
- **Communicate purpose and vision clearly**—Develop and implement a consistent and standardized project management process.
- **Garner senior management support**—A key part of the PMO implementation strategy is to understand the best ways to involve senior management. Common methods are through sponsorship or direct reporting relationships. It is essential that senior management understands the value of the PMO and serves as a champion for the PMO purpose.
- **Learn from pilot projects**—Many successful PMO implementations start with well-defined pilot projects for a given business area or type of project. The project(s) relies heavily on the feedback from the project managers and senior management involved to tailor the PMO approach.
- **Evolve over time**—Many PMOs have started with a support focus and then moved down the service spectrum over time. In other instances, a PMO implementation focuses on immediate pain areas (such as improving planning efforts) and then expands into other areas once consistency is achieved.
- **Standardize the fundamentals**—Every project is different, but the core project management fundamentals can be standardized. Effective PMOs ensure that the processes, techniques, and tools around project, planning, estimating, and reporting are consistent, predictable, and value-added. This includes providing a repository of project templates and checklists.
- **Focus on value-added deliverables**—Effective PMOs want to streamline paperwork and reduce the document approval cycles in a given project. As a result, they seek to combine deliverables when possible and attempt to leverage online, collaborative project management information systems.
- **Provide project administration support**—Rather than require additional project administration efforts from the project managers, PMOs that assign project administrators to work with the project managers enable the project manager to focus on leading the project team, resolving issues, and clearing the path of obstacles.
- **Focus on getting projects done**—Effective PMOs encourage and support their project managers to be "project leaders," to be people on the ground, with the troops, and focused on project execution.
- **Bring objectivity to the project initiation process**—The last thing the PMO needs is to have people believe that projects are subjectively approved.

When this happens, people circumvent normal channels for getting projects approved, resulting in increased lobbying and political end-runs; both of which do not work in favor of the organization's well-being and long-term success. By adopting a pragmatic approach that is based on quantifiable criteria for evaluating, approving, and prioritizing the project, the PMO can stand above the fray and avoid getting caught in political crossfire, while still acknowledging and balancing the political realities of the process.

- **Justify projects on pessimistic scenarios**—This is an organizational executive management decision. However, when it comes to estimates for budget, work effort, and completion dates, the PMO should encourage the development of multiple scenarios for any project request, especially pessimistic or "worst-case" ones. This is especially important because most project estimates are way too optimistic. Because project portfolios should be managed like investments, this allows for safer, more conservative financial projections. The key here is to understand the difference between "justifying" (or funding) a project investment and the expectations for the actual execution of the project. A pessimistic basis for justification can be totally independent from the assumptions and estimates used to guide the delivery of the project.
- **Allocate resources intelligently**—Effective PMOs monitor resource schedules and limit, if not prevent, resources from being over-allocated and from having to focus on more than one major initiative at a time. Although this ties into our discussion of Critical Chain Project Management later in this chapter, it really is common sense. Results have shown that multitasking is not productive and leads to longer work days and weeks, which can lead to frustrated workers.
- **Align strategy with delivery**—Effective PMOs partner closely with the executive team to make sure the project portfolio investments are aligned with the corporate goals and strategies.

Portfolio Project Management

Portfolio Project Management (PPM) describes various approaches to managing projects as part of an overall project investment portfolio. PPM focuses on project initiation (determining which projects should be funded), aligning projects with corporate strategy, aligning resources with those project priorities, and monitoring performance of the project portfolio throughout the year. The practice evolved out of the growing reality that more and more business is accomplished through projects, the concern that too many projects did not succeed, and the lack of visibility that many executives had on ongoing project performance.

Here's a list of additional insights and observations to help you better understand portfolio project management topics:

- **Portfolio project management is NOT program management**—This is a natural point of confusion due mainly to the terms used and to the role of many PMO organizations. Portfolio project management is focused on the "investment" aspect of the project funding decisions. Program and project management is focused on the delivery (execution) of those projects in the portfolio.
- **Never be totally objective**—Implementing portfolio management is political by nature. Most portfolio project management advocates emphasize the dimension of objectivity and the focus on quantifiable metrics introduced into the project request evaluation and approval processes for an organization. To their credit, portfolio project management processes do reduce the degree of political influence. However, people make these final decisions and the profit centers still carry tremendous influence in determining what projects are funded.
- **Element of corporate governance**—In many organizations, project portfolio management is closely tied to the corporate governance process. The senior management (or executive) group that determines the project portfolio is the same group checking project performance status on a periodic basis.
- **PPM software**—A full PPM solution manages demand (work requests) and resource allocation, prioritizes requests, and monitors investment performance.
- **May or may not include resource management**—Some organizations include resource management as part of PPM while others do not. This is something to clarify when starting in a new organization. If it is not included, there should be tight integration with the corporate resource planning and allocation processes.
- **Separate reporting process**—In most organizations, the status reporting you do for your PPM tool and the corporate governance process is different than what you do for the project leadership team. This occurs because of the limitations of the PPM tool and because of the amount of detail that the executive committee wants to see. From the advancements I see in PPM solutions and the current state of many web-based project management software offerings, I think this will change in the future.
- **Finding the balance**—You have to find balance for your given organization. While most senior management types do not want (nor have time for) the details of your project, they also do not want to be surprised. They do not

want to see a project "green" (it's going great) one reporting period and then "red" (help me, I'm in big trouble) the next. This is one of the main advantages of exception-based or stoplight-based status reporting approaches. From my experience, I tend to go "yellow" on any dimension with a high-impact risk or current issue.

Governance Processes

Okay, corporate governance is not exactly a hot (or new) concept, but it is term that gets thrown around a lot and often not explained to people who are new to the scene. Because it is closely associated to portfolio project management (PPM) and project management offices (PMOs), I thought it would be helpful to put this concept in proper context too.

Here's a few insights and observations from my experience that can help you better understand corporate governance topics:

- **Portfolio project management is part of corporate governance**—This is discussed in the previous section.
- **Other elements of corporate governance**—Corporate governance can include more than just project portfolio management. In most cases, the additional governance scope is needed to ensure compliance with strategies, standards, policies, and regulations. Specifically, other corporate governance processes can include:
    - IT Governance (compliance with architectural standards)
    - Procurement
    - HR
    - Resource management
    - Legal
    - Regulatory
    - Quality Assurance

Critical Chain Project Management

Critical Chain Project Management (CCPM) is a management practice beginning to gain momentum. As a relatively new project manager, you may find yourself working in an organization using CCPM, or you may be hearing more about it and just wondering what is so different about it. My objective is to give a brief synopsis of CCPM, clarify the key unique features, and provide you a basis for further discussion and discovery.

CCPM is a method of planning and managing projects based on Eliyahu M. Goldratt's Theory of Constraints. It is a method that emphasizes resource management and speed. It is a method that aims to remove the slack that is built in to most schedules. It is a method that requires a different approach to schedule development, project execution, and to monitoring project performance. Let's take a closer look at some specific features to help you better understand the principles and uniqueness of CCPM:

- **Critical chain**—CCPM identifies and focuses on the critical chain, as opposed to the critical path. Resources are then assigned to each task, and the plan is resource leveled using the 50% estimates. The longest sequence of resource-leveled tasks that lead from the beginning to the end of the project is then identified as the critical chain. If there are no resource constraints (and resources are leveled), then the critical chain and the critical path are the same.
- **System**—In CCPM this term refers to all tasks in the schedule.
- **Two estimates for each task**—When estimating the work effort or duration for a task, two estimates are developed. One estimate is called the 50% probability estimate, the other one is the 90% probability estimate. The 50% probability means exactly that; the task has a 50-50 chance of completing within that effort/time estimate. The assumption is that most schedules are based on 90% probability estimates.
- **Schedule on the 50% probability estimate**—A CCPM schedule is built based on the 50% probability estimates. The justification for using the 50% estimates is that half of the tasks will finish early and half will finish late, so that the variance over the course of the project should be zero.
- **Pool the differences into a buffer**—The difference between the two estimates are pooled into a buffer, called the *project buffer*. This buffer is added to the end of the project schedule to protect the targeted completion date.
- **Feeder buffers**—In addition to the project buffer, CCPM also uses a series of feeder buffers to further protect the critical chain. Any non-critical chain task that feeds into the critical chain sequence has a buffer, a *feeder buffer*, inserted between the non-critical chain task and the critical chain.
- **Resource focus**—CCPM is focused on resource constraints and on resource productivity. You will read and hear a lot about "throughput." It is a requirement that schedules are resource leveled, in order to reduce, if not avoid multitasking.
- **Resource transition**—The CCPM references discuss a third buffer type—a *resource buffer*. This is a bit confusing, because it is not a buffer in the same sense of the project buffer and the feeder buffers. The resource buffer focuses

on project execution and on the process of transitioning a task sequence from one resource to another. The process involves direct communication between the resources (performers) assigned to the two tasks. The predecessor task resources notify the successor task resources on regular, predetermined intervals about their expected completion date. Further, a final confirmation should be given a day or two before task completion so all successor task performers are ready to start work exactly when needed. Goldratt calls this notification process the *resource buffer*. It is a simple, yet effective method to ensure that a task starts exactly when it should. Early finishes are not wasted.

- **Relay runners**—As hinted at in the previous section, the mode that resources operate in a CCPM project is that of a relay runner. The resource knows when the baton is coming (predecessor task completed), as soon as the baton arrives the resource stays focused and gets the task completed as fast as it can, and then hands off the baton to the next runner (resource assigned to successor task).
- **Efficiency of pooled buffers**—This is a strong component of CCPM. By pooling the usual slack found in task estimates into buffers and setting up task management procedures that encourage and reward speed, a project can take advantage of the time gains that would normally be hidden or eaten up from multitasking, student syndrome, Parkinson's Law, inbox delays, lack of prioritization, or task handoff inefficiencies. If any particular task is delayed or completes later than the 50% estimate, the project manager "borrows" time from the project buffer and adds it to the offending activity. On the other hand, if an activity finishes early the gain is added to the project buffer.
- **Monitor the buffers for project health**—Overall project health is measured by monitoring the feeder and project buffers. If the rate of buffer consumption is low, the project is on target. If the rate of consumption is such that there is likely to be little or no buffer at the end of the project, then corrective actions or recovery plans must be developed to recover the loss. When the buffer consumption rate exceeds some threshold value (a rate that puts the buffer at risk of being consumed before the project is complete), then those response plans need to be implemented. CCPM advocates feel that buffer management is better than earned

Student syndrome is the term used to describe the common tendency is to procrastinate until the last moment. *Parkinson's Law* states that work expands to fill the allocated time.

value management (EVM) for measuring project performance, because the earned value management technique can be misleading. EVM does not distinguish progress on the project constraint (the critical chain) from progress on non-constraints

Web-Based Project Management Software

As much as I appreciate Microsoft Project, and as popular as it is, and as much I have used it in the past and certainly will for some time in the future, the purpose of this section is to make sure you are aware of the other options are available to you. If your project requires (or could benefit from) sharing project information with clients, vendors, subcontractors, a mobile or geographically dispersed team, or anyone located outside your corporate networks, you should consider web-based project management software solutions. Some of the attractive features of web-based project management software solutions include:

- No software installation required except your web browser.
- It can be much less expensive than Project. Depending on the features you require and ability to leverage open source options, it can even be free.
- Ability to update tasks and project plans from anywhere.
- Automatically creates more of a team collaboration environment.
- Provides for better visibility and openness.
- Can be deployed within a day, depending on need and licensing arrangement.
- Most vendors offer Software as a Service (SaaS) models.
- Many vendors offer hosted or installed "On Premise" options for environments that have tight security requirements.
- Faster and enhanced working processes.
- Short learning curves.

There are many options available now, and the list continues to grow. If you can consider web-based solutions, here are key elements to consider in your selection and evaluation process:

- Project management feature set required
- Enterprise visibility
- Cost
- Return on Investment
- Ease-of-use; training required

- Platform independence
- Scalability
- Integration ease
- Ability to focus on work and not status reporting effort
- Level and granularity of security needed
- Ability to use for client access
- Disaster recovery services offered (backups, prevention of data loss)

Mind Mapping Tools

Mind mapping software allows you to build, modify, and share mind maps electronically. A mind map is a diagram that contains information pieces (words, ideas, pictures, tasks, etc.) arranged radially around a central theme (key word or idea).

A mind map allows you to do visual thinking. It allows us to capture and communicate related information in a manner that is more aligned with how the brain organizes data and information. They have been used successfully in brainstorming environments to generate, visualize, and structure ideas. They have also been used as powerful aids in learning new concepts, note taking, problem solving, decision making, and in writing. I have provided basic, simple mind maps at the end of each chapter using the MindManager tool from Mindjet (www.mindjet.com).

caution

While visual thinking is exciting and most people prefer it, it will seem awkward to others, especially those who are more comfortable with linear organization structures.

So, why do I include this in a project management book? Why is the use and acceptance of mind mapping tools growing rapidly? Why are more and more organizations adding mind mapping tools to their productivity tool arsenal? To help answer these questions, let me offer these insights based on my own experience:

tip

One simple, but powerful, productivity enhancer for project managers is to use mind maps for meeting notes.

- **Ability for one-page communications**—The ability to communicate large amounts of information and the most complex concepts on a single page in an easy-to-understand manner is powerful.
- **Visual appeal**—There is a "wow" fac-

tor. It's different, but at the same time more natural for many audiences. It catches your attention and draws you in.

- **Collaborative nature**—It was built for collaborative work sessions. For a project manager, it is a powerful medium for planning a project.
- **Integration power**—Mind maps provide a portal-like home base for all documents, deliverables, or artifacts associated with the subject of the mind map. In addition, the best mind mapping software provide for easy integration with your other productivity suite software (like Microsoft Office and Project).

Tony Buzan, a British psychology author and educational consultant, is regarded as the modern father of mind mapping techniques.

- **Streamline paperwork**—Due to the organizational power and visual appeal of mind maps, information can be shared and communicated effectively simply by sharing the mind maps. There is a reduced need for additional documents to be created.
- **Working smarter**—As the pace of work increases and the nature of work becomes more collaborative, organizations, and knowledge professionals continuously look for ways to work smarter and to be more productive. Mind mapping tools can facilitate these goals.

Value of Certifications

This is always a hot topic, and not just in the project management circles. What is the value of certifications? What does having one mean? What does it really measure? These questions are fair, especially in a profession like project management that requires skills and talents that are difficult to measure in standardize testing approaches. The most popular project management certification is the Project Management Professional (PMP) from the Project Management Institute (PMI). In addition, PMI has added new certifications listed here:

- **PgMP**— Program Management Professional
- **PMI-RMP**—PMI Risk Management Professional
- **PMI-SP**—PMI Scheduling Professional

Okay, I may not be the most objective person in the world, because I am a PMP, but I think I can offer helpful insight on the value of project management certification.

- **Get serious**—By earning a certification, you demonstrate a mindset that says to others that you take your work and your profession seriously.

- **Common understanding**—A certification does not guarantee performance or results, but it does ensure that you share a vocabulary and a common understanding of fundamental project management processes.
- **Differentiator**—In a competitive marketplace, any method to further differentiate yourself from your peers never hurts, and earning a credential is good way to do that.
- **Marketability**—More and more employers are using the PMP credential as a base requirement for their project management positions.
- **Compensation**—Studies have shown that the average compensation level of certified professionals is higher than their non-certified counterparts.

Current PMI certifications—www.pmi.org:

CAPM—Certified Associate Project Management Professional

PMP—Project Management Professional

PgMP—Program Management Professional

PMI-RMP—PMI Risk Management Professional

PMI-SP—PMI Scheduling Professional

Project Management Training

When it comes to project management training, there is a wide variety of options out there. In the same way, it can be difficult to test for project management skills, it can be equally challenging trying to "train" someone to be a project manager. From my experience, here are a few insights and observations I've accumulated over the years on project management training:

- **Mentoring**—The absolute best way to learn project management is to observe it being done well. When possible, newer project managers should serve on a project team with a more senior project leader. This could be as a project manager with a senior program manager, or it could be as a project coordinator, a project administrator, a business analyst/lead (if skill set applies), or as a technical lead (again, if the skill set applies) with a senior project managers who enjoys the opportunities to mentor others.
- **Focus on specific skills**—Another worthy training strategy is to focus on one skill set at a time. In most cases, professionals have specific areas they need to improve, and often when these skills are improved, it will have a cascading effect on other areas of performance.
- **Simulations**—Given the nature of projects, it is difficult to anticipate the

specific situations and scenarios that a project manager will face or to bring the reality of projects to the classroom environment. Due to the improvements in technology over the years, a tremendous advancement in training is the use of computer and gaming simulations. I am convinced this is the future for all training efforts.

- **Computer based**—I find computer-based, web-based, virtual training offerings (webinars, online seminars, and so on) to be an efficient and convenient method for staying informed on current trends and tools and for refreshing key fundamentals.
- **PMI Special Interest Group Conferences**—I have received a lot of benefit from attending the educational conferences provided by the PMI special interest groups. I believe the main reason for this is the presentations are provided by practitioners from the field and the content is very current and relevant.
- **Skills to target**—As you gain experience in project management and attain a certain mastery of the project management fundamentals, it can be more difficult to find project management training that offers a lot of value to you. Well, one of the great things about project management is that it covers almost all aspects of business, management, and your industry, so there is never a shortage of things to learn about or improve upon. For most people, there is value in acquiring additional training in the following areas:
    - Business management
    - Procurement
    - Leadership
    - Quality techniques
    - People management
- **Tool-specific**—Especially tools used for project management, communication, and collaboration.

THE ABSOLUTE MINIMUM

At this point, you should have a solid understanding of the following:

- Agile project management approaches are characterized by change expectant, iterative development, phased deployments, collaboration, people focus, customer focus, timeboxing, detailed near-term schedules, frequent feedback loops, and constant risk management.
- The scope and responsibility of a PMO varies by organization and maturity level.
- Common traits of successful PMO implementations include alignment with corporate culture, clear purpose, senior management support, evolution over time, focus on getting projects done, and a focus on aligning strategy with project delivery.
- Project portfolio management focuses on project initiation, aligning projects with corporate strategy, aligning resources with those project priorities, and monitoring performance of the project portfolio.
- Unique features of critical chain project management include the focus on throughput, task execution speed, resource constraints, scheduling on 50% probability task estimates, and the use of buffers to protect the completion date and to monitor project performance.
- Web-based project management software solutions are excellent options for virtual, geographically dispersed teams.
- Mind mapping tools foster collaboration, simplify communication, and provide potential for increased work productivity.
- Certifications demonstrate that you take your work and profession seriously.
- Effective project management training approaches include mentoring and simulations.
- For additional information on agile project management approaches:
  - Agile Project Leadership Network: apln.org
  - www.dougdecarlo.com
  - www.jimhighsmith.com
  - Flexible Development by Preston Smith: www.flexibledevelopment.com

Figure 25.1 summarizes the main points we reviewed in this chapter.

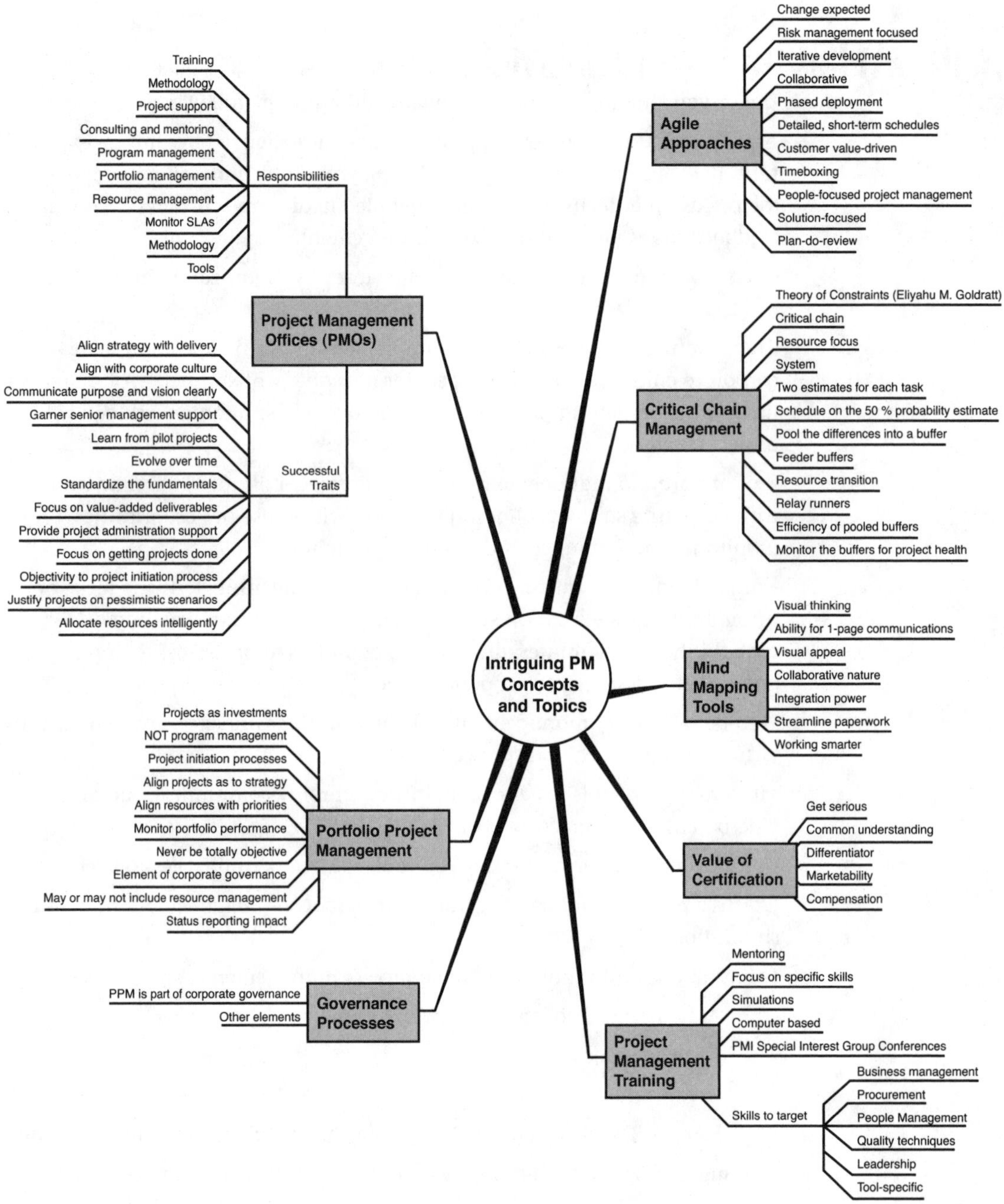

FIGURE 25.1

Intriguing project management concepts and topics summary.

Index

Numerics

A

C

How can we make this index more useful? Email us at indexes@quepublishing.com

How can we make this index more useful? Email us at indexes@quepublishing.com

D

How can we make this index more useful? Email us at indexes@quepublishing.com

F

G

How can we make this index more useful? Email us at indexes@quepublishing.com

J–K

L

How can we make this index more useful? Email us at indexes@quepublishing.com

N

O

P

Q

R

How can we make this index more useful? Email us at indexes@quepublishing.com

S

How can we make this index more useful? Email us at indexes@quepublishing.com

T

U

V

W–Z

How can we make this index more useful? Email us at indexes@quepublishing.com

Renew materials using your Touch-Tone phone.
Call 630-961-0460 or via the web at
www.naperville-lib.info

#350 10-29-2013 1:40PM

TITLE: Disaster recovery planning : prep
BARCODE: 31318010780640

DUE DATE: 11-19-13

TITLE: Managing business change for dumm
BARCODE: 31318010719135

DUE DATE: 11-19-13

TITLE: Absolute beginner's guide to proj
BARCODE: 31318019039220

DUE DATE: 11-19-13

95th Street Library
Renew by phone at 630-961-0460

Our Library now offers a mobile app. search
Naperville Public Library in your phone's
app store and download the app. You can also
access it at http://naperville.boopsie.com/

LearnIT at InformIT

Go Beyond the Book

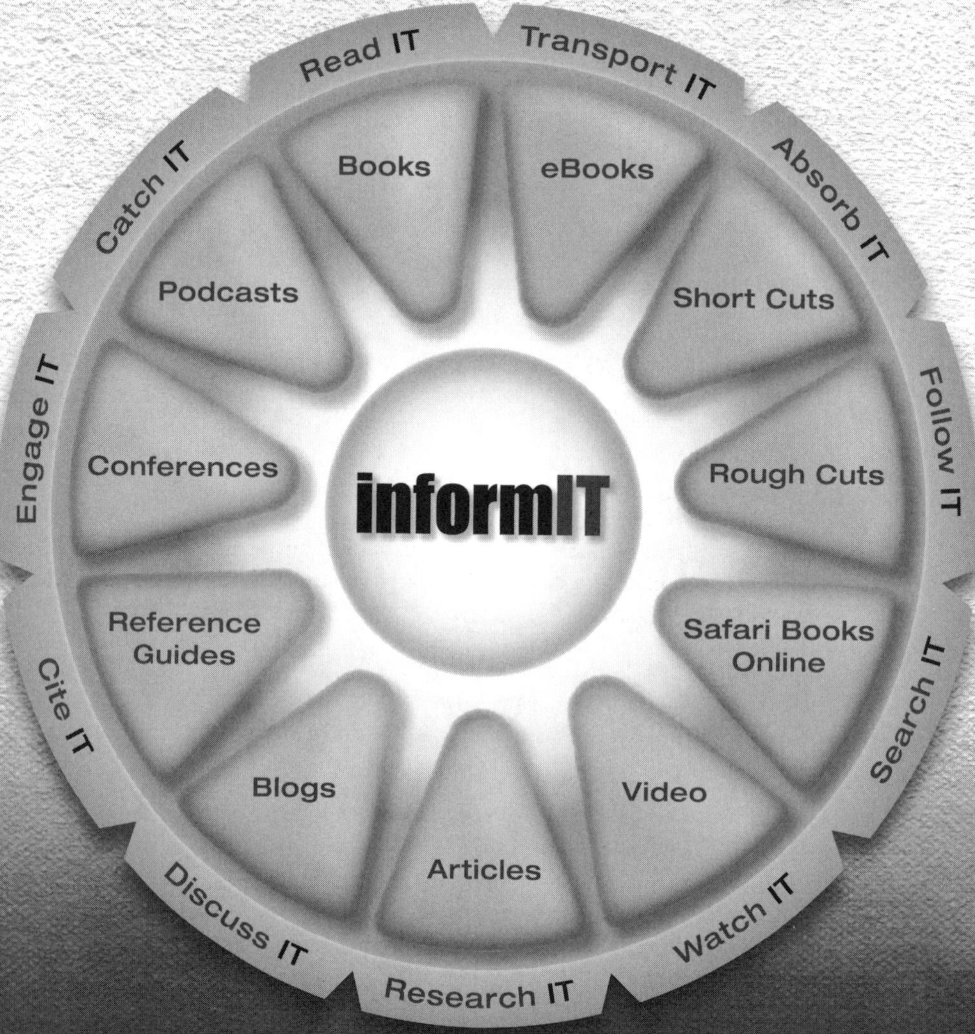

11 WAYS TO LEARN IT at **www.informIT.com/learn**

The digital network for the publishing imprints of Pearson Education

Addison Cisco Press IBM SAMS

Try Safari Books Online FREE

Get online access to 5,000+ Books and Videos

Safari Books Online

FREE TRIAL—GET STARTED TODAY!
www.informit.com/safaritrial

Find trusted answers, fast

Only Safari lets you search across thousands of best-selling books from the top technology publishers, including Addison-Wesley Professional, Cisco Press, O'Reilly, Prentice Hall, Que, and Sams.

Master the latest tools and techniques

In addition to gaining access to an incredible inventory of technical books, Safari's extensive collection of video tutorials lets you learn from the leading video training experts.

WAIT, THERE'S MORE!

Keep your competitive edge

With Rough Cuts, get access to the developing manuscript and be among the first to learn the newest technologies.

Stay current with emerging technologies

Short Cuts and Quick Reference Sheets are short, concise, focused content created to get you up-to-speed quickly on new and cutting-edge technologies.

Addison Wesley · Adobe Press · Alpha · Cisco Press · FT Press · IBM Press · lynda.com · Microsoft Press · New Riders · O'Reilly · Peachpit Press · Prentice Hall · Que · Redbooks · Sams · SAS Publishing · Sun Microsystems · Wiley

FREE Online Edition

Your purchase of **Absolute Beginner's Guide to Project Management, Second Edition,** includes access to a free online edition for 45 days through the Safari Books Online subscription service. Nearly every Que book is available online through Safari Books Online, along with more than 5,000 other technical books and videos from publishers such as Addison-Wesley Professional, Cisco Press, Exam Cram, IBM Press, O'Reilly, Prentice Hall, Que, and Sams.

SAFARI BOOKS ONLINE allows you to search for a specific answer, cut and paste code, download chapters, and stay current with emerging technologies.

Activate your FREE Online Edition at www.informit.com/safarifree

STEP 1: Enter the coupon code: RLJKTYG.

STEP 2: New Safari users, complete the brief registration form. Safari subscribers, just log in.

If you have difficulty registering on Safari or accessing the online edition, please e-mail customer-service@safaribooksonline.com

Safari Books Online